Paul and Hel

CW00486259

PAUL
AND
HELLENISM

Hyam Maccoby

SCM PRESS
London

TRINITY PRESS INTERNATIONAL
Philadelphia

First published 1991

SCM Press
26-30 Tottenham Road
London N1 4BZ

Trinity Press International
3725 Chestnut Street
Philadelphia Pa. 19104

Copyright © Hyam Maccoby 1991

British Library Cataloguing in Publication Data
Maccoby, Hyam *1924–*
Paul and Hellenism.
1. Bible. N. T. Paul, the Apostle, Saint
I. Title
225.92

ISBN 0–334–02485–4

Library of Congress Cataloging-in-Publication Data
Maccoby, Hyam, 1924–
Paul and Hellenism / by Hyam Maccoby.
p. cm.
Includes bibliographical references and index.
ISBN 1–56338–014–5
1. Paul, the Apostle, Saint. 2. Bible. N.T.
Epistles of Paul–Theology. 3. Gnosticism.
4. Antisemitism–History. 5. Mysteries. Religious.
6. Lord's Supper–History–Early church, ca. 30–600.
7. Hellenism. 8. Judaism–History –Post-exilic period,
588 B.C.-210 A.D. I Title.
BS2506.M29 1991
225.9′2–dc20   90–44765

Typeset at The Spartan Press Ltd, Lymington, Hants
and printed in Great Britain by
Billing & Sons Ltd, Worcester

For
Ed Sanders
sho'el u-meshibh shomea' u-mosiph

Contents

	Preface and Acknowledgments	ix
1	Gnostic Antisemitism	1
2	Paul and Gnosticism	36
3	Paul and the Mystery Religions	54
4	Paul and the Eucharist	90
5	Paul and Pharisaism	129
6	The Gaston-Gager-Stendahl Thesis	155
7	Paul, Hellenism and Antisemitism	180
	Notes	185
	Bibliography of Secondary Literature	203
	Index of Quotations	211
	General Index	217

Preface and Acknowledgments

On the last page of my *The Mythmaker* (1986), I promised a further volume which would supply a 'more academic treatment' of certain aspects. I have been gratified, if at times somewhat embarrassed, by the number of readers who have written to ask me when the promised book would be available, but must apologise to them for keeping them waiting so long because of various unavoidable delays.

The Mythmaker caused a storm of controversy, in the form of reviews, television programmes, meetings, seminars, and continuing correspondence. I hope that I have benefited from the arguments of others. Particularly useful were a seminar organized by Dr Nicholas de Lange at the Oriental Centre of Cambridge University, and a seminar arranged by the Philosophical Society of the University of Newcastle upon Tyne.

I must thank Professor W.D. Davies and Dr Christopher Rowland with whom I have had the privilege of discussing some of the matters contained in this book. Though I have been compelled to express my disagreement with them in the following pages, I much appreciate their courtesy and kindness.

An article comprising a shorter form of Chapter 4 has appeared in *New Testament Studies* under the title, 'Paul and the Eucharist'.

I have been helped greatly by the support of a grant from the Vidal Sassoon International Centre for the Study of Anti-Semitism, the Hebrew University of Jerusalem and from the Solon Foundation. I must thank Professor Yehuda Bauer, Chairman of the Academic Committee of the Centre and Mr Felix Posen, for their personal kindness and support of my work.

Passages quoted from the Gnostic writings have been taken from the translations in *The Nag Hammadi Library in English*, edited by James M. Robinson and M. Meyer (E.J. Brill, Leiden, 1977). My grateful thanks go to my son, David Maccoby, for his help with the General Index.

My heartfelt thanks go to my wife and fellow-worker, Cynthia Maccoby. Without her criticism, advice and help, it would have been impossible to complete this book.

Paul and Hellenism

1

Gnostic
Antisemitism

In the study of the history of antisemitism, Gnosticism presents facets of extraordinary interest and importance, which may well throw light on the problem of the nature and origin of antisemitism itself. In particular, Gnosticism presents a fully-developed antisemitic myth, in which the Jews are given an evil role not in a limited way, but in the central story of the cosmos. What is the relationship between the Gnostic antisemitic myth and other antisemitic myths, particularly that of Christianity? By analysing the structure and motivation of Gnostic antisemitism, can we make any contribution to the question of historical priority? In other words, does this much neglected approach to Gnosticism help us to decide whether Gnosticism preceded the birth of Christianity, or was, on the contrary, an outgrowth of Christianity? The vexed problem of priority has given rise to much fluctuation of scholarly opinion in recent years, and many lines of approach are valid in the attempt to arrive at a solution, none of which may be neglected, though, of course, none may be regarded as providing exclusive information. At the same time, the study of Gnostic antisemitism is important in considering the relationship between Gnosticism and Judaism, a relationship which, in turn, is involved in any attempt to understand the relationship between Gnosticism and Christianity.

The basic Gnostic myth gives an explanation of the evil of this world, and provides a way to overcome it, or at least escape from it. In essence, the explanation is that this world was created by an inferior deity, the Demiurge, whose claims to be the Highest God are false. The object of religion is to make contact with the true High God, whose dwelling-place is far beyond the skies. This contact can be made through the *gnosis*, the secret knowledge, which has been handed down through a succession of teachers since the beginning of the world. Through this teaching, thraldom to this world and to its evil, or limited, ruler, may be escaped, and union with the authentically divine may be achieved.

Psychologically, the essence of this doctrine is a feeling that we are strangers in this world, which is not our true home. Most of us have forgotten our origins, and the aim of *gnosis* is to awaken us from our amnesia. The doctrine is thus associated with a feeling of despair about the process of ordinary living, or with programmes of social amelioration. The world is essentially evil (acosmism), and spirituality is concerned with escaping from it, not improving it. Since such a programme requires a world-denying attitude that is alien to the great majority of people, or beyond their capacity, Gnosticism tends to be an elitist doctrine, which envisages salvation for the spiritual elect only, though the moderate forms of Gnosticism did provide a role, albeit inferior, for less gifted souls, provided that they accepted the Gnostic doctrine in principle.

Since the above definition of Gnosticism would not command universal assent, some justification of it is required. It may be objected that some essential features of Gnosticism, e.g. The Gnostic Saviour, or the ascent of the initiate to heaven, have been omitted. Some would argue (e.g. Gershom Scholem[1]) that the essential feature of Gnosticism is not its acosmism, but the mystical programme of an ascent through the heavens, in which dangers are experienced from hostile powers which must be placated by specially-learnt expressions. On this definition, rabbinic mysticism may be correctly designated as Gnostic, even though it is not acosmic.

Definitions, of course, are not inherently 'correct' or 'incorrect', but have to be justified by their usefulness. A mystical ascent is not in itself a religious phenomenon which tells us very much about the religious orientation in which it occurs, for such an ascent may serve very different religious purposes. In rabbinic mysticism, the ascent does not occur at the heart of the religion, for it is not a means of salvation, but a kind of virtuoso performance, admired but also somewhat deprecated as fraught with unnecessary risks. In the systems normally called 'Gnostic', however, the ascent, however risky, is of central importance, for without it the main purpose of religion cannot be achieved. Consequently, these systems are best described by some label signifying their central purpose, rather than a mechanism which, in other systems, has a different purpose. If we extend the term 'Gnosticism' to cover all systems which employ the mystical mechanism of the heavenly ascent, we shall still need a label for those systems which employ it in the service of an acosmic theology. Rather than seek such a new label, it seems best to confine the term 'Gnosticism' to the acosmic systems to which it has been applied traditionally, even though the adherents of such systems did not always call themselves 'Gnostics', and even though it is possible to find embryonic elements of acosmism in earlier philosophical or religious systems, such as those of Parmenides, Empedocles and Plato.[2] The exclusion of rabbinic mysticism from the category of 'Gnosticism' does not, of course, exclude the possibility of influence on rabbinic mysticism from Gnosticism or vice versa. Motifs of various kinds are constantly being picked up from very different religious systems, and being used for very different purposes. The vital thing is to distinguish between the central theme or motivation of a religion, which define it, and its mechanisms, which are transferable and malleable.

Similarly, it would be unhelpful to define Gnosticism in terms of its possession of a Saviour figure. Gnosticism certainly cannot do without the figure of the teacher bearing *gnosis*, but this figure need not be a divine personage descending from heaven, nor indeed need there be a special teacher who uniquely brings salvation. In its Christian forms, Gnosticism does give special significance to one teacher, namely Jesus, but even here, the uniquely saving quality of this figure is reduced by the denial of his sacrificial role and the insistence that his mission is to teach *gnosis* rather than to suffer vicariously. He becomes simply the supreme teacher of *gnosis*.

Thus, the defining characteristic of Gnosticism being its acosmism, Gnostic antisemitism is not peripheral but arises out of the core of the movement. For Gnosticism, seeing the world as evil and as ruled by an evil supernatural power, naturally looks for the earthly representatives of this power and finds them in the Jews. In theory, Gnosticism could have lighted on some other group as earthly representatives of the Demiurge, but historically this was impossible because of the special relationship of Gnosticism to Judaism. This relationship is one we shall have to explore, but first let us examine the extent and nature of Gnostic antisemitism.

In essence, Gnostic antisemitism consists of a disparagement of the Jewish claim that the Jews are the chosen people of God. The disparagement can take milder or more severe forms: sometimes the Jews are merely demoted, but sometimes they are given a position of negative election, as the acolytes of an evil deity, or Devil. The latter option is clearly antisemitic. The former option, however, is also antisemitic in effect, for, since the Jews do not accept their demotion, they are represented as sinning against the light by refusing to acknowledge the superiority of the *gnosis* to their own Torah. Thus, by their misplaced pride and failure to acknowledge their limitations, they become the chief obstacle to the progress of *gnosis*. The two antisemitic options reflect the two similar options in the Gnostic attitude towards the Demiurge himself: either he is regarded as an evil deity or Devil, or, more moderately, as a limited deity, who, however, by refusing to acknowledge his own limitations, becomes, in effect, evil. The Jews are characteristically regarded as the people of the Demiurge; and therefore attitudes towards the Demiurge are naturally reflected in attitudes towards the Jews, and vice versa. The question, indeed, is which disparagement is historically or psychologically prior, that of the Demiurge or that of the Jews? Does a feeling of resentment towards the Jews and their claims lead to disparagement of their God, or does a disillusionment with the biblical claims of the Jewish God (caused by his failure to keep his promises) lead to his demotion, entailing the demotion of the Jews? The answer to this question will go far towards answering the question, 'Who were the Gnostics?'

Again, Gnostic disparagement of the Jewish Law, or Torah is closely bound up with the disparagement of the Jews themselves. Gnostic antinomianism, to be sure, arises from the core of Gnostic acosmism, since law is rooted in an acceptance of the world and the body. In theory, The Gnostics were against every form of law, not just the Torah; the *gnosis* was to release the free spirit, or *pneuma* from the bondage of law. Those who were in thrall to the law were to be reckoned as at best *psychics* and at worst *hylics*. But in practice, the Jews were regarded as the supreme example of law-governed behaviour, and the Torah as the supreme example of legal thraldom. Here again we may ask which is psychologically prior, the rejection of law, or the rejection of the Jews. At any rate, the rejection of law was always associated with rejection or demotion of the Jews, and is thus a factor in and indicator of Gnostic antisemitism.

Let us then approach more closely the data of Gnostic antisemitism. We shall do this by considering various topics or aspects which contribute towards the demotion or reprobation of the Jews.

The Demotion of the Jewish Historical Record

An example is the following:

And Abraham and Isaac and Jacob were a laughingstock, since they, the counterfeit fathers, were given a name by the Hebdomad, as if he had become stronger than I and my brothers. We are innocent with respect to him, since we have not sinned. David was a laughingstock in that his son was named the Son of Man, having been influenced by the Hebdomad, as if he had become stronger than I and the fellow members of my race. But we are innocent with respect to him; we have not sinned. Solomon was a laughingstock, since he thought that he was Christ, having become vain through the Hebdomad, as if he had become stronger than I and my brothers. But we are innocent with respect to him. I have not sinned. The twelve prophets were laughingstocks, since they have come forth as imitations of the true prophets. They came into being as counterfeits through the Hebdomad, as if he had become stronger than I and my brothers. But we are innocent with respect to him, since we have not sinned. Moses, a faithful servant, was a laughingstock, having been named 'the Friend', since they perversely bore witness concerning him who never knew me. Neither he nor those before him, from Adam to Moses and John the Baptist, none of them knew me nor my brothers.

For they had a doctrine of angels to observe dietary laws and bitter slavery, since they never knew truth, nor will they know it. For there is a great deception upon their soul making it impossible for them ever to find a Nous of freedom in order to know him, until they come to know the Son of Man. Now concerning my Father, I am he whom the world did not know, and because of this, it (the world) rose up against me and my brothers. But we are innocent with respect to him; we have not sinned.

For the Archon was a laughingstock because he said, 'I am God, and there is none greater than I. I alone am the Father, the Lord, and there is no other beside me. I am a jealous God, who brings the sins of the fathers upon the children for three and four generations.' As if he had become stronger than I and my brothers! But we are innocent with respect to him, in that we have not sinned, since we mastered his teaching. Thus he was in an empty glory. And he does not agree with our Father. And thus through our fellowship we grasped his teaching, since he was vain in an empty glory. And he does not agree with our Father, for he was a laughingstock and judgment and false prophecy.

O those who do not see, you do not see your blindness, i.e. this which was not known, nor has it ever been known, nor has it been known about him. They did not listen to firm obedience. Therefore they proceeded in a judgment of error, and they raised their defiled and murderous hands against him as if they were beating the air. And the senseless and blind ones are always senseless, always being slaves of law and earthly fear.

The Second Treatise of the Great Seth (VII, 2, 62-64)

This is from a second-century Christian-Gnostic document, but it may serve as a starting-off point for discussion of earlier Gnostic attitudes too. The passage is spoken by Jesus Christ, who is apparently identified with 'the Great Seth' (though only the title of the work tells us this). The document, then, may belong to the sect of Sethians, or Sethian-Ophites, described by Irenaeus (Heresies, 30). Here the Gnostic scorn for the key characters of the Old Testament is expressed. Such scorn would certainly be experienced by Jews as a denigration of the Jewish role and religion. The pretensions of all the figures most revered by the Jews are dismissed. Even Moses is declared to be a 'laughingstock' in the eyes of the bearers of the true *gnosis*. The claim that Moses was 'the Friend' of God is denied, and declared to be a false statement made by those lacking true acquaintance with the divine. The God of the Jews, the source of the authority of their prophets and leaders, is identified as the 'Hebdomad', i.e. the seventh heaven, of which he is the ruler. He is called, in the same treatise, Yaldabaoth and 'the Cosmocrator'. This figure is a powerful evil god or angel, whose domain is over inferior souls only; not only is Jesus Christ superior to him, but even the saved gnostic believers, the 'brothers' of Jesus Christ, are spiritually superior to this flawed God of the Jews.

The attitude expressed towards Solomon is particularly interesting, since he is treated as a rival Messiah-figure to Jesus Christ, claiming the titles 'Son of Man' and 'Christ' which are regarded as rightly belonging to Jesus alone. There are certainly Jewish sources, both intertestamental and rabbinic, which give Solomon a quasi-Messianic role (just as there are sources which give Hezekiah a similar role).[3] Actually, the title 'Messiah' or 'Christ' ('anointed one') is regarded in Jewish sources as belonging to every king of the Davidic dynasty (as well as to every High Priest of Aaronic stock). Nevertheless, the role of the final redeemer of Israel was a special one; he was the Messiah *par excellence*, who, though still a human, not a supernatural figure, would establish the reign of God and the spiritual dominance of the Jewish people over the world. Solomon was regarded as having given a foretaste of this future glory, though his reign was marred, in the end, by sin. Hezekiah, too, was regarded as foreshadowing, by his reign, the glorious reign of the final Messiah. Neither of them, however, is called in the Jewish sources 'Son of Man', though Solomon was given the appellation, if not title, 'son of God', in virtue of I Chron. 17.3 and 22.10. The latter texts, indeed, seem to have been in the mind of the author of our tractate, since he alleges that it is David who becomes a laughingstock in virtue of Solomon's claim, and it was actually to David that Solomon's sonship was announced. It appears, then, that our author, aware of Jewish traditions about the Messiahship of Solomon, wrongly imagines that these traditions constitute a claim to divine status for Solomon; and he also confuses the title or appellation of 'son of God', applied to Solomon, with that of 'son of Man', associated with Jesus (an appellation which in Jewish tradition belonged not to the Messiah but to the guardian angel of Israel, of Daniel 7.13, who, unlike the guardian angels of the other nations, took human form in Daniel's vision).

There is a similar half-familiarity with Jewish sources in the assertion that Moses was given the title 'friend of God'. In fact, it was not Moses who was given this title, but Abraham (see Isa. 41.8; II Chron. 20.7; James 2.23). The titles that Moses does have are 'man of God' (Deut. 33.1; Josh. 14.6) and 'servant (or slave) of God' (I Chron. 6.49; II Chron. 24.9). On the other hand, the title 'fathers' is correctly attributed to Abraham, Isaac and Jacob, and the expression 'a faithful servant' is attached to Moses, showing awareness of his usual title (see Numbers 12.7).

We note, then, that our Gnostic author shows some familiarity with Jewish sources and traditions, which, however, he is inclined to garble. He finds in the Hebrew Bible a chain of authority, both prophetic and kingly, and he wishes to assert that this authority is spurious, being derived from an inferior supernatural source. Instead, he announces an alternative source of authority, that of Jesus Christ and his 'brothers', the enlightened Gnostics. But this authority is not without a historical continuity. Like the Jewish chain of authority, which it supplants, it has a succession and a tradition, beginning with Seth, the first bearer of *gnosis*, who, though possibly identified with the timeless Christ, has a historical identity fixed in the Jewish record, the Bible. Moreover, the twelve prophets are asserted not to be the 'true prophets', of whom they were merely 'imitations'; this implies an alternative line of Gnostic prophets covering a historical time-span equivalent to that of the biblical prophets. Here we see a characteristic tension or conflict in Gnosticism: a dependence on the Hebrew Bible, combined with a rebellion against it. The Gnostics find in the Hebrew Bible both the tradition which they repudiate, and the alternative tradition which they assert. This close relationship to the Hebrew Bible and other Jewish sources is our chief clue to the identity and status of the people who became Gnostics.

Of course, our passage has a relationship to the New Testament too, and it could be argued that the Gnostic authors of our document, being Christian, are related to the Hebrew Bible and the Jewish tradition only through the mediation of the New Testament which has its own links with the Jewish sources; and that any observable differences are an outcome of Gnostic reaction against orthodox Christianity. However, we shall see that Gnostic documents that are pre-Christian or at least non-Christian show an orientation to the Jewish sources that is similar to that of the Christian-Gnostic document now under consideration, and that this type of orientation differs in important respects from that of the New Testament to its Jewish background. It will be argued here, therefore, that our document, while showing some direct influence from the New Testament, also shows influences bypassing the New Testament, and deriving from pre-Christian or non-Christian Gnostic sources. The Gnostic attitude towards the Jews and Judaism thus has an independent history, not explicable as arising out of Christianity, either by positive or negative influence.

First, the details of New Testament influence should be noted. The allegation that the observance of dietary and other laws by the Jews is a 'doctrine of angels' can be traced to Galatians 3.19 (see also Acts 7.53), though the category 'angels' can have a pejorative significance in Gnostic thought that is foreign to the New Testament. It is an indication of New Testament influence that our document uses the word 'angels' here rather than a more usual Gnostic term, such as 'powers' or 'archons'. There is no possibility of direct influence from Jewish tradition, for the notion, advocated by some scholars, that Jewish biblical or extra-biblical tradition contains a doctrine that the Torah was given by angels is certainly wrong.[4]

The expression, 'I am he whom the world did not know', seems derived from John 1.10. The Gospel of John, indeed, was the most congenial of the Gospels to the Gnostics, and is frequently quoted by them.

In general, however, there is a great difference between the Gnostic attitude to the Jewish tradition, as shown in our passage, and that of the New Testament. The New Testament does not denigrate the Hebrew prophets, but on the contrary recruits them into Christianity by making them into proto-Christians, who foresaw the coming of Jesus. In a sense, the New Testament does demote the Hebrew prophets, since it assigns them to an obsolete dispensation, but they are conceived as predicting and acquies-

cing in their own obsolescence. There is no suggestion that the
Hebrew prophets were in the service of any power other than the
supreme God. God himself planned both their mission and their
eventual obsolescence. Even though the chief prophet, Moses, is
represented by Paul as receiving the chief prophetic work, the
Torah, not from God but from angels, this was itself an
arrangement sanctioned by God. The fact that God deputed this
task to angels shows that he meant the Torah to be authoritative
only for a time. This way of expressing the limited validity of the
Torah seems to have been originated by Paul, from whose
statement in Gal. 3.19 stemmed both Acts 7.53 and Heb. 2.2, as
well as, probably, Col. 2.18 (see note 3).

Our Gnostic document, on the other hand, adopts a tone of
dismissive contempt towards the Hebrew prophets. It is noteworthy that it even takes the same attitude towards John the
Baptist, who, in the New Testament, is the supreme example of
the submissiveness of the old dispensation to the new. Yet even in
this Gnostic document we can find a hint of the view, characteristic of the New Testament, that the Torah did once have some
validity. This hint is contained in the words 'we mastered his
teaching' and 'we grasped his teaching'. These expressions signify
that the Gnostics have not so much rejected the teaching of the
Archon (i.e. the Torah) as transcended it. It has become irrelevant
to them because they have passed far beyond its orbit, yet it was a
teaching that could not be ignored or bypassed, but, at some stage
in the progress towards enlightenment, had to be 'mastered' and
'grasped'. The same attitude can be seen in the constantly
repeated, 'We are innocent in respect to him; we have not sinned.'
This means that the Gnostics claim to have passed beyond the
sinful state which makes people subject to the Archon; but again it
is tacitly acknowledged that those who are still in a sinful state are
rightly under his rule and would incur further guilt by rebelling
against him.

Thus the undoubted difference between the New Testament
and the Gnostic writings on the question of the authority of the
Hebrew Bible and the Jewish tradition is a matter of emphasis
rather than fundamental disagreement. Both regard the Hebrew
Bible as obsolete, but the Gnostics allow themselves much more
contemptuous language in dismissing the Hebrew authorities

(prophets and kings) than is found in the New Testament. The real difference lies in the Gnostic view that the Archon, and his followers the prophets, remained unaware of their own limitations. In the New Testament, on the other hand, the 'angels' who gave the Torah were fully aware of their subordination to God, and the prophets were similarly aware that their pronouncements would be superseded one day by greater authority. There is thus a curious similarity between the Gnostic attitude to the Jews generally and the Christian attitude to the Jews *after* the coming of Christ. For the Gnostics, the Jews denied Christ throughout their history, and this denial rendered both their god, the Archon, and themselves, a 'laughingstock', despite the validity, up to a point, of their doctrine. For the Christians, the Jews, or at least the Jewish prophets and other leaders, acknowledged Christ until his coming, and then denied him, thus becoming the bearers of a Torah which had become falsified by being elevated into an absolute. In the Gnostic attitude, on the other hand, while a little room has been left for acknowledgment of the positive aspects of the Torah, the negative aspects are so much more deeply felt that they almost always slide into outright condemnation and rejection, even when the pre-Christian period is under consideration.

To complete the picture of the contrast between Gnosticism and Christianity in this area, it is necessary to point out that the anti-prophetism of Gnosticism is not entirely without parallel in normative Christianity. Thus the treatment of the non-Jewish figure of Melchizedek in the Epistle to the Hebrews has much in common with the Gnostic glorification of the non-Jewish figure of Seth. Both are intended to devalue the Jewish chain of authority by demonstrating the existence of an alternative and superior historical continuity. While Seth heads a chain of Gnostic teachers outshining the Hebrew prophets, Melchizedek heads a priesthood that transcends the Aaronite Jewish priesthood. This topic will receive more extended treatment on later pages.

We may now turn to tracing the history of the Gnostic attitude to the Jewish tradition by considering the evidence of documents that can reasonably be supposed to be earlier, at least in part, than the Christian-Gnostic document so far examined. It was one of the great surprises of the Nag Hammadi documents that some of them, while displaying all the characteristics of Gnostic belief,

show no obvious Christian influence, and yet are clearly influenced by the Old Testament and other Jewish writings or traditions.
The conclusion that Gnosticism existed independently of Christianity, and did not arise as a heresy out of Christianity, but rather
(at least in the case of *some* Gnostic sects[5]) out of Judaism, is still
being resisted by some scholars. The present enquiry may help
towards a solution of this controversy. But as Birger Pearson has
argued,[6] we may trace Jewish influences, unmediated by Christianity, not only by concentrating on supposedly non-Christian
texts, but by isolating passages in Gnostic works, whether Christian or non-Christian, which utilize Jewish traditions not found in
Christian sources, and unavailable through normal Christian
channels, e.g. traditions found only in Midrashic works. Such
passages indicate a direct historical connection between Gnosticism and Judaism, and thus may derive from a period in the
history of Gnosticism before it amalgamated with Christianity, in
the form of the Gnostic-Christian sects. In the passage from *The
Second Treatise of the Great Seth* analysed above, the concept of the
Messianic status of Solomon may be such a tradition, though this
example is not unchallengeable, since this concept could have
been derived from the Old Testament itself. If we find unmediated
Jewish traditions in a work believed to be probably non-Christian,
this may be taken as further evidence of the independent nature of
the work; if in a Christian-Gnostic work, this may be taken as
evidence of a non-Christian stratum, especially if the work in
question is regarded, for other reasons, as being a Christianized
version of an originally non-Christian work. Gedaliah Stroumsa
has given an extended example of the use of unmediated Jewish
material in his treatment of the Gnostic theme of the seed of Seth.[7]

The theme of the demotion of the Jewish pretensions to be the
chosen people can similarly be found to involve the use of much
unmediated material taken from Jewish traditions, despite the fact
that this theme runs counter to the whole trend of Judaism. Thus
this theme must be regarded as one of the earliest and most basic
of Gnostic doctrines, predating the Gnostic involvement with
Christianity. The fundamental nature of this theme implies that
Gnosticism first arose as some kind of protest against Judaism,
though as yet we do not know the basis or sociological motivation
of this protest, or how deeply embedded in Judaism the protesters

were: whether they were disillusioned Jews or people on the fringes of Judaism (e.g. lapsed converts or disappointed aspirants to conversion) motivated by cultural rivalry or resentment. Whatever the status of the protesters, their attitude bespeaks considerable anger against both Jews and Judaism; a determination to relegate these arrogant Jews to a low position in the universe and to explode their claims to be the most significant people alive.

An example of Gnostic denigration of the Jewish historical record is the following:

> They become wicked in their action, and some of them fall away to the worship of idols. Others have demons dwelling with them as did David the king. He is the one who laid the foundation of Jerusalem; and his son Solomon, whom he begat in adultery, is the one who built Jerusalem by means of demons, because he received their powers. When he had finished building, he imprisoned the demons in the temple. He placed them into seven waterpots. They remained a long time in the waterpots, abandoned there. When the Romans went up to Jerusalem they discovered the waterpots, and immediately the demons ran out of the waterpots as those who escape from prison. And the waterpots remained pure thereafter. And since those days they dwell with men who are in ignorance, and they have remained upon the earth.
>
> _Testimony of Truth_ (X,3), 69-70

The redaction-date of the _Testimony of Truth_ is probably third century, but the above extract bears the marks of an early Gnostic polemic against the biblical record, handed down as a standard reproach-topos. It is reminiscent of the antisemitic reinterpretations of the biblical story by Alexandrian Greeks such as Manetho, as preserved in Josephus. The attack on Jerusalem and the temple, however, suggests a Samaritan, rather than an Alexandrian, origin for this polemic. Samaria, of course, is a much-favoured candidate for the origin of Gnosticism, or at least some varieties of it, especially in view of the prominence of Simon Magus, the Samaritan, in the heresiologists' accounts.

Yet the above attack also shows familiarity with normative Jewish traditions. Apart from the obvious use of vulnerable aspects of the biblical story itself (the disparagement of Solomon as the fruit of David's adulterous union with Bathsheba[8]), legends known also from the rabbinical or Hellenistic-Jewish sources are employed. That Solomon had power over demons is the theme of many rabbinic stories which are told to his glory; here it is a theme used to his discredit. A rabbinic story tells how Solomon enslaved Asmodeus (Ashmodai), the king of the demons, and learnt from him how to find the *shamir*, a magical rock-splitter that would enable the temple to be built without iron tools (Babylonian Talmud, Gittin, 68b). This story has been modified above into the accusation that Jerusalem was built by demons, which makes it into a demonic city. The statement that Jerusalem's foundation-stone was laid by David, and that it was completed by Solomon, appears to be Samaritan propaganda, showing the parvenu status of Jerusalem compared with Shechem; rabbinic tradition identified Jerusalem with Salem, the holy and ancient city of Melchizedek, thus giving the city awesome historical authority. The Bible, of course, makes David the conqueror of Jerusalem, not its founder (II Sam. 5.6). The story about the demons imprisoned in seven water-pots, and liberated by the Roman destruction of the Temple, has no rabbinic parallel, and appears to derive from some Hellenistic antisemitic source. (The authors of this story appear to have been unaware of the fact that the Second Temple was not built by either David or Solomon). While in the Jewish sources, the demons whom Solomon rules are inferior powers of no cosmic significance (rather like elves in later folklore), the Gnostic attack sees them as related to the evil power which Gnosticism identifies as the Creator God of Judaism. The attack on Solomon, in particular, seems designed to combat his Jewish status as a Messianic figure, as in the passage previously quoted, and to associate him with the power of evil.

Other texts, as in our first passage, attack the authority of the biblical prophets, e.g.:

> Because of this race famines will occur and plagues. But these things will happen because of the great incorruptible race. Because of this race temptations will come, a falsehood of false prophets.
>
> *Gospel of the Egyptians* (III,2), 61

This work seems only superficially Christianized. The 'race' referred to is that of the Sethian 'seed', and in a reversal of the biblical story which is nevertheless fully parasitic on the Bible, the people of Sodom and Gomorrah are declared to belong to 'the great incorruptible race' persecuted by the evil Demiurge. Similarly, our extract says, other disasters come from the Demiurge, seeking to destroy the Gnostic elect. The Hebrew prophets were inspired by the evil deity, and were sent to tempt people to evil. In contrast, there is another succession of prophets who are truly inspired by the High God, 'the prophets and the guardians who guard the life of the race'. The concept of the Gnostics as a 'race' is itself a distorted version of the Jewish self-understanding as a 'chosen people'. The racialism of the Gnostic concept, however, (related as it is to the Gnostic doctrine of predestination) with its conviction that all the enlightened are of the divine seed of Seth (though requiring to be awakened to awareness of their divine descent by *gnosis*), is in contrast with the Jewish concept of a chosen people to which anyone, of whatever birth, may attach himself by conversion. The Gnostic concept, however, serves the purpose of providing an alternative 'chosenness', and of nullifying the Jewish claim to special status. Just as the unnamed Gnostic prophets are provided to oust the biblical prophets from their high role, so the claim to Sethian descent ousts the Jews from what was seen, from a hostile standpoint, as a position of cosmic aristocracy. This aspect, however, needs further study in relation to the question of whether the Gnostics came from within the Jewish fold, or rather from Judaism's penumbra, consisting of such varied groups as the 'God-fearers', prospective or lapsed converts, or ambivalent observers.

Here it may be noted that the theme of privileged Sethian descent is itself partly derived from Jewish sources, as Birger Pearson has pointed out.[9] Philo, in his treatise *On the Posterity and Exile of Cain*, (L), speaks of Seth as 'the seed of human virtue'. This, however, is not meant in any literal sense, but in the allegorical sense that Seth, in contrast to Cain, is to be regarded as an exemplar or type of virtue. Philo can hardly have meant that all righteous people are physically descended from Seth, since, according to the biblical record which Philo revered as holy writ, Seth was the ancestor of *all* mankind, since the Cainites did not survive the Flood, and only Seth's descendant, Noah, together with his family, survived to continue the human race. This makes

Seth the physical ancestor of all the wicked people of post-
Diluvian times, as well as of all the righteous. Philo meant,
therefore, that whenever a person is found to be righteous, he is
being true to the spirit of his ancestor Seth, while wicked people
are being false to Seth, who is equally their ancestor.[10] The
Gnostics, on the other hand, were able to avoid the apparent
absurdity of deriving only the 'perfect' from Seth by their concept
of a heavenly Seth, whose seed is implanted anew into every
person predestined to acquire *gnosis*.[11] Thus the Gnostics have
applied a Jewish-Hellenistic idea in a new way, giving it a twist
that it never had in Philo, who would never have thought of the
Sethian seed as rivalling the Jewish claim to chosenness, since for
him the Jews, like everyone else in the world, were Sethian seed.

While it is possible to find the germ of the Sethian idea in
Philo, it is even more interesting to note the virtual *absence* of Seth
in the pseudepigraphic literature which has provided so much of
the thematic structure of Gnosticism.[12] The same virtual absence
can be noted in the rabbinic literature. The attractiveness of Seth
to the Gnostics as a central figure, we may surmise, was partly
because of his detachment from Jewish tradition. Here is a non-
Jewish figure who can be used to head a chain of authority
entirely separate from that of Judaism. Other pre-Jewish figures
(i.e. figures presented in the Bible as pre-Jewish), e.g. Enoch and
Noah, were not so suitable for this role because they had been
given an established status in post-biblical Jewish literature as
precursors of Judaism.[13] Here the suggestiveness of the phrase
'another seed' (Gen. 4.25) helped to recruit Seth to the cause of
alienation from the forces of this world and from the Jews. An
indication of the positive value given to alienation is the title
'Allogenes' which was bestowed on Seth and other Gnostic
redeemers. While this title literally just echoes the theme of
'another seed', the term has associations which further repel the
Jewish tradition; for *allogenes* is a Septuagint term for 'gentile'.
The Gnostics by their choice of this sobriquet are drawing
attention to the non-Jewish and anti-Jewish nature of their
doctrine. Yet at the same time, the figure of Seth, chosen for his
remoteness from Judaism, was known to the Gnostics only from
the Jewish Bible.[14] Even to distance themselves from Judaism,
the Gnostics are dependent on Jewish material. This astonishing

paradox shows that, whatever may be the solution of the question, 'Who were the Gnostics?', they (or at least those of them who belonged to Gnostic sects that produced biblically-based texts) were people who felt a strong tie with Judaism even when rebelling against it.

The Demotion of the God of Judaism

Even more pervasive in the Gnostic writings than the denigration of the Jewish historical record is the theme of the evil and inadequacy of the Demiurge. In so far, however, as the Demiurge is identified in the Gnostic writings as the Creator-God of Genesis and as the giver of the Torah and the other prophetic writings, the disparagement of the Demiurge is also a disparagement of the Jews and Judaism and a powerful ingredient in Gnostic anti-semitism.

We may begin again by examining a typical passage:

And when Aldabaoth noticed that they withdrew from him, he cursed his earth. He found the woman as she was preparing herself for her husband. He was lord over her though he did not know the mystery which had come to pass through the holy decree. And they were afraid to blame him. And he showed his angels his ignorance which is in him. And he cast them out of paradise and he clothed them in gloomy darkness. And the chief archon saw the virgin who stood by Adam, and that the luminous Epinoia of life had appeared in her. And Yaldabaoth was full of ignorance. And when the foreknow-ledge of the all noticed (it), she sent some and they snatched Life out of Eve.

And the chief archon seduced her and he begot in her two sons; the first and the second (are) Eloim and Yave. Eloim has a bear-face and Yave has a cat-face. The one is righteous but the other is unrighteous. (IV 38. 4-6 adds: Yave is righteous but Eloim is unrighteous.) Yave he set over the fire and the wind, and Eloim he set over the water and the earth. And these he called with the names Cain and Abel with a view to deceive.

Now up to the present day sexual intercourse continued due

to the chief archon. And he planted sexual desire in her who belongs to Adam. And he produced through intercourse the copies of the bodies, and he inspired them with his opposing spirit.

And the two archons he set over principalities so that they might rule over the tomb. And when Adam recognized the likeness of his own foreknowledge, he begot the likeness of the son of man. He called him Seth according to the way of the race in the aeons.

The Apocryphon of John (II, 1), 23-25

This is from a Christian-Gnostic work of the second century, but the above passage is clearly the fruit of the independent meditation on the Hebrew Bible from a standpoint very different from that of the New Testament and in no way derived from it. It shows points of departure that are situated within the Jewish, not Christian, tradition, yet the bizarre ingenuity with which the themes are radically transformed shows no continuity with biblical modes, such as is found in the rabbinic literature even at its most imaginative. It seems impossible to suppose, as some scholars do, that this kind of improvization on biblical themes could come from people rebelling against Judaism from within. Rather it seems the work of people coming to the Bible fully equipped with an alien tradition of thought, and adapting the biblical story to conform to this pre-posited structure. Yet the points of contact with Jewish tradition, and the need to give a Jewish clothing to non-Jewish theologoumena, in such a way as to dethrone the Jewish God and Judaism, argue that we have to do with people whose relationship to Judaism is more than purely external.

The Creator of the world, Yaldabaoth, is earlier described as having been born 'imperfect' because of a kind of primal sin by his mother, the high divinity Sophia, who gave birth to him 'from herself' without proper union with the supreme male principle. She then repented and cast away her monster-child, but he set up his own kingdom and created powers to serve him. He is described as a mixture of light and darkness, and is said to have three names: 'The first name is Yaldabaoth, the second is Saklas, and the third is Sammael. And he is impious in his madness which is in him. For he said, "I am God and there is no other God beside me", for he is ignorant of his strength, the place from which he had come.' The three names all have a Hebrew, or Aramaic, derivation, Yaldabaoth meaning (possibly) 'child of the abyss' (though Scholem disagrees[15]), Saklas meaning 'fool', and Samael being the well-known name of Satan in the Pseudepigrapha and rabbinic writings, explained by the Gnostics as meaning 'blind god'. We thus have here an identification of the Creator-God of Genesis with Satan, a frantic blasphemy in Jewish eyes, and the ultimate repudiation of Judaism.

This drastic reversal of values can be seen working through the interpretation of the biblical story in the above-quoted passage. The light of knowledge which is in man is regarded as deriving from a higher power than the Creator. The latter, indeed, seeks to frustrate the higher aspects of man, though not entirely success-fully. The expulsion from Eden and the curse of barrenness on the earth was due not to the sin of Adam and Eve, but to the jealous rage of the Demiurge when he saw that human beings possessed spiritual capacities beyond his reach, and were able to act or think independently of him.

Some of the logical difficulties encountered by the Gnostics in their programme of reversal of biblical values can be seen in the above extract. One of these is the puzzle created by the charac-ter of Abel. If Seth was of 'another seed' and thus superior to all Adam's other progeny, what are we to make of the good/evil dichotomy represented by Abel and Cain? How good was Abel, if he had the approval of the evil Demiurge, and how evil was Cain, if he had the Demiurge's disapproval? Many different attempted solutions to this problem can be found in the Gnostic writings, including the radical, yet in some ways logical, solu-tion adopted by the Cainites, who regarded Cain as good and Abel as evil.[16] In our present extract, the solution cannot be regarded as very successful. Abel's goodness is retained, but without sufficient grounding in Gnostic reasoning. The uncer-tainty of the texts shows that some difficulty was felt; in one text, it is not clear which of the two, Cain and Abel, was 'righteous'. Cain and Abel, also, are identified with heavenly powers, of an inferior kind, and given the names Eloim (Elohim) and Yave (Yahveh), two names belonging, in the Bible, to the supreme God of the universe, but here regarded as not even belonging to

the jealous Creator-God, but only to his progeny, who are
further degraded by being given an animal aspect. The added
detail that both Cain and Abel were engendered through a
seduction of Eve by the 'chief archon' (echoing Jewish legends
about the seduction of Eve by Satan in the form of the
serpent[17]), completes the demonization of the Creator-God and
also marks off the evil descendants of Cain from the high-born
descendants of Seth.

We note, then, that this value-reversal of the biblical story
shows a familiarity with Jewish traditional *aggadah* (especially in
the motif of the seduction of Eve), combined with an animus
against Jewish religion that is pathologically intense (especially in
the treatment of the sacred divine names, Elohim and, even more
strikingly, YHWH, the revered Tetragrammaton). What kind of
people, we may ask, could combine such knowledgability with
such hatred? The answer given by Grant, Pearson, Stroumsa,
Green and other scholars that these were Jews rebelling against
their own religion gives a sufficient explanation of the first factor,
but not, it may be thought, of the second. One can imagine a
disillusioned Jew becoming an atheist; but it is hard to imagine
him adopting a fantastic scheme of mythology in which the Lord of
Being has become a cat-faced minor deity.

The Denigration of the Torah

It is an essential doctrine of Judaism that the commandments of
the Torah are God-given (even though their practical implement-
ation in the *halakhah* is left to a large extent to human decision).
The Torah ('teaching') in which the commandments are embodied (chiefly the Pentateuch) is extolled as wise and holy, and the
way of life based on the Torah as the highest and most beneficial
possible for human beings. Gnosticism constitutes the negation of
these valuations: the Torah was not given by God but by a demon,
and adherence to its commandments is not righteousness but
abject slavery.

Yet it is somewhat remarkable that the Gnostic writings do not
contain any sustained polemic against the Torah. There are a few
casually contemptuous remarks such as, ' . . . they had a doctrine
of angels to observe dietary laws and bitter slavery' (see above,

p. 6). The observance of the commandments of the Torah is quite
frequently referred to as 'slavery', but there is no detailed polemic
against circumcision, observance of Sabbath and festivals, or even
dietary laws. Moreover, the ethical aspect of the Torah is not even
mentioned: it is not explained in what ways the Ten Commandments or the *mishpatim* dealing with reparation for injuries are to be
regarded as failing in their object or as unnecessary. Here the
Gnostic writings differ from the Pauline epistles, which are much
concerned to expound the rejection of the commandments of the
Torah, and to provide an alternative foundation for ethical
behaviour. Paul's agonized struggle against sin, his conviction
that the struggle cannot be resolved by conformity to rules,
however admirable, and his resort to the sacrifice of Jesus as a
solution to the ever-present problem of moral evil, have no
counterpart in the Gnostic writings, since the Gnostic do not
regard moral evil as a problem at all.

The tone of the Gnostic writings towards the Torah is one of
amused contempt, not of agonized rejection. Only unen-
lightened people, they suggest, could be so concerned about
petty details of everyday life, such as which foods to eat, which
days to celebrate, or which actions to avoid. The truly enlightened find such questions irrelevant, for they live on a god-
like plane in which life is a matter of being, not of doing, and
the basic experience is bliss, not anxiety. There is nothing in the
Gnostic writings, also, corresponding to the Pastoral Epistles of
Paul, in which day-to-day problems, including moral problems,
of the ostensibly saved are tackled, with the unwilling
acknowledgment that despite the supposed solution of the cross,
the question of morality has not disappeared. None of the Gnostic writings gives us any impression of what it was like to live in
a Gnostic community. The inevitable frictions, petty irritations
and conflicts of principle, requiring compromise solutions or
schisms, which we know did occur in Gnostic groups, are not
reflected in the Gnostic writings, since this would lower the tone
of ineffable god-like bliss which was supposed to characterize
the true Gnostic. Any dependence on rules would impair the
freedom of the 'perfect' and would constitute the 'slavery' which
was the mark of the Torah; and the human condition of living
in a community, demanding the hammering out of ground-rules

through which the difficult business of living together can be achieved, was simply denied. The exception among the Gnostic sects was Valentinianism, which, like Pauline Christianity, worked out a compromise with the everyday world. This Valentinian compromise consisted of allowing a limited validity to the needs of the 'psychic' individuals, who could not reach 'pneumatic' status but could live good lives on their own plane, while maintaining community relations with the 'perfect'.[18] This compromise was also adopted by later Gnostic sects, the Manichees and the Albigensians, and is the characteristic pattern of any Gnostic sect that was able to have more than an ephemeral existence. But this compromise was not invested with any positive spiritual fervour, being a matter of practicality not basic theory, and so does not find any expression in the Gnostic writings, which all assume that the only way deserving respect is that of the 'perfect'.

The only biblical commandment that receives extended discussion in the Gnostic writings is not any of the practical commandments of Jewish community living, but, as one might expect, one belonging to mythology. This is the commandment given to Adam and Eve by God to refrain from eating the fruit of the tree of knowledge of good and evil. The way in which this commandment is treated, however, illustrates well the Gnostic attitude to commandments or rules in general.

A typical passage is:

But of what sort is this God? First [he] envied Adam that he should eat from the tree of knowledge. And secondly he said, 'Adam, where are you?' And God does not have foreknowledge, that is, since he did not know this from the beginning. [And] afterwards he said, 'Let us cast him [out] of this place, lest he eat of the tree of life and live for ever.' Surely he has shown himself to be malicious envier. And what kind of God is this? For great is the blindness of those who read, and they did not know it. And he said, 'I am the jealous God; I will bring the sins of the fathers upon the children until three (and) four generations.' And he said, 'I will make their heart thick, and I will cause their mind to become blind, that they might not know nor comprehend the things that are said.'

But these things he has said to those who believe in him [and] serve him!

The Testimony of Truth (IX, 3), 47-8

This passage is in a Christian Gnostic text of the second or third century, but its attitude towards the God of Genesis is certainly not derived from the New Testament, or conceivable as an outcome or development of New Testament teaching. Whereas the Pauline epistles take for granted that Adam was sinful in disobeying God, and indeed regard his sin as more heinous and devastating in its effects than either the Genesis narrative or Jewish tradition support, the Gnostics do not regard Adam's disobedience as sinful at all. It was the Gnostic aspect of Adam, his possession, however partial, of heavenly insight, that enabled him to defy the envious prohibition of the evil, or limited, Demiurge, and show himself superior to his commandments. Texts from the Hebrew Bible are used to prove this interpretation. Did not the Creator-God call himself 'jealous' (Ex. 20.5)? Did he not show himself to be lacking in knowledge, or foreknowledge, when he failed to foresee Adam's action? Was not even his prohibition of the fruit of the tree of life evidence of his envy and malice towards mankind? The author uses the words of Isaiah 6. 9-10 to show that the Creator-God deliberately set out to prevent his followers, the Jews, from discovering the Gnostic truth. The same verses are used in the New Testament (Mark 4. 11), not to denigrate the Creator-God, but to denigrate the Jewish people, who are regarded as so far gone in sin that God despairs of enlightening them and thus speaks to them obscurely (as Jesus does in his parables). This example illustrates a general difference between Gnostic and Christian antisemitism: the Gnostic attack is mainly against the Jewish God, rather than the Jewish people, who are regarded as his dupes and victims (yet despicable as such), while the Christian attack is entirely against the Jewish people themselves, as inveterate sinners and wilful rejecters of God and his prophets.

In other Gnostic writings, the picture of Adam's disobedience as an act of enlightenment is given further elaboration. We are told that all the trees which Adam and Eve were allowed to eat were in fact harmful: 'their trees are godlessness and their fruit is deadly poison and their promise is death' (Apoc. John, 21). When Adam

was disobedient to the Chief Archon this was 'due to the light of
the Epinoia which is in him, which corrected him in his thinking
(to be) superior to the chief archon'. The serpent who tempted Eve
is regarded in some texts as inspired by the High God, in others as
only temporarily inspired and reverting afterwards to earthliness,
and in yet other texts as being wholly evil, and acting for ulterior
motives of its own. (Here again the puzzle of how to treat
characters presented as evil in the biblical narrative proves
difficult to solve; see above, in relation to Cain.)

The main point, however, is that the commandments of the
Creator God are regarded as evil, being 'envious' and enslaving.
This attitude must obviously apply to the whole Torah revealed
by this same Creator God to his people Israel, though the Gnostics
do not attempt to explain what code of morality is to be substituted
for the Torah (all codes being unnecessary), or even to distinguish
between acceptable and unacceptable, or outmoded, laws (in the
manner adopted by Christian legists, in their distinction between
the ethical and the ceremonial laws of Judaism).

An interesting treatment of the Torah is found in the text quoted
above, the Testimony of Truth:

For many have sought after the truth and have not been able to
find it; because there has taken hold of them [the] old leaven of
the Pharisees and the scribes [of] the Law. And the leaven is
[the] errant desire of the angels and the demons and the stars.
The Pharisees and the scribes are those who belong to the
archons who have authority [over them].

For no one who is under the Law will be able to look up to the
truth, for they will not be able to serve two masters. For the
defilement of the Law is manifest; but undefilement belongs to
the light. The Law commands (one) to take a husband (or) to
take a wife, and to beget, to multiply like the sand of the sea. But
passion which is a delight to them constrains the souls of those
who are begotten in this place, those who defile and those who
are defiled, in order that the Law might be fulfilled through
them. And they show that they are assisting the world; and they
[turn] away from the light, who are unable [to pass by] the
archon of [darkness] until they pay the last [penny].

The Testimony of Truth (IX, 3) 29-30

Clearly, this passage owes much to the New Testament, and such explicit reference to the Law is unusual, but the Gnostic emphasis is characteristic. The objection to the Law is that it accepts this world, instead of rejecting it as evil. In particular, the Law accepts sexual passion as legitimate and propagation as desirable. This shows that the Law is the creation of 'the archons' and is a source of 'defilement'. The Jews, therefore, and their religious guides, the Pharisees and scribes, are irredeemably worldly and removed from the light and 'defiled'. The denigration of the Torah is explicitly connected to a denigration of the Jews that (in its emphasis on dirtiness or 'defilement' in relation to sexual disgust) has strong echoes in later antisemitism, including that of the Nazis. But this kind of personal attack on the Jews is found only in a text that is much influenced by Christian antisemitism; earlier Gnostic texts stress rather the blindness and gullibility of the Jews in allowing themselves to be duped by the Demiurge.

The Gnostics and Antisemitism

We may now attempt to draw the threads together and come to some conclusions about the nature of Gnostic antisemitism, and also about the kind of people who composed those Gnostic groups that felt a strong interest in interpreting the Jewish Bible in an anti-Jewish sense.

The evidence leads to the conclusion that the Gnostics were primarily interested in attacking, not the Jews, but the Jewish God. Remarks are certainly found in the Gnostic writings that denigrate the Jews as a people, but these remarks are always desultory and incidental to the main attack on the Demiurge and his associated archons. The Gnostic writings do not contain sustained diatribes against the Jews such as are found in Christian writings from the New Testament on. While the Christian writings constantly reiterate the theme that the Jews are persecutors (of their own prophets as well as of Jesus and Christian figures), the Gnostic writings seldom picture the Jews as persecutors of Gnostics, but constantly portray the Demiurge in this role. The Jews, in the Gnostic myth, are mere pawns of the Demiurge, characterized by supine over-obedience, while in Christian antisemitism, on the contrary, the chief characteristic of the Jews is stubborn disobedience. Thus the Jews are colourless figures in the Gnostic writings, not by any means the actively demonic figures found in the Christian writings. This is not to say that the Gnostic writings are free of antisemitism, but that their antisemitism does not seem central or emotionally important in their thought. The Demiurge seeks to destroy the Gnostics by sending the Flood and by sending fire and brimstone over Sodom and Gomorrah, but Jewish persecution of later Gnostics is not given vivid narrative form, though it is sometimes mentioned. Of course (an important consideration) the fact that the Demiurge is always frustrated in his purposes and never has any serious success in his attempts to destroy the Gnostics (who are always brought to safety by higher powers) defuses the conflict and ensures that no accumulation of bitter resentment against the Jews, the Demiurge's acolytes, occurs. The Gnostic myth lacks the element of repeated successful violence that characterizes the Christian myth. Consequently, even the Demiurge is regarded with contempt, or even amusement, rather than hatred.

What kind of people are likely to have produced this almost comic version of the Jewish Creator of the universe, who reminds us of nothing so much as the 'villain' character in an animated cartoon, repeatedly attempting to annihilate the hero, and always failing? The view that has found favour with scholars in recent years is that Gnosticism arose out of Judaism and was especially motivated by the disappointment of Jewish apocalyptic hopes. In order to explain the defeat of the Jews by Rome, the Jewish God was demoted to the status of a national angel, and the transcendent High God, far above worldly battles, thus remained unaffected by defeat.[19] Or, more profoundly, disillusionment led some Jews to a conviction that this world was irredeemable by any apocalyptic solution, that the creator of such an evil world must be himself evil, or at least limited, and that salvation must be sought through escape from this world into the realm of the pleroma (a concept derived from Platonism, but coloured by Jewish conceptions of the transcendence of the divine). An alternative explanation has been put forward by Henry A. Green on class-sociological rather than national-historical lines.[20] This is that Gnosticism arose among a marginal class of assimilated Jews in Alexandria whose hopes of upward mobility had been dashed by the displacement of their patrons, the Ptolemaic upper class, on the advent of Roman power. On this theory, the Demiurge is a substitute for the resented Roman power itself, which lorded over a world made hateful to certain Jews by their disappointed ambitions and their displacement from both Jewish and Hellenistic religio-political structures, while the mystical orientation of Gnosticism expresses their longing to escape from an intolerable social situation.

The theory of a Jewish origin of Gnosticism certainly provides an explanation of the most puzzling feature of some, at least, of the Gnostic writings, namely the knowledge of Judaism displayed in them (even including a knowledge of haggadic tradition found in intertestamental or rabbinic texts). This knowledge does not come to the Gnostics through Christianity, but appears to have come directly from Judaism; this is shown both by the direct engagement with biblical passages, especially from Genesis, without the mediation of Christian concepts, by the use of haggadic traditions not found in Christian sources, and by the absence, in many important contexts, of reference to Christianity, or the superficiality (where Christian references do exist) of the Christian framework, showing that Christianization of an originally non-Christian text has occurred.

There seems little doubt now that some forms of Gnosticism arose out of Judaism, but the question remains how, and through what kind of experience of Judaism. The conclusion appears unescapable that these Gnostics were at most marginal Jews. The theory that they were Jews of a central kind, brought up in the full discipline of Judaism, but reduced to despair by their earnest meditation on the failure of the biblical promises, hardly bears examination. If this were the case, we would expect to find in the 'Jewish' Gnostic writings a much fuller engagement with Jewish tradition. What we do find is a great interest in the early chapters of Genesis, and hardly any interest in other parts of the Hebrew Bible. The prophecies of Isaiah, Jeremiah, Ezekiel, or Zechariah, which we would expect people who had once been committed Jews to quote with anguish or to re-interpret in some new sense are passed over in silence. The commandments of the Torah, which were of the utmost importance to committed Jews as the basis of

their ethics and communal practices, and as the substance of their
Covenant with God, are hardly mentioned, and there is no
evidence of any struggle experienced in achieving freedom from
them. Clearly even Pauline Christians of Gentile background were
far more conscious of prophetic and prescriptive texts than the
Gnostics were. There does not appear to have been any emotional
investment by the Gnostics in specifically Jewish hopes or
practices, either in the form of disappointed repudiation or in the
form of reinterpretation. They are merely dismissed with casual
disdain.

On the contrary, it seems that the Gnostics came to the
Hebrew Bible with already-formed interests and fastened on
that part of the Bible that was relevant to these interests, since
it was concerned with cosmology and was susceptible of theo-
sophical interpretation. It is true that the Jewish mystics who
produced the Hekhalot literature also displayed special interest
in Genesis in their study of *ma'aseh bereshit*, but these same
mystics were also deeply rooted in prophetic and halakhic Judaism, as their writings amply show, and indeed regarded their
mystical exercises as secondary to their main loyalty to the
Jewish Covenant, through which, and not through mysticism,
they expected to achieve salvation. Even the Jewish apocalyptic
writers, whose mystical visions were much more central to their
beliefs, did not hope for salvation through their actual visions,
but through what those visions foretold, namely the fulfilment
of the biblical prophecies and the establishment of the kingdom
of God on earth; thus the core of their belief was still the Covenant of Sinai. Only the Gnostic writers show no interest in Covenant, and regard mysticism as an end in itself and as the chief
end of man.

It might be argued (and this seems to be the unspoken
argument of certain scholars) that Gnosticism arose precisely
because some disillusioned Jews turned from the central doctrine
of Judaism to what had previously existed in the periphery,
making it central. One can imagine someone starting from Philo's
premises and moving to a standpoint in which the contemplation
of God becomes far more important than the satisfaction of earthly
moral demands or the fulfilment of earthly eschatological hopes.
Indeed, Philo complains that some Alexandrian Jews did not take

this step, regarding the literal fulfilment of the commandments of the Torah as unnecessary. But this would result in something very different from Gnosticism. It would not lead to the denigration of the Creator-God or even to the condemnation of the Torah, which would rather be regarded as a propaedeutic leading to the higher contemplative life – the step-ladder that could be thrown away once its object had been achieved. Jewish mysticism was the contemplation of the Creator-God and his works, not the repudiation of them, which is something radically different. The case of Elisha ben Abuyah, which has often been adduced to show that a person could move from the heart of rabbinic Judaism to a Gnostic stance, is unconvincing. There is no evidence that Elisha became a Gnostic; what evidence there is points rather to his secularization.

The closest analogy to the Gnostic demotion of the Jewish Creator-God is the familiar process by which various polytheistic systems of the ancient world attempted to explain and incorporate the God of Judaism. Sometimes he was identified with Zeus or Jupiter; at other times, he was identified with Saturn, because of the holiness of Saturday to the Jews, and also probably to indicate that he was an outmoded god. Alternatively, he could be given minor status within the Roman system, as when the Emperor Hadrian proposed to include the Jewish god, whom he regarded as identical with the Jewish progenitor Abraham, in his pantheon. All these attempts were aimed at a syncretism that would break down the isolation of Judaism and give it an intelligible place in the pattern of polytheistic religion, but they also had the effect of reducing the status of the Jewish God and denying the claim that he was the One God whose only relationship with other gods was one of repudiation.

On the other hand, Philo's theology can be regarded as an attempt of a similar kind undertaken from the Jewish side. In addition to the systems of polytheism, the Hellenistic world contained the conception, largely deriving from Plato and Aristotle, of a supreme reality beyond all human categories, transcending both gods and men. Philo's work, and that of other Alexandrian Jews, consisted of an attempt to identify this supreme reality with the God of Judaism; on the face of it, a difficult task, since the Hellenistic conception was abstract and impersonal, while the

Jewish God was portrayed in the Bible as both active and emotional; yet not impossible, since the Jewish God was invisible and transcendent and had a name signifying abstract being. It may be fruitful to consider the possibility that Gnosticism, partly at least, represents a hostile reaction to Alexandrian Jewish theology; a repudiation of the audacious attempt of Jews to annex the God of Plato and Aristotle.

The Gnostic method of repudiation was to deny the identification of the Jewish God with supreme reality, and to assert instead that the Jewish God was to be identified with a lower deity, the Demiurge, a figure who performs a role in a complicated cosmological and mythological system explaining how the lower forms of existence evolved out of the higher. This is not to say that the Gnostic mythology was an *ad hoc* theory concocted to combat Judaism. On the contrary, the whole Gnostic mythology already existed, and the strategy used was simply to find a place in this mythology for the Jewish God; a strategy strictly parallel to that used by the polytheists, when they identified the Jewish God as, say, Saturn. Indeed, one of the strongest objections to the theory that Gnosticism arose out of Judaism is the sheer complexity of the Gnostic myth, which shows a development independent of Judaism. It is quite incredible that this mythology with all its ramifications could have come into being simply through the need for some disillusioned individuals to create an alternative to Judaism, especially as some of its most essential elements, such as the fall and redemption of the female divinity, have no parallel in early Jewish mysticism (though they did finally enter mediaeval Jewish mysticism, probably through the influence of Cathar Gnosticism).[21]

Again, this is not to say that Gnosticism is a very old religious phenomenon; it seems to have arisen no earlier than the first century BCE, and perhaps only in the first century CE, as an acosmic and salvationist version of the pleroma philosophy that stemmed from Plato. The same pleroma philosophy inspired apocalyptic and rabbinic mysticism, though in forms very different from Gnosticism, and not sharing its mythology. A transition from Judaism straight into Gnosticism thus appears far too abrupt and unlikely. Far more likely is that Gnosticism (or rather, the biblically-inspired versions of Gnosticism) functioned as a *rival* to Judaism, and as a counter to the Jewish attempt to appropriate the Hellenistic supreme deity as identical with the God of Judaism.

Here it is necessary to insist that not all Gnosticism was biblical. There are two extremist schools of scholarship in the field of Gnosticism. One school refuses to accept that any form of Gnosticism preceded, or was independent of, the advent of Christianity, and thus denies that there was any significant encounter between Gnosticism and Judaism in isolation from Christianity. The other school is so insistent on the Jewish provenance of Gnosticism that it refuses to accept the existence of forms of pre-Christian Gnosticism that were independent of Judaism. Both schools become involved in unconvincing exegesis of documents that are awkward for their respective theses: one school reading a Christian meaning into documents that have no (or superficial) Christian reference, the other reading a Jewish meaning into documents that appear to be neither Jewish nor Christian. A view that escapes these extremisms is that there was *one* form of Gnosticism that represents an encounter between Gnosticism and Judaism, without the intervention of Christianity. Other forms of Gnosticism were Gnosticism pure and simple, an entirely Hellenistic phenomenon, and, of course Christian Gnosticism, the kind of which we have the most numerous examples.

We may now return to our question about the identity of the biblical Gnostics and put the question rather differently. What kind of people were attracted to the Gnostic viewpoint, but felt that they had to express it, partly at least, in terms derived from the Jewish Bible? What kind of people wished to reduce the pretensions of Judaism, but could do so only by engaging fully in the Jewish sacred writings which they found it imperative to reinterpret, rather than to ignore?

The most likely place to find our quarry is in the penumbra surrounding Judaism, consisting of people on their way in or on their way out.[22] These are basically Gentiles who are attracted by Judaism enough to study it or to seek acquaintance with knowledgable Jews. Some pursue their study far enough to become actually converted to Judaism, but find Jewish observance too strenuous or too alien, and lapse. Others only reach the status of 'God-fearers', attend the synagogues in this capacity, but eventually become resentful of the inferior status accorded them. Others never actually declare or renounce allegiance to Judaism, but, having become the targets of Jewish missionary activity, acquire a considerable smattering of Jewish knowledge, and feel constrained to formulate some attitude towards Judaism. Such marginal people develop ambivalent feelings towards Judaism. On the one hand, they feel it to be a force to be reckoned with; on the other hand, they feel a certain resentment at the impudence of this barbarian faith in professing to be superior to the spiritual claims of Hellenistic culture; or, if they have gone so far as to succumb to Judaism for a while, they feel a corresponding need, after lapsing from Judaism, to justify their reversal of attitude and to reassert the superiority of the Hellenism from which they had temporarily defected. The most likely place to find such people in numbers sufficient to give rise to a distinctive religious grouping is Alexandria, where Jewish missionary activity was confident and even sometimes aggressive. The unease at such activity and the need to fight susceptibility to it, or to justify withdrawal from it after initial acceptance, could lead to a religious movement that contrasted the superior spiritual quality of Hellenism with the materiality and this-worldly stance of Judaism, while at the same time accounting for Judaism and explaining its proper place in the scheme of things.

Thus biblical Gnosticism (a more accurate term, it may be suggested, than 'Jewish Gnosticism') should be considered in relation to other hostile Alexandrian reactions to Judaism employing some knowledge of the Jewish Bible. Thus the Alexandrian writers criticized by Josephus in *Against Apion*, i.e. Manetho, Chaeremon, Lysimachus and Apion himself, clearly had some acquaintance with the biblical story of Moses and the Exodus, though not such detailed knowledge as is shown by the Gnostic writers of early Genesis. Knowledge of the Bible clearly does not prove the Jewish origin of the knowers, since such knowledge is a requisite too for enemies of the Jews if only to act as a basis for misrepresentation. Even knowledge of haggadic traditions does not mean that the knowers were of Jewish origin, since such knowledge could easily be picked up in the course of conversation with Jews, or by attending Jewish ser-

mons, as many non-Jews did. An interesting later parallel is the
case of Muhammad, who shows, in the Koran, a preoccupation
with the Jewish scriptures and a rather garbled knowledge of
haggadic traditions very reminiscent of the Gnostics. The arguments used by some scholars to prove the Jewish origin of the
Gnostics could be used just as well to prove the Jewish origin of
Muhammad. Muhammad seems to have been on the margins of
Judaism in his early life, when he learnt much from Jewish
merchants and missionaries. He reacted eventually by develop-
ing his own religion, based mainly on Judaism, and partly on
Christianity. He thus avoided the indignity of succumbing to
Judaism and abandoning his own Arabian cultural history,
which he elevated to a dignified role as a background to his new
religion. His rejection of Judaism was far less radical than that
of the Gnostics. Yet the resultant style of antisemitism also
shows some interesting parallels to that of the Gnostics (see
below).

We may now turn to the question of priority. In the light of
the above analysis of the level of Gnostic antisemitism and the
type of marginality shown by Gnosticism, what light has been
thrown on the question, 'Which came first, Gnosticism or
Christianity?' While a full answer to this question must await
the investigation of Christian antisemitism in forthcoming chapters, it may be said at once that the relationship of Gnosticism
to Judaism is so much more central and vital than its relationship to Christianity that it seems clear that Gnosticism in its
basic and original form was the result of an encounter with
Judaism, not of an encounter with Christianity. The Gnostic
myth as it developed in the biblical Gnostic sects was chiefly
concerned with the early chapters of Genesis not with the New
Testament. Even in the Christian Gnostic writings, the figure of
Jesus does not appear integrally, but is grafted on to the figure
of the Gnostic Redeemer in a way that denies the basic Christian belief about Jesus, that his death was an atoning one for all
mankind. The Gnostics deny that Jesus died an atoning death,
or even that he died at all. It is hard to see how this attitude
could have arisen out of Christianity, but easy to see how it
could have arisen as an adaptation of a previously-existing
Gnostic scheme to the advent of Christianity.

Similarly, Gnostic antisemitism is hard, if not impossible, to derive from Christian antisemitism. It is only in the latest of the Christian Gnostic writings that we can see any personal attack on the Jews as the opponents of the Saviour or as a nation dedicated to evil. In all the earlier Gnostic writings, the Jews are portrayed as deluded, rather pitiable figures, enslaved to the Demiurge and unable to understand true freedom or spirituality. This attitude of contempt, rather than hatred, arises from the fact that the Jews, in the Gnostic myth, never accomplish anything evil because they are always easily frustrated by the superior power of the Gnostics. This attitude derives from the Gnostic view of the Demiurge, who figures so much more prominently in their imagination than the Jews. The Demiurge is always plotting evil, but never succeeds. Since the true Gnostic exists on the spiritual plane, he is immune to physical attack. In Christianity, on the other hand, physical damage is recognized as a true evil, especially in its supreme instance, the crucifixion of Jesus; the opponents of Jesus are therefore regarded with horror and hatred, not contempt. Here again, the tone of Gnostic antisemitism is much closer to Islamic than to Christian antisemitism. While Muhammad is represented as being opposed by the Jewish tribes of Arabia, he invariably wins all battles against them, unlike Jesus who, in the Christian myth, suffers horribly at the hands of the Jews.[23] In keeping with this attitude, Islam, though very far from being a Gnostic religion, took over the Gnostic version of the crucifixion, by which not Jesus, but a substitute, suffered, while Jesus was wafted away. The milder antisemitism of contempt always characterized Islam until very recent times, when the shock of military defeat by a people traditionally and even doctrinally regarded as unmilitary turned contempt into hatred. The transition from contempt to hatred is understandable, especially when the despised persons prove more effectual than was thought possible; a transition from hatred to contempt is much less conceivable. Consequently, it is difficult to accept that Gnostic antisemitism was an outgrowth of Christian antisemitism. Rather it was the result of an independent encounter with Judaism, which took on a Christian colouring only at a later stage.

All our enquiries, then, lead to the conclusion that Gnosticism existed either before the advent of Christianity, or simultaneously with it, and, in either case, independently of it. But this opens the possibility that the influence actually went the other way; that it was Christianity, and in particular, Pauline Christianity, that was influenced by Gnosticism.

2

Paul and Gnosticism

We have seen that Gnosticism sets the stage for cosmic antisemitism by giving the Jews the role of acolytes of the Demiurge. This is
a most important step in the history of antisemitism, for it moves
beyond mere vilification of the Jews, as found in the accusations of
Hellenistic antisemites such as Manetho or Apion, and gives the
Jews a key role in the cosmic drama of good and evil. Yet Gnostic
antisemitism remains somewhat mild, since for the Gnostics, the
chief drama does not take place on earth but in the heavens, and
therefore the Jews, as mere earthly representatives of the Demiurge, have, after all, a very insignificant role. Nothing of any real
importance takes place on earth, and the Gnostics themselves,
once they have achieved enlightenment, become utterly superior
to earthly vicissitudes and achieve a cosmic status that is actually
divine – and even super-divine, for they become superior to the
Demiurge, who is a kind of deity. Thus the actions of the Jews,
even if they should manage to do some harm to the unimportant
physical shell or body of a Gnostic, would not merit great
indignation, but rather amused contempt.

Further, even the Demiurge himself is not a figure of unequivocal evil, for he too is often treated with contempt rather than
loathing. He is regarded as an inferior deity, who has his own
sphere of authority and his own powers. Sometimes he is regarded
with considerable tolerance, as the appropriate deity for limited
human beings (psychics) who are constitutionally incapable of
reaching pneumatic status. This toleration of the Demiurge and

his followers reaches its apex in Valentinianism, though it is
doubtful whether, as some scholars argue, this means that
Valentinianism is a form of Gnosticism that is not acosmic. At any
rate, in all forms of Gnosticism, the Demiurge is an equivocal
figure, ranging from being the chief cause of cosmic evil (the Devil)
to being the god of the limited. Consequently, the Jews too have
the same range of evaluation, and are sometimes regarded not as
evil but only as irredeemably mediocre.

Yet undoubtedly the dualism of Gnosticism and its location of
the Jews in the camp of evil is the beginning of a sinister
development in the history of antisemitism. Mere dislike of the
Jews, or resentment of their religious pretensions, could lead to
some vicious antisemitic attacks by authors writing in Greek and
Latin; but once the idea appeared, as it did for the first time in
Gnosticism, that the Jews were the representatives of the wrong
side in a war of cosmic scale, the way was opened to the
diabolization of the Jews and to schemes for their suppression or
elimination. If the Gnostic dualistic scheme were to be taken over
by some group who placed a higher valuation than the Gnostics on
events taking place in this world, the Gnostic disdain could easily
be transformed into a bitter enmity fraught with drastic consequences.

This is precisely what happened in Christianity. In the fully-
developed scheme of Christian antisemitism, as found in the
church Fathers and in mediaeval passion-plays, the Jews are the
people of the Devil, who malevolently brought about the death of
the Saviour, and continually seek to frustrate the purposes of God
and of his church. We are concerned here, however, not with the
full development of this scenario in later times, or even in the
Gospels, but with its earliest adumbration in the writings of Paul.

At first sight, there seem to be fundamental differences between
Paul's religious scheme and that of Gnosticism. Paul accepts that
the Creator of this world was the highest God, not an inferior
deity, as in Gnosticism. Paul accepts too that the Torah and the
writings of the Prophets came from the high God. Yet these
acceptations are both qualified to such an extent that it may be
useful to consider Paul's views as a kind of moderate Gnosticism,
modified in such a way as to avoid direct confrontation with
Judaism, but instead to incorporate it as a necessary step towards

the final truth. And yet this very watering-down of the basic concepts of Gnosticism results in a sharpening of the antisemitism that is built into the Gnostic fabric. It is possible to consider Paul's views in this way because of the evidence that has been accumulating that in Paul's time Gnosticism already existed, having begun as an encounter with Judaism, not with Christianity. The fact that Paul was at times in conflict with certain types of Gnosticism does not prove that the label of 'Gnostic' is entirely unapplicable to Paul himself, or that he was unaffected by Gnostic influences. There were many differences of opinion, and at times sharp altercations, between the various Gnostic groupings, despite their sharing of basic concepts.

God and Satan

We may begin by considering Paul's views on God and Satan. The usual scholarly procedure is to regard these as chiefly akin to Jewish doctrines or attitudes found in the apocalyptic writings and in the Qumran literature. But Paul's doctrine of the role of Satan departs so radically from that of any Jewish tradition, however sectarian, that it is more to the point to consider the relationship between Paul and Gnosticism in this area.

A key passage is II Cor. 4.4: 'In their case the god of this world (or age) has blinded the minds of the unbelievers, to keep them from seeing the light of the gospel of the glory of Christ, who is the likeness of God.' As Bultmann says, 'It is Gnostic language when Satan is called "The god of this world".'[1] The expression *ho theos tou aionos toutou* is typically Gnostic, but it has been transferred from the Demiurge to Satan. To call Satan a 'god' is extraordinarily bold language for someone allegedly brought up in Judaism, even though the evil god has been demoted from his usual position in Gnosticism as Creator and represented instead as the usurping ruler of this world who has his appointed 'age' until the time comes for the high God to resume sway over his creation. No such expression for Satan is to be found in the apocalyptic or Qumran literature, nor, of course, in the rabbinic literature. It may be argued that Paul is not really calling Satan a 'god', but saying that he is regarded as a god by the benighted people of this 'age'. But this explanation cannot be reconciled with the context. Paul is

saying that the Jews, who are the object of his attack, show their
blindness by their adherence to the Law and failure to recognize
Christ. This blindness is caused by Satan. But Paul is not saying
that the Jews actually worship Satan. This would be the full
Gnostic position which Paul repudiates. The Law to which the
Jews cling was not given by Satan, but by God, but only for a time,
and it is Satan who works on the Jews to prevent them from
acknowledging the temporary nature of this God-given Law. Thus
it is Paul, not the Jews, who designates Satan as a 'god'.

MacRae argues that, on the contrary, this passage shows Paul's
fundamental opposition to Gnosticism, because, having incauti-
ously described Satan as a 'god', he then realizes the possible
misunderstanding to which this may give rise, and quashes the
Gnostic notion of a Demiurge by referring in verse 6 to the 'God
who said, "Let light shine out of darkness".' This, by its evocation
of Genesis 1.3, reaffirms the Jewish doctrine that the God of
Creation was not an inferior god, or Demiurge, but God himself.[2]
It seems inadequate, however, to say, as MacRae puts it, that Paul
'sees the danger of his own language', and then corrects it. Paul,
writing to people recently converted from polytheism, would
surely have taken all pains to avoid polytheistic language if he had
not been convinced that Satan was indeed a kind of god whose role
in the cosmos was far greater than that accorded to him in Jewish
tradition.

Indeed, Paul's picture of the cosmic role of Satan is fundamentally different from that found even in the most dualistic of Jewish
writings, i.e. the Pseudepigrapha and the Qumran writings. In
addition to the passage quoted above, describing Satan as a 'god'
(which taken on its own might be regarded, even if somewhat
implausibly, as a momentary lapse), there are other important
passages in Paul's writings which show that Paul's view of Satan
was far more akin to the Gnostic view of the Demiurge. An
important passage is the following:

> Put on all the armour which God provides, so that you may be
> able to stand firm against the devices of the devil. For our fight is
> not against human foes, but against cosmic powers, against the
> authorities and potentates of this dark world, against the
> superhuman forces of evil in the heavens (I Cor. 6. 11-12).

In another important passage, Paul refers to Satan as 'the commander of the spiritual powers of the air' (Ephesians 2.2). These and similar passages in Paul's writings and in those of his disciples (e.g. Rom. 8.38; I Cor. 15.24; I John 5.19; Col. 2.15) show that the Pauline view of Satan went far beyond that of the Jewish dualistic writings. Instead of regarding Satan as, at most, a fallen, renegade angel, working surreptitiously against the purposes of God in a world which, on the whole, was under God's domination, Paul regarded Satan as the ruler of this world and of the regions of the heavens contiguous to the earth. Though God would eventually recapture the territory occupied by Satan and his hosts, He had allowed, for his mysterious purposes, the whole region of earth and its environs to be taken over by the forces of Satan, so that the saints were in the position of a secret resistance movement in occupied territory, working against the mighty occupying power and awaiting the moment of liberation from the outside.

The Torah

Further important similarities may be noted between Paul's attitude towards the Torah and that of the Gnostics. The difference, of course, is that Paul accepted that the Torah was given by God, while the Gnostics denied this, alleging that it was given by the Demiurge, who only deceived himself and others into thinking that he was God. Nevertheless, there is a strong structural and verbal correspondence between Paul's concept of the Torah as a limited, partial revelation and the Gnostic concept of the Torah as having only limited authority.

1. *The Torah given by angels*

Paul actually goes some way towards limiting even the authority of the Torah by saying that it was given not by God but by angels (Gal. 3.19, echoed in Acts 7.53 and Heb. 2.2). This does not go so far as Gnosticism, for angels act under the authority of God, not against it; yet this does distance God from the Torah in a way that is contrary to all Jewish thinking. There have been many attempts by scholars, however, to show that this distancing is not un-Jewish, and that parallels can be found in intertestamental or rabbinic thinking. We may take as an example the treatment of this subject by W.D. Davies.[3]

Davies first argues that the reliance of previous scholars on Josephus *Ant.* 15.136 is incorrect, since Josephus may be speaking here not about angels but about human intermediaries, i.e. Moses and other prophets. This destroys a great stand-by of scholars seeking to prove that it was a Jewish commonplace in the first century that the Torah was given by angels. I would only disagree here with Davies' caution in saying that the argument based on this passage of Josephus *may* be incorrect; Davies' own arguments show it to be definitely wrong.

Davies, however, goes on to say that there is a 'well-attested' Jewish tradition about the giving of the Torah by angels, but that this was not intended to diminish the importance of the Torah but, on the contrary, to enhance it. Only in Gal. 3.19 and Heb. 2.2 'does this mediation imply any inferiority and is therefore associated with the notion that it (the Torah) was to change, and this is a specifically Christian development.' In Acts 7.53 and 58, Davies argues, the mediation of the angels still has its traditional Jewish implication of privilege rather than inferiority.

It is necessary here to define the word 'give' in the expression 'to give the Torah'. If it means merely 'to take some part in the handing over of the Torah to the Israelites', then there are certainly Jewish traditions that the angels took some part in this (e.g. Canticles Rabbah I.2). But if it means 'to compose and promulgate the Torah', there is no Jewish tradition that comes even remotely near this concept. In Jewish tradition, it is always God who is the sole author of the Torah.

What Paul is saying in Gal. 3.19, however, is that the angels, not God, were the authors of the Torah. The expression he uses is *diatageis di'angelon*. The word *diatageis* means 'ordained' or 'commanded', not 'transmitted'.[4] It implies unequivocally the authorship of the angels.

Only if the angels are conceived to be the authors and commanders of the Torah does their participation convey a sense of inferiority in the Torah itself, as not proceeding directly from God. If, however, God himself ordained and composed the Torah, then the participation of angels in the role of conveyors of God's message to the individual Israelites does not in the least diminish the authority of the Torah, but only adds to the glory and splendour of the occasion when it was transmitted. This is the only role assigned to angels in the rabbinic traditions about Sinai.

There is thus great confusion in Davies' account of the matter. He notes (like Kittel) that in the Jewish traditions the participation of angels actually adds to the authority of the Torah rather than diminishing it, but he fails to realize that this is because the angels are firmly excluded from the role of authors. In Acts 7.53 (and also Acts 7.38), the angels take the role of ordainers, not transmitters, and so we must conclude that in this passage too (contrary to Davies' opinion), the intention is to allot the Torah an inferior status. It is true that this is not the main point of Stephen's alleged speech (which is to denounce the disobedience of the Jews to the Torah). But it is an incidental hint that this Torah was valid only for a time, and that the time has now come when disobedience to it has become a virtue instead of a sin. There can be little doubt that Acts 7.53 has been directly influenced by Paul's statement in Gal. 3.19, since there is the verbal similarity of *diatagas* corresponding to Paul's *diatageis*.

In Acts 7.38, however, a different expression is used. Here it is said not that angels ordained the Torah, but that an angel 'spoke' to Moses on Mount Sinai. A similar expression is found in Hebrews 2.2, where the same verb *laleo* is used, this time of angels in the plural. This is rather different from the concept of the angels as authors of the Torah; here the voice that spoke from Sinai becomes an angel's voice, instead of that of God. This is a daring concept, since it emends the plain text of the Bible which insists on the voice of Sinai as the voice of God himself (Deut. 4.12; 4.36). It shows the lengths to which Pauline Christians were prepared to go to deny the divine authority of the Torah. This rare instance of emendation of scripture by Christian authors reminds us of the emendations more frequently employed by Gnostics, and later by Muslims. Christians had far more to lose by emending the Hebrew scripture, since they depended on it (suitably re-interpreted) for their own authority. We can therefore judge by this uncharacteristic emendation how important it was for Christians to deny full authority to the Torah.

It goes without saying that no rabbinical writing shows the slightest doubt that it was God himself who spoke on Mount Sinai, any more than that it was God himself who was the author of the

Torah. The claim that there is a 'well-attested Jewish tradition that the Law was given by angels' rests on mere confusion of thought. The biggest role given to angels in the matter was that of carrying the words spoken by God on Mount Sinai to the ears of individual Israelites; some rabbis refused to allow even this role to the angels.[5]

Having cleared away the misconceptions discussed above, we can now turn back to Paul's words in Galatians with a fuller sense of their daringness and newness. Paul is saying, contrary to all Jewish thought, that the Torah was composed by angels, not by God. The only parallel to this is to be found, not in any Jewish source, but in the Gnostic writings. Later writers, in Acts 7.38 and Hebrews 2.2, drew the logical conclusion that it was an angel, not God, who spoke on Mount Sinai; for if the Torah was composed by angels, they could hardly have used God as their announcer. Paul himself, however, did not go so far as to draw this conclusion, which directly contradicts scripture.

The likeness of Paul's doctrine to the Gnostic teaching that the Torah was composed by the Demiurge is not, of course, a complete identity, for the Demiurge is not exactly an angel. He acts not as an emissary of the High God, but in ignorance of him, sometimes even in defiance of him. If the Torah was composed by angels, this gives it validity of a kind, for angels act in accordance with the will of God. Thus Paul's doctrine that the Torah was composed by angels gives it just the status that he wants for it: a limited validity which lasts only for a period. In some of the Gnostic writings, the Torah has no validity, even for a period; yet there were Gnostics who were prepared to grant the Torah a limited validity that was not even restricted in time. This was the view that the Torah was intended for those who could never achieve the status of pneumatics. This latter Gnostic view was more tolerant, in a way, than Paul's view, which declared that after the coming of Christ, the validity of the Torah ended completely. Thus, though there are differences in detail between Paul's view and that of the Gnostics (who in fact differed amongst themselves), the structural similarity is very great. Paul's strictures against honouring the Torah *after* the coming of Christ are just as severe as those of the most anti-Torah Gnostics, and in general he gives the same definition of the Torah as limited and issuing from a limited authority.

The above discussion allows us to understand a difficult passage that has often been interpreted to express opposition to the Gnostics, whereas it actually confirms a debt to Gnosticism. This is the passage in Colossians referring to an alleged 'heresy' (Col. 2.16-19; whether Colossians was written by Paul or by one of his disciples is here immaterial). The passage runs:

> 16. Allow no one therefore to take you to task about what you eat or drink, or over the observance of festival, new moon or sabbath. 17. These are no more than a shadow of what was to come; the solid reality is Christ's. 18. You are not to be disqualified by the decision of people who go in for self-mortification and angel-worship, and try to enter into some vision of their own. 19. Such people, bursting with the futile conceit of worldly minds, lose hold upon the Head . . .

Much discussion has been devoted to the question of who exactly are the people criticized here. According to a typical view, they formed 'one of the strangest of syncretistic cults. It seems to have been compounded of pagan philosophy, angel-worship and rigorous Judaism. Like the mystery cults, it professed an inner secret knowledge, and, like them, it upheld various forms of asceticism. But it also placed in the forefront of its creed an exact observance of the Jewish ceremonial Law, with all its rules for circumcision, sabbath-keeping and festivals.'[6] It is agreed by most commentators that this strange sect was a variety of Gnosticism, and therefore the above passage is often quoted to show that Paul's views and those of Gnosticism were poles apart.

It makes much more sense, however, to interpret the passage as referring not to some strange syncretistic cult, but to the Jerusalem church. The features of the above passage that have been interpreted as a bizarre form of worship simply refer to the continued practice of Judaism viewed in a pejorative light. Thus the accusation of 'angel-worship' should be understood in the light of Paul's doctrine that the Torah was composed by angels. Thus the Jerusalem church, by continuing to practise Jewish rituals even after the coming of Christ, were failing to recognize the temporary nature of the Torah. They were giving the kind of honour or worship to angels and their production, the Torah, that ought to be reserved for God and for Christ, both of whom had cancelled the temporary validity of the angel-derived Torah. Thus so far from the mention of 'angel-worship' showing opposition to a form of Gnosticism, it is evidence that that the writer of the above passage took a Gnostic, or near-Gnostic, attitude towards the Torah as having been composed by angels. What has prevented recognition of this simple explanation is the totally incorrect assumption that there is nothing un-Jewish about the claim that the Torah was composed by angels.

There is thus nothing puzzling about the fact that the criticized group were devout practisers of Judaism. This is just what the members of the Jerusalem church were, and it was this that brought Paul into conflict with them (Gal. 2.11-14; Acts 15.1-2; 21.18-21). As for the 'self-mortification' practised by the criticized group, this does not refer to any outlandish Gnostic practices, but is simply a pejorative way of talking about the normal Jewish practice of refraining from eating certain foods, an abstention which, in Paul's view, was a needless asceticism. The next phrase is translated by NEB as ' . . . and try to enter into some vision of their own' and by AV as ' . . . intruding into those things which he hath not seen'. The earliest reading is *ha heoraken embateuon*; both the foregoing translations adopt the later reading in which the word *me* ('not') is inserted in the text. The earlier reading, however, is preferable, the simple meaning being, ' . . . adhering to things that he has seen', i.e. failing to appreciate the unseen, spiritual things. This reading, unlike the later reading, fits well with the ensuing words ' . . . bursting with the futile conceit of worldly minds'. In other words, the criticism is not that the group has some false 'vision', but that it has no vision at all. This is the familiar criticism against Judaism, as voiced by the Gnostics, that it is a religion of this humdrum, earthy world and has no apprehension of the spiritual world.

Thus the accepted picture of the author of Colossians, as battling against some Gnostic sect, falls to pieces on examination. He was battling with the Judaizing Nazarenes of the Jerusalem church, and his criticisms tally closely with the kind of criticisms urged against Judaism by the typical Gnostic. Whether Colossians was written by Paul himself or by a disciple, its alignment is with the Gnostics, not against them.

A somewhat similar controversy has surrounded a passage

undoubtedly written by Paul, his attack on Judaizing opponents in Gal. 4.9-10. Here too some scholars have seen evidence of a syncretistic Jewish-Gnostic sect, because this group is associated by Paul with worship of the 'elements' (*stoicheia*). Most scholars, however, have recognized that the context as a whole necessitates the interpretation that Paul is opposing Judaizing Christians of the Jerusalem church. This means that Paul regards obedience to the Torah as a worship of inferior powers. Indeed, in Gal. 4.3, Paul says distinctly that before the coming of Christ, 'we' (by whom he clearly means the Jews, i.e. those 'under the law', v.5) were 'in bondage under the elements of the world'. This is pure Gnostic language. Indeed, Paul seems to go even further, and to identify the angels who gave the Torah with the pagan gods previously worshipped by his correspondents. He hints this by reproving his correpondents for 'turning back' (*epistrephete*) to the 'elements' when they succumb to persuasion to observe the Torah. Thus again this passage, far from showing Paul in controversy with Gnostics (the minority opinion), shows him arguing against Judaism in typical Gnostic fashion by ascribing the authorship of the Torah to inferior powers.

Indeed, in the heat of controversy, Paul here oversteps his usual mark and fails to allot his usual degree of authority to the Torah. Angels are after all, in Paul's usual thinking, not gods, but servants of God. But Paul, angry about the Judaizing defection of some of his followers, falls back into a kind of Gnostic antisemitism that is hardly distinguishable from that of the regular Gnostic writings. His very language ('bondage under the elements of the world' and 'weak and beggarly elements to whom you desire again to be in bondage') could have come straight out of a Gnostic treatise. His animus against Judaism is especially strong in his treatment of circumcision, the sign of the Abrahamic Covenant. He equates this, in a way typical of Hellenistic and Roman antisemitism, with mutilation (5.12). This brutal passage is usually bowdlerized in translation. It should be translated, 'I wish they would have their penises chopped off completely' (rather than AV, 'I wish they were even cut off' or NEB, 'They had better go the whole way and make eunuchs of themselves').

In the context of discussion of Paul's relationship to Gnostic, or allegedly Gnostic, movements, it remains to discuss his opponents in I Cor. 6.12-20. As has often been pointed out, there is a similarity between these libertarians and such Gnostic cults as the Carpocratians, who argued that since they had been released from sin by Christ, they were at liberty to do anything. Here, indeed, Paul may well be in opposition to Gnostics or gnosticizers. But it would be a mistake to conclude from this that Paul himself cannot be characterized as a Gnostic or gnosticizer. The extreme libertarian Gnostic groups were opposed by the more moderate Gnostics, such as the Valentinians. It was a perennial problem for Gnosticism, as for all antinomian sects, to explain why a moral code was still required. This puzzling problem faces Paul in I Corinthians, and the very fact that it is a problem for him places him among the Gnostics. Thus the fact that he does occasionally have Gnostic opponents certainly does not prove that his own viewpoint was anti-Gnostic.

Paul's attitude towards the Torah (except in his more impatient moods) was that it had a limited and temporary validity, leading up to the fuller revelation of Christ. Even after the advent of Christ, Paul was willing to concede that Jewish-Christians might, if they so wished, continue to observe the precepts of the Torah, though he regarded such observance as not making any contribution to salvation. But he angrily opposed the notion that Gentile converts to Christianity should adopt the Torah; this he regarded as a betrayal of the principle that the crucifixion of Jesus was sufficient to produce salvation. Even Jewish-Christians who regarded their observance of the Torah as salvific, rather than a matter of custom, were, in Paul's view betraying the basic Christian principle. He evidently thought that eventually the empty observance of the Torah by Jewish-Christians would die out and his compromise would then become unnecessary.[7] It was thus a correct interpretation of Paul's attitude when the later church banned Jewish observances altogether for Christians, including those of Jewish origin: Paul's compromise had never been intended to be permanent.

Paul's attitude to the Torah may thus be characterized as a moderate Gnosticism, of a kind that can be roughly paralleled in those Gnostic writings that regarded the Demiurge as a limited rather than an evil deity.

It should be noted however that Paul's attitude to the Torah varied within certain limits. Sometimes he takes a hostile view towards it that is hardly different from that of the Gnostic writings, as in the passage from Galatians just discussed. Occasionally, however, at the other extreme, he regards the Torah as a code of ideal conduct that cannot be faulted, except that it is impossible for the individual to live up to it except by rebirth through Christ. In this mood, he sees the Torah not as an imperfect code, but as so perfect that it convinces us, by its impossibility, of our need for salvation (Rom. 7.7).[8] How can we reconcile Paul's scorn for certain aspects of the Torah (e.g. the law of circumcision, and the calendar of festivals) with his respect for it as a daunting demand for an impossible virtue? The later church reconciled this contradiction by distinguishing two aspects of the Torah, the moral and the ceremonial, the former eternal and the latter temporary or symbolic. This distinction certainly seems to fit Paul's pattern of dismissal and retention. But Paul himself nowhere makes this distinction. The moral aspect of the Torah seems to him usually to be a natural system of ethics that will be observed as a matter of course by those who are saved. The ceremonial aspects are seen as the badges of adherence to the Torah rather than to Christ, and are rejected as such. Here as in so much else, Paul lacks systematic thought, and works out a policy in reaction to circumstances. But his general attitude towards the Torah is that it has been rendered obsolete by the advent of Christ, and his scheme of explanation of this is broadly Gnostic; i.e. that the Torah emanates from inferior authority and its adherents lack true spirituality, being in thrall to inferior powers.

2. The interpretation of the Torah

Those Gnostics who based their doctrine on the Bible (i.e. those characterized in Chapter 1 as 'biblical Gnostics'), did so by a radical reinterpretation of the Bible, by which normal Jewish interpretations were subverted. Thus, for example, the overthrow of Sodom and Gomorrah, instead of being understood as a punishment by the Most High God for heinous sin, was interpreted as an act of tyranny by the Demiurge. Most notably, the line of authority in the Bible was changed. Those who appear to be the heroes of the biblical story, such as Abraham, Moses, Joshua, Samuel, David or Solomon, are declared to be inferior personages, and another line of heroes is unveiled, such as Seth, Enoch, Melchizedek and many unnamed persons, all characterized by their non-Jewishness and lack of relation to the Jewish religious tradition.

The Gnostics, however, regard the Bible as a flawed record, emanating from the Demiurge, and do not hesitate to amend it when they feel this necessary. They do not explain how it is that this flawed record is the basis of their doctrine, or why the Demiurge included so much material in the Bible that was useful to Gnosticism. They treat the Bible in a way somewhat similar to that of modern scientific biblical critics: as a valuable historical record in which the bias of the author has to be discounted. Another analogue can be found in the Q'uran, in which the Hebrew Bible is used as a source, but as requiring emendation in the light of the superior inspiration of Muhammad. The difference is that Muhammad regarded the Bible as having been altered by corrupt Jewish editors, while the Gnostics regarded it as corrupt at source.

Paul's reinterpretation of the Hebrew Bible is just as radical, but, despite his claim that it derives from angels not directly from God, he regards it as a totally inspired work which he is not at liberty to alter in any way. His strategy is different from that of the Gnostic writings, but while more reverent to the Hebrew Bible, his strategy is even more subversive of the Jewish tradition. For he takes over all the main Jewish figures of authority (dismissed by the Gnostic writers as inferior) and recruits them as supporters of his own reinterpretation. This leaves the Jews as misinterpreters of their own holy writings, and their dislodgment from the position of the people of God is even more complete than in regular Gnosticism.

Yet there are also some passages in which Paul's strategy is closer to that of the Gnostics. As an example, we may take his use of a contrasted pair in the biblical narrative, Hagar and Sarah (Gal. 4.21-31).[9] This technique of expressing the alleged rejection of the Jews by identifying them with the inferior figure in a contrasted biblical pair was further extended by the church Fathers Maximinus, Tertullian, Augustine and Chrysostom in their writings against the Jews, in which, for example, the Jews were identified with Cain and the Christian church with Abel.

Tell me now, you who are so anxious to be under law, will you not listen to what the Law says? It is written there that Abraham had two sons, one by his slave and the other by his free-born wife. The

slave-woman's son was born in the course of nature, the free
woman's through God's promise. This is an allegory. The two
women stand for two covenants. The one bearing children into
slavery is the covenant that comes from Mount Sinai: that is
Hagar. Sinai is a mountain in Arabia and it represents the
Jerusalem of today, for she and her children are in slavery. But
the heavenly Jerusalem is the free woman; she is our mother (Gal.
4.21-27).

This passage has much of the tone of the Gnostic writings, since it
characterizes the Torah as a law of slavery, as opposed to the Jewish
tradition which regarded the Torah as a law of freedom, marking
the evolution of the Israelites from slavery in Egypt to the status of a
free people. As in the Gnostic writings, there is a reinterpretation of
the Bible that Jews would regard as perverse. For nothing is clearer
in the Bible than that Sarah, not Hagar, is the physical and spiritual
mother of Israelite nationhood and religion. The biblical narrative,
explaining the election of the Israelites, shows how unelected
branches of the human and Semite family are hived off into their
own separate nationhoods: out of all Abraham's numerous progeny, only Isaac is chosen, while Ishmael, the son of Hagar,
becomes the progenitor of the unelected (though not rejected)
Arabs. Similarly, later, Esau becomes the progenitor of the Edom-
ite nation, which consoles him for the loss of the main religious
birthright. Thus, to regard the Jews and the Sinaitic covenant as
stemming from Hagar flies in the face of the biblical narrative in a
way that is reminiscent of Gnostic emendation of the Bible.

    Paul, however, avoids emendation of the Bible by saying that his
interpretation is an 'allegory'. He is not denying that the Jews are
physically descended from Sarah, not Hagar. He is only saying that
the contrast between Sarah and Hagar prefigures the contrast
between the two covenants, that of Sinai and that of Christ. But the
dislodgment is nevertheless tremendous. The revered Matriarch of
the Jewish people is being made alien to them and is attached
instead to the Christian church. The Jews, instead of being central
to the biblical narrative, become associated with its marginal
figures. Sarah becomes a proto-Christian, like all the main figures of
Jewish authority. The covenant of Sinai is declared to be an
Arabian event.

If the 'biblical Gnostics' had been handling the contrasting pair, Sarah and Hagar, they would have done so by elevating the status of Hagar and denying the superiority or election of Sarah. This would have shown their scorn for the conceit of the Demiurge in exaggerating, in his flawed composition, the Hebrew Bible, the importance of his acolyte, Sarah. This, however, would have left the Jews in possession of their own tradition. Paul's technique dispossesses the Jews while preserving the authority of the Hebrew Bible as a source of allegorical truth. Yet we may think that an interpretation that denigrates the Sinai revelation does in fact dislocate and amend the meaning of the Hebrew Bible as much as any Gnostic text.

In another passage, Paul comes even closer to a Gnostic treatment of a biblical figure. This is in his treatment of Abraham in Romans 4. Here Abraham is treated as a pre-Israelite figure, the father of many nations other than Israel, and therefore as the type of the saved Gentile. He points to a way of salvation superior to that of the Torah, since he is the exemplar of 'faith' rather than 'works'. He thus plays a role similar to that of Seth or Enoch in the Gnostic writings; figures who can be detached from the Jewish tradition by reason of their Gentile status, and who carry a *gnosis* that is superior to the limited prescriptions of the Torah. Paul's treatment of Abraham leads on to the even more characteristically Gnostic treatment of the figure of Melchizedek in the pseudo-Pauline Epistle to the Hebrews.

Normally, however, Paul does not treat the Jewish figures of authority as by-passing the Jewish tradition, but as integrally belonging to it, but with an awareness of its limited and temporary validity. Thus Moses (II Cor. 3.13-18), wearing a veil over his face, thereby deliberately withholds the full truth from the Israelites, since the time has not yet come to remove the veil and reveal the glory of Christ.

The allegorical method used by Paul preserves the validity of the Hebrew Bible while rejecting, or declaring no longer relevant, its literal meaning. Thus the crossing of the Red Sea, in Jewish tradition, and in the plain meaning of the Bible, signifies the liberation of the Israelites, their election as the people of God, and their transition to the Promised Land. This meaning, however, is irrelevant to Paul's message of individual salvation. So he interprets the crossing of the Red Sea as an allegory of baptism (I Cor. 10.1-2), an interpretation that destroys the whole political dimension of Judaism as a religion of liberation and this-worldly Utopianism. The question here, however is, 'What is the background of Paul's allegorical method?'

The obvious analogy is with Philo, whose allegorical method, combined with that of Paul, stimulated the vast allegorical activity of Christian literature from Origen onwards. But Philo is always careful to explain that he does not abandon the literal meaning. His allegorical method is intended to uncover a deeper dimension of meaning supplementing and not superseding the plain meaning of the text. But Philo informs us, with indignation, that there were other Jews in Alexandria who used the allegorical method as a means of destroying the authority of the commandments. The philosophical meanings derived from the text were to take the place of the plain meaning and thus cancel the obligation to fulfil the commandments. It is these contemporaries of Philo who should be regarded as the precursors of Paul's allegorical method. We cannot see here the influence of Gnosticism, since the allegorical method is not consistent with the negative Gnostic approach to the Bible. The Gnostic method is either to amend the Bible, declaring its account of events to be wrong, or to re-interpret the words of the Bible to give an unusual but non-allegorical meaning – an example is the interpretation of 'another seed' (Gen. 4.25) to mean 'seed from another, supernatural, race'. Paul's use of allegory, therefore, must be reckoned as part of his programme of radical re-interpretation of the Hebrew Bible combined with retention of its authority. In many ways, this leads to a greater negation of the biblical narrative than that found in the Gnostic writings. For the latter are on the whole accepting the narrative at face value, with some corrections and exegetical innovations; while Paul is rejecting the narrative as such, declaring it to be unimportant to salvation except as allegorically conveying spiritual truths.

Thus, Paul is basically a Gnostic thinker in his view of God, Satan and the Torah, though he has distinctive traits that differentiate him from other Gnostics. It is in his scheme of salvation, however, with its basic theme of the descent of the divine saviour to a fallen world, that the deepest affinities of

Pauline with Gnostic thought can be located. Yet here the sacrificial element in Paul's thinking, aligning him with the mystery cults rather than the Gnostics, produces an amalgam of Gnosticism and mystery religion that is unique. It is therefore best to discuss the theme of salvation in Paul's thought in relation to both Gnosticism and mystery religion simultaneously.

3

Paul and the
Mystery Religions

The question of whether, or how far, Paul was influenced by the mystery religions has been much debated. The History-of-Religions school of scholarship, including Richard Reitzenstein, Wilhelm Bousset and Rudolf Bultmann, were struck by similarities between Paul's doctrine of salvation and that of the mystery religions, and felt constrained to see an influence on Paul from this Hellenistic source. Their view, however, came under attack from many angles. Paul's doctrine, it was argued, despite superficial similarities, differed fundamentally from that of the mystery religions. Further, such elements of similarity that existed could have arisen from influence in the other direction: mystery religions might be influenced by Christianity. It was especially argued that the doctrine of a dying-and-resurrected god could not be proved to have existed in mystery religion until after the advent of Christianity. Another line of argument was that Paul's whole doctrine could be sufficiently explained as deriving from Jewish sources, though it was admitted that the latter might have been influenced by Hellenism. Thus even elements in Paul's thinking that came ultimately from Hellenism did not prove any immediate Hellenistic influence on Paul, and did not cast doubt on his account of himself as coming from a strictly Pharisee background.

We may begin by considering the latter claim. Can Paul's doctrine of salvation be derived from Jewish sources, either by way of direct derivation or of logical development, or is it something entirely new and unprecedented in relation to Judaism? If the latter, we shall have to consider whether Paul's doctrine was entirely his own creation, or whether other, non-Jewish, influences were at work in it. In either case, we shall consider what effect Paul's doctrine of salvation, combined with the Gnostic influences discussed in the last chapter, had on the growth of Christian antisemitism.

Paul's doctrine of salvation may be summarized as follows. Mankind is in the grip of sin and Satan. This thraldom cannot be broken by any moral effort on the part of man, since his moral nature is too weak. Consequently, mankind is doomed to everlasting punishment. God, however, in his mercy, has provided a way of release by sending his divine Son into the world to suffer a cruel death, which atones for mankind's sin. By accepting this death with faith and thankfulness, mankind can mystically share in it and also share in the resurrection and immortality of the Son of God. Those who do not have faith, and persist in thinking that they can escape condemnation by their own moral efforts (guided by the Torah) are doomed to eternal damnation.

The myth contains the following elements: (1) the hopeless moral condition of mankind; (2) the descent of the divine saviour into a human body; (3) the violent death of the divine saviour; (4) the resurrection, immortality and divinity of the crucified Saviour; (5) the vicarious atonement effected by the divine death for those who have faith in its efficacy; (6) the promise of resurrection and immortality to devotees of the Saviour. The question now to be addressed is whether these elements, or any of them, are to be found in the Judaism of Paul's time or before.

1. The hopeless moral condition of mankind

Paul's radically pessimistic view of man's unredeemed moral condition is expressed as follows:

> I discover this principle, then: that when I want to do the right, only the wrong is within my reach. In my inmost self, I delight in the law of God, but I perceive that there is in my bodily members a different law, fighting against the law that my reason approves and making me a prisoner under the law that is in my members, the law of sin. Miserable creature that I am, who is there to rescue me out of this body doomed to death? God

alone, through Jesus Christ our Lord! Thanks be to God! In a word, then, I myself, subject to God's law as a rational being, am yet, in my unspiritual nature, a slave to the law of sin.

The conclusion of the matter is this: there is no condemnation for those who are united with Christ Jesus, because in Christ Jesus the life-giving law of the Spirit has set you free from the law of sin and death. What the law could never do, because our lower nature robbed it of all potency, God has done: by sending his own Son . . . (Rom. 7.14-8.1)

The psychology expounded here is as follows. We are rational beings, but our reason has no active, only a percipient, power. By it we recognize what we ought to do, but are powerless to do it. Our actions are dictated by our bodily constitution, which impels us to sin. We are prisoners in our bodies, helplessly watching what our bodily nature (the 'law' of our bodies) dictates to our actions. The principle of our identity, which lies imprisoned in our bodies, is our spiritual nature (defined and governed by the 'law' of the Spirit), which can only be freed by outside divine intervention. This liberation has come about through the death and resurrection of Jesus Christ, for those who become 'united' with him.[1]

At one time, many scholars claimed to have found this whole conception in rabbinic Judaism. Paul's 'dilemma', it was claimed, was that of the typical Pharisee, desperately trying to fulfil the whole Law, and always aware of his failure, since the omission of even one precept will plunge him into damnation.[2] Recent scholarship, however, has become increasingly aware that this is a caricature of Pharisaism, or at least of the rabbinic Judaism which was used by the earlier scholarship as providing information about Pharisaism too.[3] Rabbinic Judaism has an entirely different psychology, not a hint of which is to be found in Paul's writings. In this, the human psyche contains both a 'good inclination' (*yetzer ha-tob*) and an 'evil inclination' (*yetzer ha-ra'*), and man has the power not only to choose between them, but to transform the energies of the 'evil inclination' into good, with the guidance of the Torah. If a sin is committed, the remedy lies in repentance (a concept never mentioned by Paul, though it figures largely in Jesus' teaching in the Synoptic Gospels). The idea of the impossibility of doing good is directly opposed to the entire spirit of rabbinic Judaism, which, basing itself on Deut. 30.11-14, regards virtue as within the capacity of ordinary people – and accordingly does not pitch its definition of virtue so impossibly high that it becomes beyond the reach of normal humanity (while still allowing for supererogatory aims for a minority). Nor does rabbinic Judaism equate the evil impulse with the body or the 'flesh', or regard the aim of religion as liberation from the body. It regards the body as an inseparable part of the personality, not as its prison, and bodily acts are regarded as the locus of righteousness and liberation from sin.

Since the effort to ground Paul's moral pessimism in rabbinic Judaism failed, new efforts were directed to ground it in pre-rabbinic Judaism. It has been argued that Pharisaism and rabbinic Judaism are by no means the same thing, and that it was a mistake to look for corroboration of Paul's attitudes in the post-Destruction rabbinic movement rather than in pre-Destruction literature such as the Pseudepigrapha and the Qumran literature. Here, it is argued, a moral pessimism and reliance on supernatural help similar to Paul's may be found.

The chief evidence adduced has been that of IV Ezra, particularly as there are grounds for belief that the author of this work, written in the first century, was a Pharisee. Passages such as the following, from IV Ezra, have been held to show a strong similarity to the moral pessimism of Paul in Romans:

> For the first Adam, clothing himself with the evil heart, transgressed and was overcome; and likewise also all who were born of him. Thus the infirmity became inveterate; the Law indeed was in the heart of the people, but with the evil germ; so what was good departed and the evil remained. (IV Ezra 3.21-22)

> For the grain of evil seed was sown in the heart of Adam from the beginning, and how much fruit of ungodliness has it produced unto this time, and shall yet produce until the threshing-floor come! (IV Ezra 4.30-32)

> And I answered and said: This is my first and last word; better had it been that the earth had not produced Adam, or else having produced him, (for thee) to have restrained him from sinning. For how does it profit us all that in the present we must

live in grief and after death look for punishment? O thou Adam, what hast thou done? For though it was thou that sinned, the fall was not thine alone, but ours also who are thy descendants! For how does it profit us that the eternal age is promised to us, whereas we have done the works that bring death? (IV Ezra 7.116-18)

Such passages, it is argued, show the same sense of the inveterateness of sin, of the impossibility of moral regeneration by human effort, and of the irreversible consequences of Adam's sin, that are found in Paul. It is concluded, therefore, that these were characteristic of first-century Pharisaism (though not of second-century rabbinism). The only difference is that Paul saw some escape from his dilemma, while the author of IV Ezra did not.

Seen in the context of the entire work, however, the similarity vanishes. The book is modelled, to some extent, on the plan of the book of Job: here, it is Ezra who addresses a long complaint to God about his handling of the world. Unlike Job, however, Ezra's main complaint is not about God's injustice in awarding rewards and punishments, but in his deeper injustice in giving man a moral task without giving him the moral equipment to fulfil the task successfully. The final part of the book, spoken by an angel, gives the answer to Ezra's complaint. This answer contains three aspects: God's inscrutability, the coming eschaton which will put things right, and (most important for the comparison with Paul) a rebuttal of the charge of man's moral helplessness. In this section, the angel asserts unequivocally man's power of free will and his responsibility for his own actions (7.19-29, 70-74, 127-31). Thus the passages adduced to show similarity with Paul are actually there in the book to be refuted, and the book would be better described as anti-Pauline. Written in the wake of the Destruction, the writer had more cause than Paul for despair of human effort, yet he asserts its validity. The book does attest the existence of despairing views in the period, but the author, from a traditional Jewish standpoint, firmly quashes them. The same remarks apply to the attempted recruitment of II Baruch on the side of Pauline moral pessimism. Thus the alleged gulf between Pharisaism and rabbinic Judaism on this issue does not exist.

On a different tack, some writers have tried to show that Paul too does not, after all, rule out the possibility of human moral effort, but has the same blend of consciousness of human evil and acknowledgment of ultimate human responsibility as the author of IV Ezra. This line, if established, would also place Paul in first-century Pharisaism. Thus, W.D. Davies (after describing the rabbinic doctrine of the *yetzer ha-tob* and the *yetzer ha-ra'*): 'When we compare such speculations with what Paul describes in Romans 7 the similarity is obvious. It is difficult not to believe that the Apostle is there describing his experience as a Jew suffering under the *yetzer ha-ra'*. There is, it is true, no exact equivalent in Romans 7 to the rabbinical idea of the *yetzer ha-tob* . . . '[4] Later, writing about the fall of Adam and Paul's doctrine of original sin, he writes, 'Nevertheless, every man fell because of his own sin as is clearly implied in Romans 7.'[5] Davies' reasoning seems to be: Paul's references to 'the sin of the flesh' are equivalent to the rabbinical *yetzer ha-ra'*. Therefore the whole rabbinical doctrine of the struggle between the *yetzer ha-ra'* and the *yetzer ha-tob* is implied, with its assertion of human freedom and responsibility, and denial of original sin. This is eisegesis with a vengeance. A passage which, on any dispassionate reading, is all about human helplessness in the face of sin has been turned into a declaration of human freedom, and is to count as such in further discussion. This kind of sleight of hand is all too prevalent in Pauline studies, in the writings of those unwilling to face the evidence of Paul's complete moral pessimism and its radical difference from the basic attitudes of Judaism, whether pre-Destruction or post-Destruction.[6]

2. *The descent of the divine saviour into a human body*

Paul states clearly the doctrine of the pre-existence of Jesus as a supernatural being. The question of whether Paul went so far as to regard Jesus as co-partner with God in the creation of the universe depends on whether Colossians is regarded as an authentic epistle of Paul, a question still being debated (see Col. 1.16-17). Also, the question of whether Paul regarded Jesus as God depends on the problem of the punctuation of Romans 9.5. (Most scholars agree, however, on stylistic grounds, that Paul is here calling Jesus 'God', not inserting a sudden blessing of God the Father.) But certainly Paul ascribes divine status and pre-existence to Jesus in I Cor. 8.6: ' . . . yet for us there is one God, the Father, from whom all being comes, towards whom we move; and there is one Lord, Jesus Christ, through whom all things came to be, and we through him.' The upshot seems to be that Paul took a 'subordinationist' view (later regarded as heretical), by which Jesus was divine and pre-existent (i.e. existed from all time before his descent into human form), but was an inferior deity to God the Father, though sharing with Him the work of creation, revelation and redemption. For a fairly clear statement of this subordinationist view, see I Cor. 15.28, though Paul was too little of a systematic theologian to hold such a view in a consistent form, or to be worried about the problems it raises for monotheism. The best explanation, how-ever, of Paul's untroubled ability to believe in both a High God and a subordinate divine 'Lord', without abandoning his belief in monotheism, is to be found in the influence of Gnosticism. For it is in Gnosticism that we find a monotheistic belief in a High God combined with a vast mythology of lower deities; the philosophical justification lies in the doctrine of emanation and pleroma, by which the lower deities all 'proceed' (in the later Christian phrase) from the unknowable High God.

Does such a concept have any antecedents in Judaism? (The pleroma theory of the Kabbalah is here, of course, irrelevant, since it did not enter into Jewish mysticism until the Middle Ages.) Certainly, there are many instances in the Hebrew Bible of the descent of supernatural beings, i.e. angels, to earth, in human form (e.g. Judg. 13.16, where Manoah thinks the angel is a human being, or the angels who came to deliver Lot, Gen. 19), in order to give some message or perform some task. But such angels play no continuing part in the story, but perform their commission and disappear. Paul's conception of Jesus thus departs completely from the Jewish conception of heavenly visitants. Paul's Jesus is the main actor in the story, to whom all the human characters are subordinate. Instead of a human story with occasional appearan-ces of heavenly visitants in walk-on parts, we are concerned with a heavenly visitant whose story dwarfs in importance the human events of the time. Such a story has affinities with pagan myth, not with the Hebrew Bible.

It is argued, however, that Jewish conceptions of the End-time did contain the scenario of a central heavenly visitant, and that there is evidence of this in the Jewish apocalyptic literature. Here we must make some distinctions. There were Jewish conceptions of the End-time in which the glorious appearance of a liberating angel played a part, though (contrary to the assertions of some scholars) this redeeming angel was never identified with the Messiah, who was always regarded as a human leader.[7] But nowhere in the Jewish writings do we find the idea of a heavenly power who descends into matter in order to perform a salvific agon of humiliation and suffering. This kind of figure, however, is characteristic of Gnosticism. In some Gnostic writings, Seth himself is regarded in this light: he is not a mere human bearer of *gnosis*, but a high heavenly power who has self-sacrificingly adopted human shape in order to bring enslaved humans the means of spiritual liberation.[8] Relevant too is the Gnostic figure of Eve, Norea or Sophia, the female heavenly power whose descent into matter, evil and humiliation causes her to combine the roles of *salvator* and *salvanda*.[9]

Here we must consider two figures in the Hebrew Bible who have often been identified as precursors of the Pauline conception of Jesus: the figure of Wisdom, and the figure of the Suffering Servant. Some attempts have been made to argue that the personified Wisdom of Proverbs and the intertestamental writings was identified in Jewish thought with the Messiah, thus giving the Messiah divine status as at least an aspect of God. This would make the claim of Jesus' divine status intelligible in Jewish terms: as the Messiah, he was the embodiment and incarnation of the Wisdom of God. Moreover, certain passages in Jewish literature seem to imply a descent of Wisdom to earth: e.g. 'She crieth at the gates, at the entry of the city, at the coming in at the doors' (Prov. 8.3). All this, however, as W.D. Davies has shown, is very vague and unconvincing.[10] There is nothing to show that Wisdom was anything other than a poetic personification. She was never given concrete mythical status such as to make her either an object of worship or identifiable as that political, historical figure (in Jewish terms), the Messiah.

The Suffering Servant of Isaiah, on the other hand, is certainly an earthly figure, but there is no hint that he has descended from on high. Christian exegesis has always made much of him as a prophecy of the crucified Christ, but, as Jewish exegesis has pointed out, the actual passage refers to his sufferings and threatened death, but not to his actual death. On the contrary, the natural meaning of the passage is that he is rescued without undergoing death. There is no evidence that the passage has ever been understood in Jewish circles as referring to a heavenly visitant. Interpretations in the Targum and later Jewish literature understand the figure of the Suffering Servant either as a human Messiah, or as the Jewish people personified, or as both simultaneously.[11]

Some writers have attempted to find a link between Judaism and Paulinism by pointing to the translation of certain humans into angels or near-angels in some Jewish traditions (e.g. Elijah, Enoch, Moses, Melchizedek). These instances, however, are beside the point, since none of them is pre-existent. It is not a matter of the descent of a divine figure, but of the promotion of a deserving human to supernatural status after death, or in some cases before death. This is, after all, merely a natural development of the idea that all righteous people achieve immortality: these especially righteous people achieve immortality plus. Out of all the literature searched for the idea of a pre-existent being, the only passage with any claim to consideration is in the Prayer of Joseph, which is extant only as a fragment quoted by Origen in his commentary on John. This appears to convey the idea that Jacob was the incarnation of an archangel called Israel. It is much more likely, however, that the idea is the Platonic one that influenced later Jewish mysticism: that everything on earth is a reflection of something in heaven. Thus Jacob is not the archangel Israel descended to earth; he is the earthly counterpart of the archangel Israel. This idea is more clearly expressed in Joseph and Asenath, 14, in the resemblance between Joseph and the angel who appears to Asenath. If this interpretation is correct, Jacob was no more an incarnation than everyone and everything else on earth. Indeed, the idea that all humanity is the incarnation of God is certainly a Jewish one, since it stems from the biblical statement that God breathed life into Adam (Gen. 2.7). This means that human life is of the substance of God, or divine. But to say that all humans are incarnate God by the mere fact of their normal bodily birth is to exclude the hypothesis that this applies only to certain individuals, who have descended especially from heaven to don human bodies.

We conclude, then, that the Pauline concept of Jesus as a pre-existent heavenly visitant to earth performing a salvific role in human form through humiliation is entirely alien to Judaism. It arises from the basic Pauline notion that rescue must come from above, since this earth and the moral nature of man are too corrupted to be saved by human effort. The descent into evil matter of a divine being is characteristically Hellenistic, being prominent in Gnosticism. It derives, in a mythopoeic way, from Plato himself, and his conception of the Guardian who eschews the pursuit of perfection and escape from matter in order to help lower mortals; and in the background of Plato we may discern Orphic and Indian ideas of the same kind. Judaism never developed such notions because it never regarded matter as evil.

3. The violent death of the divine saviour

The New Testament itself endeavours to find a Jewish background for the idea of the violent death of the Messiah by grounding it in the prophecies of the Hebrew Bible. Thus John 19.37 quotes Zechariah 12.10, 'They shall look on him whom they pierced,' as a prophecy of the execution of Jesus. Indeed, the rabbis too explained this verse in a somewhat similar way when they said that it referred to the death of the 'Messiah son of Joseph' (b. Sukkah 52a). This is a reference to a tradition that there would be two Messiah-figures, one descended from Joseph and the other descended from David, of the tribe of Judah. The Messiah son of Joseph would be killed in an apocalyptic battle, but the Messiah son of David, would then be successful in establishing a messianic kingdom. This tradition appears to be an attempt to reconcile different streams of tradition about the Last Days deriving from the Northern and the Southern Kingdoms.

But these Messiahs are purely human figures. The death of the Messiah son of Joseph, a non-sacrificial death in battle, carries no connotations of supernaturalism. The Messiah son of David, who brings salvation in a political sense, does not die, except eventually of old age.

But the Pauline conception of the death of the Messiah, or Christ, is totally removed from Jewish conceptions, since it involves the death of a heavenly visitant. The notion of a supernatural being entering human flesh, in which he suffers a

violent death, is nowhere to be found in Jewish sources. Yet this
is really Paul's central concept. It is strange that those who are
concerned to argue that Paul's ideas all have their roots in
Judaism never seem to feel the need to argue for a Jewish origin
of this central concept. It seems that this is overlooked as if it
were a merely historical event rather than an important mythological theme. That Jesus died on a Roman cross is undoubtedly an historical event; but we are concerned with the mythological use made of this event, particularly by Paul, and in this
mythological context, it invites comparison with deaths of
supernatural beings in other mythologies. Our first point must
be that in the Jewish mythology it has no analogue.

The idea that gods can die, and can sometimes die violently,
is a commonplace in pagan mythology. It contrasts profoundly
with the Jewish concept of an undying God. The dying and
rising gods of paganism correspond to a cyclic conception of
life.[12] Since nature shows continual death and rebirth, and the
gods are part of nature, we should expect a pattern of death and
rebirth in them too. The God of Judaism, however, is not part
of nature, but its Creator. He stands above and apart from the
cycle of the seasons, which continues to operate not by affinity
to him, but by the fiat and guarantee of his word (Gen. 8.22).

Paul, however, did not identify or equate Jesus with the God
of the Hebrew Bible, but thought of him as a somewhat lower
deity, whom he called the 'Lord'. Nevertheless, he thought of
Jesus as much superior to the angels. Indeed, every Christian
who was saved was superior to the angels, and would 'judge'
them (I Cor. 6.2). This conception is very similar to that of
Gnosticism, in which the Gnostic elect would rise to the status
of the higher powers of the pleroma, and be superior to the
Demiurge and his associated supernatural powers. Such beings
could very well be thought of as gods, since they had powers
and knowledge far above that of mere angels. Paul's conception
that one of the higher powers, Christ, descended to earth to
suffer death is thus not quite so far removed from Judaism as
the later Christian conception that made Jesus part of a triune
Godhead, and equal partner with God the Father. Even in this
later conception, however, the impassibility of God the Father
himself was somehow preserved by insulating him from the

suffering of the Christ (except in the heretical Patripassian doctrine).

Thus it would not be an adequate derivation of the death of Christ from Judaism to point to the fact that, in some Jewish traditions, angels are not immortal. Indeed, according to rabbinic opinion, most angels perish as soon as their commission has been fulfilled (Gen.R.s. 50). Such angels are little more than hypostatizations of the commissions themselves. Even those angels who have achieved full personality and even individual names may be obliterated by God at any time he wishes. In rabbinic opinion, angels are more powerful than human beings, but spiritually inferior, being without the power of moral choice. Thus, while in Gnosticism and Paulinism human beings may become greater than angels when liberated from the flesh, in rabbinic Judaism, human beings are already greater than angels, precisely because, being in the flesh, they have the power to overcome bodily temptation; also, the very fact that humans are in the flesh gives them opportunities for the service of God that are denied to angels.[13] In earlier Judaism, however, angels could succumb to temptation and thus become fallen angels or devils. In all circumstances, however, their deaths were those of created beings, not of gods, and cannot be compared with those of either pagan gods or the Paulinist Christ.

Where then can we find the antecedents of the death of Christ? There is no sufficient analogue in Gnosticism, because here the body is of no real significance. We have to look for embodied deities whose bodies form an important part of their personalities, so that when the body is tortured and killed, this is indeed a cosmic event, not, as in Gnosticism, a matter of indifference. A satisfactory analogue can be found only in the mystery religions. Here we find again and again the violent death of a saviour deity: a death that is experienced in its full agony and that has cosmic significance.

Dionysus is torn to pieces by the Titans; Osiris is dismembered by Set; Adonis is gored to death by a divinely-sent boar; Attis, afflicted by a divinely-sent madness, kills himself by castration; Orpheus is torn to pieces by Maenads. All these figures, and more, are the centres of rites in which their deaths are rehearsed for some salvific purpose. Nowhere in Judaism can we find such figures, though we can discern them in the pagan background of the Hebrew Bible. Thus Isaac appears to be heading for such a fate, but the sacrifice is cancelled. No doubt in the earlier story from which the Bible version was edited, Isaac did suffer death, and then experienced a resurrection and divinization, as a recently-discovered Midrashic fragment indicates.[14] But the Hebrew Bible resolutely turns its face against such a version, since its doctrine is that only the One God can save; He forbids human sacrifice, whether actual or notional, and endures no other deities or mythologies. In the figure of the Pauline Christ, however, we find a reversion to the cults outlawed by the Hebrew Bible, and a new violently-dying saviour.

We may now consider the question of whether, in the mystery cults, the victim is already a god, or only becomes one through his violent death. Is the pre-existence of the Pauline Christ as a high supernatural power echoed in the victim-figures of the mystery cults? At first sight, the answer is that the mystery cult victims are not pre-existent gods, but mortals who only achieve divine status through their deaths. This is certainly true of Attis, Adonis and Orpheus. Dionysus and Osiris are more equivocal figures, having elements of pre-existence and also of mortality. Dionysus has one divine parent, and one human parent; Osiris is a human king of Egypt, but may have descended from on high. Indeed, this equivocal status is characteristic of mystery cult saviours. Even Attis, Adonis and Orpheus have some peripheral features of pre-existent divinity.[15] The reason is that their sacrifice must be a real one; a Gnostic abandonment of an unreal shell of a body would have no sacrificial efficacy. On the other hand, someone who becomes a god must have some special quality that fits him for such a role, some affinity for godhood. The necessity for human status may be explained as deriving from a prehistoric background of the mystery cults in rites of human sacrifice; or, alternatively, if one adopts the rites-of-passage theory of the mysteries (as argued by Jane Harrison),[16] as deriving from the initiation-ceremony of a human adolescent. But whichever explanation we adopt, both human and divine quality are required, and this creates the problem of when the transition takes place. The near-ideal solution is that the victim is of demi-god status when born, having a human mother and a divine father. This prepares him for the agon through which he becomes fully divine, without reducing the reality of the sacrifice.

Paul, the pioneer of the fusion between Gnosticism and mystery religion, gives Jesus full pre-existent status, and this creates many problems in theology for later generations, and paves the way for the Docetic heresies. The problem is how to conceive of a supernatural power who dons a human body without ceasing to be god-like. If he retains self-awareness as supernatural, his suffering in the flesh lacks full reality, since his body is a receptacle rather than an integral part of his personality; here we see the germ of theories of *kenosis*. The Gospels inherit this problem from Paul and deal with it in different ways. The Synoptic Gospels, on the whole, reject Paul's doctrine of pre-existence and move the story into a fuller mystery religion dimension. The trappings of a mystery religion passion play are presented: the birth from one divine parent, the *hilaria* of the triumphal entry, the betrayal by a colleague, the donning of royal robes, the ritual scourging, the mourning by a concourse of women – all elements lacking in Paul. Only the acosmism and moral pessimism by which Jesus is presented, like a Gnostic visitant, as surrounded by malice and incomprehension, derives from Gnosticism. In the Fourth Gospel, however, Pauline Gnosticism triumphs. Jesus has become a pre-existent power of the pleroma again, and his death hovers on the border of Docetism, which the author has to ward off by polemicism, since even he is anxious to preserve the reality of the sacrifice.

Here we must also give attention to the sacramental communion meal that features in every mystery religion (for a full treatment of this topic, see the next chapter). This meal, represented in Pauline Christianity by the Lord's Supper (later re-named the eucharist), involves eating the body of the god who has died the violent death, so acquiring his divinity and immortality. This meal is relevant to our enquiry about the pre-existence of the god. For the communion meal harks back to an earlier stage in religion when an animal was torn to pieces and eaten raw in community in order to transfer its *mana* to the tribe.[17] In this earlier form of the mystery rite (traces of which still linger in the later, more sophisticated and spiritualized rites), the dead animal did not become divinized by its death. It was because it was already divinized, by the possession of *mana*, that the rite took place at all. This pre-sacrificial stage (where the victim is killed for its own sake, not as a propitiation of a higher deity) contributes a primitive element of pre-existence to mystery deities even when their myth insists that they were born as humans.

It is often said that the sacrificial death of Jesus has Jewish antecedents in the Jewish sacrificial cult, i.e. the animal sacrifices of the Temple. This argument is found in the New Testament itself, especially in the post-Pauline Epistle to the Hebrews, but also in Paul's own comparison of Jesus with the paschal lamb (I Cor. 5.7). The idea that the sacrifice of Jesus is the 'fulfilment' of the Jewish sacrificial cult is indeed ingrained in Christian thinking of all periods, but it is invalid. Elementary but fundamental distinctions need to be made between animal sacrifices and the sacrifice of a man-god. These two forms of sacrifice belong to two different worlds, and two profoundly different theories of sacrifice. In Judaism, in both biblical and rabbinic thinking, animal sacrifices were not salvific. Their function was to effect a final 'cleansing' (*kapparah*) for sin; not in the sense of removing sin itself, which could be removed only by repentance and reparation, but in the sense of making friends with God and restoring good relations with him after the breach caused by a sin. It was a meal shared with God to signalize the resumption of favour and friendship. Thus, according to the rabbis, sacrifice never atones for deliberate sin, only for unwitting sin (b. Shabb. 70a). In the case of deliberate sin, repentance and reparation to the injured party (Lev. 6.1-7) have the effect of turning a deliberate sin into an unwitting sin, which then requires the final *kapparah* of sacrifice.[18] In Pauline Christianity, however, the sacrifice of Jesus atones for sin in a much more direct way; the sacrificed person suffers the death deserved by the sinner. This is a throwback to the kind of pagan sacrifice that Judaism rejected. It is not the 'fulfilment' of the Jewish sacrificial cult, but an atavistic return to pre-Jewish notions of sacrifice.

This is not to deny, of course, that considerable change and development in attitudes to sacrifice is reflected in the Hebrew Bible. In the very earliest stratum, preceding the composition of the Bible, we can detect the practice of human sacrifice, as mentioned above in connection with Isaac. When human sacrifice was banned and regarded as an abomination, as in the denunciations of Jeremiah, animal sacrifice, which took its place, was regarded at first as a vicarious atonement; this stage appears in the ritual of the Day of Atonement.[19] Later strata of the Hebrew Bible, however, abandon the notion of vicarious atonement and substitute the idea of a shared meal of friendship and reconciliation with God.[20] This development in the direction of rationality and human responsibility is abandoned, however, in Pauline Christianity, which returns to the primitive level of vicarious atonement through a human-divine sacrifice. In answer to our question of the influence of Judaism on Paul, we might answer that there is such an influence, but only in the form of atavism. Paul responds to the Hebrew Bible, which he read in the Greek of the Septuagint, by reading back into it attitudes which it had outgrown, but vestiges of which remained in the text. Paul, in a way, sees, like a modern anthropologist, the primitive background from which the sophisticated editors of the Hebrew Bible and its Jewish commentators were trying to escape, and proceeds to assert it as the true meaning of the text. But he is enabled to do this because of the influence of contemporary pagan cults which retained as a living reality the concepts found as dead vestiges in the most primitive layer of the Hebrew Bible.[21]

4. The resurrection, immortality and divinity of the crucified saviour.

Since the death of Christ, in Paul's schema, is a sacrificial one, atoning for the sins of mankind and conferring immortality on those who believe, it is necessarily followed by a resurrection, with which the divine being, having suffered his earthly agon, overcomes mortality and resumes his previous place as the greatest supernatural power under the High Father God. Paul does not show any concern about a bodily resurrection for Jesus, such as we find in the Fourth Gospel: his resurrected Jesus is seen by various witnesses, but does not demonstrate corporeality, as to doubting Thomas (John 20.27). On the contrary, he has a 'body of glory' (Phil. 3.21). It seems, then, that even after his resurrection and ascent to Heaven, Jesus has a body, but a glorious one; this distinguishes him from God the Father, who is bodiless, and confirms Jesus' status as a power or emanation inferior to the Highest God.

Since there is no precedent in Judaism for a deity who dies, there can be no precedent for a deity who is resurrected. Yet some writers seek to find a Jewish precedent for the resurrection and translation of Jesus in such figures as Enoch and Elijah, who ascended to heaven and assumed angelic or near-angelic status.[22] We have already considered these figures in relation to the divine descent, and seen that they provide no precedent for that concept. But are they relevant, instead, to the divine ascent? Can we see in the bodily ascent to heaven of Enoch, Elijah and others a Jewish foreshadowing of the bodily ascent of Christ, as envisaged by Paul?

It has to be said that the resurrection of a divine, pre-existent, incarnate figure after a violent death is very different from the ascension to heaven of a human figure while still alive or after dying of old age. Anthropologists have become very wary of superficial parallels between cultures, where the contexts within which the apparent parallels are embedded are significantly different. Yet this kind of snatching at fleeting parallels is still the rule in comparative study of Judaism and Christianity. Here the difference is between a salvific death, followed by the return of the descended saviour to his own vacated heavenly place, and a righteous death, for which the reward is a high place in heaven. These two themes are not only different, but reflect entirely different theologies. One tells us, 'Do not despair because of your helplessness; help will come from above.' The other tells us, 'Your own efforts can achieve much; some people, through their own virtuous efforts, have even reached heaven.'

The matter is complicated, however, by the survival of pre-Pauline concepts of resurrection in Paul's own writings and also in the Gospels. The doctrine of resurrection was, of course, familiar to Jews, especially Pharisees, as a promise of reward to all deserving humans, whether Jewish or non-Jewish. The death and resurrection of Jesus could be regarded not as a divine sacrifice, but as simply a miracle. Jesus' return to bodily life was like the resurrection of Lazarus, though more important because of its eschatological significance; it was the first of many resurrections which would now happen in accordance with the prophecy of Daniel 12.2 about the Last Days. Paul refers to this Jewish concept and prophecy when he calls Jesus 'the firstfruits of them that slept'

(I Cor. 15.20); but his main theory makes Jesus' resurrection unique in its salvific power, not merely the earliest of a plentiful crop. The Jerusalem church no doubt saw Jesus' resurrection in a Jewish way as heralding the general resurrection of the righteous of the past. But if Jesus was not just a righteous man, but an incarnate deity, his resurrection takes on a totally different meaning for which it is vain to look for a Jewish parallel. We must look for a parallel in religions which had the concept of the salvific death and resurrection of a deity. The mere fact that Judaism also had a doctrine containing the word 'resurrection', but which referred to humans not to deities, does not provide any adequate derivation. It only means that in this, as in so many other cases, a Jewish word has been given a non-Jewish meaning (prominent examples are the words 'Christ' and 'eucharist'). For further discussion of the Jewish doctrine of resurrection, see section 6.

For the resurrection of a deity after a violent death, we must look again to the mystery religions. Dionysus, torn to pieces by the Titans, is brought to life again by Rhea. Adonis, killed by a boar, is raised on the third day. Baal, killed by Mot, comes back to life. Attis, after dying of his wounds, comes back to life and dances. Osiris, after being dismembered by Set, is put together again and revived, after which he becomes a god. In Mithraism, the bull killed by Mithras was not itself resurrected, but it provided life, through its body and blood, for the whole created universe.[23]

Recently, however, scepticism has been expressed about whether any of the above-mentioned figures can really be understood as dying-and-rising gods, as in the formulations of earlier anthropologists, especially J.G. Frazer and Jane Harrison. Jonathan Z. Smith writes, 'All the deities that have been identified as belonging to the class of dying and rising deities can be subsumed under the two larger classes of disappearing deities or dying deities. In the first case, the deities return but have not died; in the second case, the gods die but do not return. There is no unambiguous instance in the history of religions of a dying and rising deity.'[24] In the case of Adonis, Smith points out, the first references to joyous festivities on the third day celebrating resurrection are found in the Christian writers Origen, Jerome, Cyril of Alexandria and Procopius of Gaza; these rites, therefore, may have been copied from Christianity. The resurrection of Attis too is found only in post-Christian writings. Osiris, Smith admits, is dismembered and then 'rejuvenated', but since he then journeyed to the underworld and did not return to earth, he cannot 'be said to have "risen" in the sense required by the dying and rising pattern'. Also, his death and revival were not seasonal, but were a model for the Egyptian beliefs about mummification and the survival resulting from it.

To take the last instance first, Smith's use of the word 'rejuvenation' in preference to 'resurrection' (in the case of a dismembered corpse) is hard to understand. While it may be that Osiris's death was not seasonal, Frazer's seasonal interpretation of dying-and-rising gods was not always accepted by his school; Jane Harrison usually preferred a rites-of-passage interpretation. This is not a vital matter, as long as some kind of rebirth is postulated. Again, that Osiris 'did not return to his former mode of existence' is hardly a material point. This is not part of the definition of a dying-and-rising god. That Osiris is the model for the immortality achieved by mummification may also be true without in any way damaging his identity as a dying-and-rising god. The only essential characteristics are that 'he was dead and is alive' and that this brings salvation, however defined.

Smith's distinction between 'dying' and 'disappearing' gods is questionable, especially when they disappear to Hades. But in any case, in our present enquiry we are not concerned with disappearing gods, but only with those who are most definitely dead, since they die by extreme violence. There can be little doubt that when Dionysus was torn to pieces, or Osiris dismembered, they were thereby dead; and it is just as unquestionable that they are afterwards found to be alive, and that this revival has significance in their cult for the rebirth of initiates. Finally, Smith's remarks about the lateness of evidence about the resurrection of Adonis and Attis are not convincing. Recent evidence, as summarized by Gasparro, indicates that Attis survived his death at least in the form of an impersonal vitality suffused through nature (rather like the Mithraic bull), and that this concept was centuries earlier than the Roman Attis cult. Moreover, vases of the first century BCE found at Tarsus depict Attis dancing; and these are analysed by Vermaseren as evidence of Attis's personal resurrection. As for Adonis, Smith's doubt about his resurrection leaves us with a very unlikely cult devoted to mourning the death of Adonis and nothing else. Such a cult would seem to have very little to offer its devotees.[25]

In general, we must conclude that there is good evidence that the concept of the salvific revival or resurrection of a violently-dying god existed in the mystery cults at the time of Paul. Paul's version of this theme, with its ascent of Jesus Christ through the pleroma to the position of First Power, clearly owes much to the Gnostic schema. But the saving power of the crucifixion itself, followed by the resurrection, is not a Gnostic idea. The emphasis on bloodshed and violence as the precondition of salvation belongs to the mystery-cults alone. Resurrection cannot be said to be a Gnostic idea at all, since Gnosticism does not recognize death as a reality, in the case of pneumatic individuals. Their 'death' is merely the discarding of an illusory shell, the body.

5. The vicarious atonement effected by the divine death for those who have faith in its efficacy

Since there is no divine death in Judaism, there is nothing to correspond to the atonement effected by a divine death. Animal sacrifices in Judaism, as pointed out above, do not work in the same way as the death of Jesus in Paul's soteriological scheme. First, the animal sacrifices are not vicarious or prophylactic. Even in the case of sin-offerings, the animal does not die in the place of the offerer of the sacrifice. Since the offerer has already expiated his sin by repentance and reparation (without which no sin-offering for a deliberate sin is valid at all, see Lev. 5.23), he does not stand in need of 'salvation', but only of final reconciliation. Most sacrifices, however, are not sin-offerings, but simply gifts, offered in thanksgiving or out of piety. An exception is the sacrifice of the paschal lamb at the time of the Exodus, whose blood, smeared on the doorposts, saved the Israelites from the death-dealing Lord. But this was only one historical occasion, and did not leave its mark on the sacrifices of the Temple. The paschal lamb of Egypt is carefully distinguished in the rabbinic writings from the 'paschal lamb of the generations', which has the status of a festival celebration and has no connotation of prophylaxis or atonement.[26]

Secondly, the sacrifice of Jesus works as an atonement for all

sins indiscriminately, while the Temple sin-offerings are each
offered as final atonement for a particular sin. In other words,
Jesus dies to wipe out 'sin' in general, while the Temple sin-
offering wipes out only one sin. Even the Day of Atonement
sacrifice, which is offered for the sins of the congregation
indiscriminately, acts only in respect of sins committed in the
previous year. As soon as the Day of Atonement is over, the
problem of sin exists just as before; all that has happened is that a
kind of annual auditing has taken place, so that a new start can be
made without a back-log of sin – and even this, in rabbinic theory,
does not work without repentance and reparation. Thus there is
no magical element of 'rebirth' in the Temple sacrifices. The
problem of sin is regarded in a piecemeal manner, as a perennial
problem which nothing is ever going to abolish. As long as a
person is alive, he will face the temptation to sin day after day.
Success in the past is no guarantee of success in the future, and no
mystic initiation will transform the personality. At the same time,
sin itself is not regarded mystically as an ineradicable spiritual
stain, stemming from the sin of Adam, but as an 'inclination' that
can be handled and even channelled into good by any ordinary
person, by the exercise of his own innate spiritual resources (the
'good inclination') and with the help of the guidance of the Torah.
Moreover, if he fails, as he inevitably will from time to time, this is
not a matter for despair, for the remedy lies in repentance, or
'return' (*teshubah*), and those who stray from the way can always
return to it.

This whole mental climate is worlds away from Paul's attitude
towards sin and its cure. Paul does indeed regard sin as a mystical
stain that can be removed only by mystical means. This mystical
means consists of the death of Christ, which acts as a vicarious
atonement for mankind; and also of the 'faith' by which the initiate
makes the atonement available for himself. Both these elements
are derived from Hellenistic religion, not from Judaism, though
terminology derived from Jewish sources is used by Paul to
'judaize' his concepts. Here again it must be stressed that the use
of a Jewish term does not necessarily argue a Jewish derivation,
since such a term can often be given a meaning that is totally alien
to every form of Judaism in Paul's time. The term 'rejudaization'
has been much used in New Testament scholarship, to denote an

alleged tendency on the part of Christian communities to revert to Judaism. The value of this term is questionable, since it is often an expression of a twentieth-century *tendenz*, concerned with discounting and nullifying evidence of the essential Jewishness of Jesus and his immediate followers; but the term 'judaization' may be a useful way of referring to the tendency of Paul and his followers to camouflage Hellenistic ideas by giving them Jewish-sounding labels.

While the idea of sin as a stain on the soul of mankind deriving from the primeval Fall is not entirely absent from rabbinic Judaism,[27] it is there a peripheral notion, marginalized by conflicting conceptions, and the remedy is not a vicarious sacrifice, but the giving of the Torah. The idea of vicarious sacrifice is also not entirely absent from rabbinic Judaism;[28] but again as a peripheral idea that has no importance for the general theory of how a person achieves righteousness.

It is necessary to point out that it is the Pauline idea that Jesus died for the sins of mankind that has been rejected by Jews, as irreconcilable with the Jewish way of coping with sin and guilt. But the idea that the Jews rejected Jesus as under a 'curse' because of the manner of his death is entirely wrong. Many Jews died by crucifixion and were regarded as heroes and martyrs, not as under a curse. Paul's very individual use, in Gal. 3.13, of the biblical verse (Deut. 21.23) about hanging after death by execution, as if it applied to a Roman crucifixion, was not based on any rabbinic source. Even a criminal dying by Jewish execution was not regarded as under a curse; on the contrary, his death was regarded as an atonement for his sin. But a Jewish patriot dying by Roman oppression was not regarded as a criminal in any way, but as a martyr.[29] While some scholars, in recent years, have stressed the alleged Jewishness of Paul's ideas, this is one area in which Paul is supposed to have rejected a rooted Jewish idea, the 'curse' of crucifixion, and substituted something new and shocking – especially shocking because of the alleged previous Jewish belief that he who died on a cross incurred a curse – the redemptive power of the cross. There was, in fact, no 'curse' or 'scandal' of crucifixion in Judaism to exorcise, the 'curse' being entirely of Paul's own manufacture; what was indeed new, however, was the concept of the cross, or any form of violent death of a saviour-

figure, as the central way to atonement and redemption for
mankind. It is true, of course, that Jesus' death on the cross
demonstrated to most Jews (not believing in his resurrection) that
he was not the Messiah. But this was not because of the manner of
his death, but simply because he had not succeeded in ending the
Roman tyranny and instituting the kingdom of God. The idea that
his catastrophic failure was a success on the cosmic level was not
part of Jewish thinking, and was therefore rejected; but his death
on a Roman cross was cause for sorrow, not condemnation, like
the deaths of other Messiah-figures before and after him.[30]

For Paul, the idea of vicarious sacrifice is of paramount
importance. Again and again, he stresses that the violent death of
Jesus atones for the sins of mankind, which could find no
atonement except through this sacrifice. Relevant passages are
Rom. 3.25 and 5.8-9, which refer to forgiveness and justification
through the death and blood of Christ, and Paul's account of the
institution of the eucharist, referring to 'the new testament in my
blood' – a passage fully discussed in the next chapter. The
necessity of the death of Christ for human salvation is expressed by
Paul as follows: 'I am crucified with Christ: nevertheless I live; yet
not I, but Christ liveth in me: and the life which now live in the
flesh, I live by the faith of the Son of God, who loved me, and gave
himself for me. I do not frustrate the grace of God: for if
righteousness come by the law, then Christ is dead in vain' (Gal.
2.20-21).

W. D. Davies, however, argues that the concept of sacrifice does
not figure largely in Paul's writings (unlike in the pseudonymous
Epistle to the Hebrews). Davies is aware that first-century
Judaism did not regard the animal sacrifices of the Temple as
central to atonement for sin (see above). Paul, he argues, as one
steeped in rabbinic thought, saw the concept of sacrifice as limited
in scope, and therefore gave other concepts priority.

Paul, Davies argues, sees the death of Jesus not as a sacrifice,
primarily, but as an exemplification of the concept of 'obedience
unto death', the chief model of which, in the Hebrew Bible, is the
Suffering Servant of Isaiah 53. Thus the atonement brought about
by Jesus was not caused by his death, but by his obedience to his
mission. Davies adduces evidence from Jewish sources to show
that obedience to heavenly commandments by individuals (the

Patriarchs being the most noteworthy instance) can build up a stock of 'merits' that is available for others, and thus acts as a means of vicarious atonement.[31]

The effect of this argument is to portray Jesus, in Pauline thought, as primarily a martyr, not a sacrifice. A martyr dies because of his steadfast adherence to his moral principles even in the face of death. A sacrifice, on the other hand, dies not because of principles so strong that they overcome his instinctive desire to stay alive, but because his death itself is desirable and necessary to his aim. The Suffering Servant of Isaiah is undoubtedly a martyr, or at least one prepared to be a martyr (whether he actually suffers death is doubtful; see above). But it is very difficult to conceive Christ, in the Pauline scheme, as a martyr. Christ is certainly 'obedient unto death', but to what commandment is he obedient? The answer surely is that he is obedient to the commandment, or mission, of undergoing death (Phil. 2.8). There is certainly some precedent for this in Jewish tradition, as well as in pagan legends of willing sacrifices, for the figure of Isaac is often portrayed in rabbinic literature as one utterly obedient to the command to suffer a sacrificial death. This makes Isaac a sacrifice, not a martyr, the great difference being that the sacrifice of Isaac was cancelled.

Another strategy has been employed by some scholars to argue that the Pauline concept of the death of Jesus was not sacrificial. This is to argue that the death was not primarily atoning but 'participatory'; i.e. that the effect of the death of Christ is not to wipe out human sins, but to enable humanity to participate in the divinization and resurrection of Christ. This topic belongs to the next section, but here it is sufficient to say that sacrifices may be participatory as well as atoning. In other words, it is an unacceptable narrowing of the definition of sacrifice to confine its purpose to atonement. As we shall see, the sacrifices of the pagan world (though not of Judaism) were often aimed at divinization rather than atonement (though the two concepts are not finally separable). In any case, Paul's participationism does nothing to detach him from the notion of sacrifice, since the sacrificial death of Jesus is just as necessary to the participationist as to the atoning theory.

The general conclusion of the present section is that the idea of vicarious atonement by the death of Christ is not based on any Jewish source. Judaism has an entirely different theory of atonement, based on a radically different psychology of sin. Again the place to look for essential similarity to the Pauline view is in pagan religion. Here we find many examples of the willing sacrifical victim whose death averts the wrath of a god and saves the community from the punishment it deserves for its sins.[32] These are human figures who were 'obedient unto death' as atoning sacrifices in cases of special crisis. Even more relevant, however, are the human-divine sacrificial figures of the mystery religions, whose deaths purge their devotees of their sins and make them eligible for immortality, so rescuing them from the continuing crisis of earthly life. The mystery religion which is nearest in tone to Paulinism is perhaps Orphism, which, more than other mystery religions, had a negative attitude towards human earthly endeavour, and regarded its rites as a universal panacea for the human dilemma, rather than as merely conferring special privileges on the initiated. The death of Dionysus, in Orphism, had an atoning effect for those who shared it mystically, and the resurrection of the god was the guarantee of the entrance of the initiate into a new and superior form of life, in which moral problems were transcended. Whether there was a direct influence of Orphism on Paul, or whether he was influenced rather by the cult of Attis, as seems more probable both for geographical and cultic reasons, is difficult to decide. Further evidence, both about the diffusion of Orphic beliefs, and about the earlier worship of Attis may throw light on the question. There seems no reason, however, to reject the conclusion that some form of mystery religion was the chief influence on him, in respect to the atoning death of Christ, rather than any form of Judaism.

6. *The promise of resurrection and immortality to devotees of the saviour*

The belief in the 'resurrection of the dead' (*tehiyat hametim*) had been part of Judaism for at least two centuries before the time of Jesus. The belief is plainly stated in the biblical book of Daniel, and is found in much of the intertestamental literature. The New Testament itself attests it as a Pharisee belief which was denied by the small sect of the Sadducees. Since, as Josephus points out, the mass of the people supported the Pharisees, this belief was in fact the norm.

The Jewish belief in the resurrection of the dead, however, was poles apart from the doctrine now put forward by Paul. The Jewish belief did not make resurrection dependent on the sacrificial death of a divine visitant, or on 'faith' in the efficacy of such a sacrifice. In the Jewish belief, all human beings, whether Jewish or non-Jewish, who had led righteous lives would be brought back to life in the body in the Last Days, in order to share in the peace, prosperity and justice of the kingdom of God, conceived not as a bodiless spiritual realm but as the fulfilment of human hopes on earth. The resurrection of the dead must be distinguished sharply from the survival of the soul after death, which was also a Jewish doctrine, but one which received far less emphasis and was not regarded as an essential article of faith. The Jewish doctrine of the resurrection of the dead was thus imbued with characteristic Jewish humanism. All human history was striving towards a messianic kingdom of human fulfilment, and all those individuals who had striven during their lifetime to this end would be given the opportunity to share in the final success. Demythologized, the doctrine expresses the vital thought that in the final kingdom, all whose lives have contributed towards it will in some sense be there.

Paul's doctrine, on the contrary, is essentially anti-humanist. He is totally unconcerned with the notion of a kingdom of God on earth, which was the centre of the teaching of Jesus himself. In Paul's doctrine, resurrection implies an escape from earthly living into a different dimension, where the human problem is not solved but jettisoned. While he retains the idea of a bodily resurrection, the humanist implications of this idea are nullified by his specification of the new body as comprising a complete transformation of the human condition into something angelic or even super-angelic (I Cor. 15.50-54). Not the slightest mention is made by Paul of the establishment of a just society on earth as an eschatological aim, though this was the chief concern of the Hebrew prophets and of the intertestamental Jewish apocalyptic literature. Such an aim is abandoned by Paul as impossible of realization for corrupted mankind. He has no vision of a perfected human society; salvation is for him entirely for the individual, as in the Orphic and Gnostic religious schemes, and this salvation consists in the raising of the individual to superhuman status.[33]

This anti-humanist and apolitical conception of resurrection arises directly from Paul's central and un-Jewish doctrine of the saving power of Jesus' death on the cross. It is the death of the divine visitant that saves, not any exercise of human energies towards a just society. Consequently, individual resurrection has no societal aspect, and indeed involves the abolition of society.[34] All those who have endeavoured to show continuity between Paul's conception of resurrection and that of Judaism are ignoring an unbridgeable gulf. When Paul himself aligned himself with the Pharisee doctrine of resurrection (Acts 23.6-9), it is clear that this was merely a device and he did not really believe that his doctrine was the same as that of the Pharisees. This is another instance of 'judaization', the clothing of un-Jewish ideas with a Jewish vocabulary, which is characteristic of Paul in his endeavour to link his version of mystery religion with the Jewish tradition.

Since in Paul's thought, the idea of resurrection is connected so inextricably to a religious aim of divinization or achieving superhuman immortal status, we must surely ask where else in the ancient world this connection occurs. The answer is clearly in Gnosticism and mystery religion; but it is only in the latter that this aim is dependent on the death of a human-divine figure, whose death and resurrection are shared symbolically and mystically by the believer. A good example is the initiation of Pythagoras in Crete, as recounted by Porphyry:[35]

> . . . he lay from dawn outstretched face-foremost by the sea and by night lay near a river covered with fillets from the fleece of a black lamb, and he went down into the Idaean cave holding black wool and spent there the accustomed thrice nine hallowed days and beheld the seat bedecked every year for Zeus, and he engraved an inscription about the tomb with the title 'Pythagoras to Zeus' of which the beginning is:
> 'Here in death lies Zan, whom they call Zeus' . . .

We do not usually think of Zeus as a dying-and-rising god, and the rites of the Idaean cave are usually associated with Dionysus. But God the Son, who suffers death, is ultimately identical with God the Father, whose impassibility is normally preserved. It is clear that the death and rebirth undergone by Pythagoras is associated with a divine death and resurrection. The fact that this testimony comes from a work of the third century CE does not invalidate it, since the information given is clearly traditional.[36]

It is clear too that the immortality promised in Egyptian religion through the procedure of mummification was guaranteed by the death and rebirth of Osiris; that in Mithraic religion, the death and diffused life (rather than individual rebirth) of the divine bull brings rebirth to the initiate, after a symbolic death; and that a similar divine death and survival in the religion of Attis is the basis of initiation into the cult. Orpheus is a more complicated figure; he is himself initiated, by death and rebirth, into the mystery of the death and rebirth of Dionysus, but as the leading exemplar of the initiate, he becomes, in some areas, a dying and rising god himself.[37]

Since the notion of achieving immortality through the death and resurrection of a divine figure was so widespread in Paul's time, it is inappropriate to look for the origin of the Pauline doctrine in a Jewish concept of resurrection that is totally different in its thrust and emphasis. The difference may be summarized as follows: Jewish resurrection was the recovery of human life, while both Pauline and pagan resurrection are the achievement of supernatural status, i.e. divinization. To be resurrected, in Jewish eyes, was a miracle, but was not essentially different from the resurrections which had occurred in earlier times through the agency of Elijah and Elisha, or the raising of Lazarus by Jesus. Those resurrected did not become immortals, though they were promised prolonged health into good old age by the prophecy of Isaiah 65.20-22. Even those who believed in the immortality of the resurrected conceived this as an earthly immortality, such as Adam might have had if he had not sinned.

Divinization through a dying and rising deity involves other ideas which are also not to be found in Judaism, but which are characteristic of Paul. One of these is the Pauline concept of 'faith'. It is through 'faith' in Christ that a person shares in the crucifixion and resurrection of Christ, and thus shares in his divinization. It is through 'faith' too that a person becomes 'in' Christ, sharing in the life and personality of Christ, and thereby achieving mystical fellowship with all those who are similarly 'in' Christ, since they all form one supernatural personality together with Christ and are no longer mere individuals. This is the Pauline theory of the church, which through the 'faith' of its members transcends their human limitations and binds them into a superpersonality which is continuous with Christ himself and constitutes his 'body'.

All these ideas are alien to Judaism, which has an entirely different theory of fellowship. 'Faith' in Judaism (*emunah*) means loyalty to the Covenant made between God and Israel; and this covenant was made between two partners each of whom retains his original status, one divine, the other human, without intermingling of their natures. It is true that there is a strong sense of fellowship in Judaism, but this does not arise from any mystical transcendence of the bounds of human personality, and does not involve any theory of divinization. It is the fellowship of human beings embarked on a common enterprise and having a common tradition which stresses the value of human status as a God-given condition which it is not the business of religion to transcend: 'The secret things are for the Lord our God, and the revealed things are for us and for our children for ever, to perform the words of this Torah' (Deut. 29.28). W. D. Davies argues that there is a Jewish background for Paul's theory of community 'in Christ' in the Jewish concept of the unity of Israel as shown, for example, in the injunction that 'in every generation, everyone should regard himself as having personally taken part in the Exodus from Egypt'.[38] But this concept of community is at the opposite pole to Paul's. It means an attachment to an enterprise spanning many generations but firmly rooted in an historical event of liberation giving rise to an earthly project of communal living as outlined in the Torah. This is the kind of loyalty by which, for example, Frenchmen make vivid to themselves the ideals of the Revolution, or Americans immerse themselves in the liberating events which created their project of human development. It is not a programme of divinization but a dedication to a human aim inspiring enough to transcend normal selfish concerns, and to create a sense of comradeship with all those engaged in the same enterprise, whether of previous or coming generations.

Paul's project, on the other hand, is directed towards individual salvation and transformation into a supernatural state of being which is indeed shared with others but has nothing to do with the establishment of a just society on earth. The aim, on the contrary, is to transcend the need for justice to others by breaking down the barriers which divide one human personality from another, so that all form part of one supernatural entity. Paul is not entirely unconcerned with morality and justice, but he regards these as interim matters affecting the transition-period of waiting for the time when all will be transformed and only Christ will exist. W. D. Davies attempts to show a Jewish background for even these conceptions by pointing to Paul's use of the Exodus theme as symbolically foreshadowing the Pauline scheme of salvation.[39] But the use of Jewish expressions is not evidence of a genuine link with Jewish religion. Radical reinterpretations of Jewish material were the main method by which Gnostics reversed the meaning of Judaism. Paul too by regarding the crossing of the Red Sea, for example, as a symbol of Christian baptism (I Cor. 10.2), is reversing the meaning of Judaism, turning it into a scheme of individual, rather than communal or political, salvation. The depoliticization of the Exodus story robs it of its Jewish meaning, while at the same time, of course, aiming at the annexation of Jewish authority for an alien message.

The true source of ideas of merging of human personality with the divine is in Hellenistic mystery religion, mysticism and philosophy. In Orphism, in particular, the aim of the initiate is to achieve divine status by merging with the divinity of Dionysus. In Gnosticism, itself much influenced by mystery religion, the achievement of *gnosis* brings with it a supernatural status higher than that of the angels associated with the Demiurge. Thus the obvious place to look for the origins of Paul's notions of 'faith' and its supernaturalizing effects is in the Hellenistic religious environment, while all attempts to find these notions in Judaism are tortuous and unconvincing, since they conflict with Judaism's essential humanism.

Even more important, however, is the fact that the divine sacrifice which, in Paulinism, brings about the divinizing effects, mediated by 'faith', is nowhere to be found in Judaism. As has been noted, the violent death of the divine figure is just as necessary to the divinizing effect as to that of atonement. There has been some tendency recently to argue that the atoning effect of the cross is not very important in Paul; but even if this is so, the pattern of a divine sacrifice is not any less strong. A 'participationist' interpretation of Paul does nothing to lessen the importance in his thought of the violent divine death, and this, in the last resort, is what divides him utterly from Judaism.

The Divine Death and Antisemitism

Paul undoubtedly makes a great effort to ground his doctrines in Judaism, and this has made it unthinkable for many commentators to see him as a Hellenistic rather than as a Jewish figure. The picture of Paul as the 'Jewish rabbi', who continues to 'think like a Pharisee', while carrying the implications of Judaism to new unexpected levels foreshadowed by the teaching and life of Jesus himself is so rooted in New Testament studies that the most obvious aspects of his debt to Hellenistic religion have been discounted. There has been a natural reluctance to disbelieve Paul's own account of his origins, and a disposition to see evidence of Pharisee learning in the Epistles where none exists.[40] The conviction of Paul's deeply Jewish roots has also made it unthinkable that it was he who laid the foundations for Christian antisemitism. Yet the evidence for this is unmistakable; and the most potent ingredient in the antisemitism arising from Paul's amalgamation of Jewish and Hellenistic religious elements is the notion of the divine death, which comes in its entirety from Hellenism. Without this element, Paul's antisemitism would have remained at the relatively mild level of Gnostic antisemitism, as described earlier in this book. The Jews would have been despised as the worldly uncomprehending people who failed to appreciate the *gnosis* brought by Jesus and thus stamped themselves as mediocrities who could never achieve divinization. Even violence believed to have been offered against Jesus by the Jews would have been dismissed as a laughable and impotent attempt to destroy what was indestructible, the immortal spirit of Jesus. For such violence had no positive meaning in Gnosticism, as it had in the mystery cults, which transmitted to the Hellenistic world the belief, going back to prehistoric times, that only through violence and the shedding of blood could salvation and rebirth be obtained.

For Paul, the divine death of Christ was indeed the key to salvation. A death which, historically speaking, was that of a Jewish messiah-figure, heroically but unsuccessfully attempting to bring about the era of the kingdom of God on earth in fulfilment of the prophecies of the Hebrew Bible, was mythologized into a divine sacrifice through which eternal life could be achieved. In Greek religion, we come across, again and again, the figure of the guilty sacrificer, who performs a necessary sacrifice for the community, but is obliged to flee under a hail of curses or stones.[41] Whenever sacrifice, whether of humans or animals, is required, the community needs to transfer its guilt for the terrible deed to some scapegoat figure. Remnants of such scapegoat figures survive even in the Hebrew Bible, including Cain; but heavily disguised and transformed, since Israelite religion outlawed human sacrifice and transformed the theory even of animal sacrifice in such a way that no guilt was necessary.[42]

In Paul's writings, the Jewish people does not yet function in this role of Sacred Executioner. They have already become a mysterious people who somehow contribute to the salvation of mankind by their 'blindness' in rejecting Jesus. But it is their rejection of Jesus' message, not their role in Jesus' death that Paul emphasizes.

But this outline of rejection is later filled in by the Gospel-writers in an impressive mystery-story in which Jesus is surrounded by forces of evil and hounded to his death by all the factions of the Jewish people, Pharisees, Sadducees and Herodians, united only by their common hatred of the divine figure who is destined for sacrifice. Above all, the figure of Judas Iscariot (unknown in the role of betrayer by Paul) is developed to incapsulate in one person the guilty role of the Jewish people: he is possessed by Satan, yet designated by Jesus himself to perform his fated role. He is a figure of total guilt and evil, yet his deed produces the salvation of mankind. The more he is hated, the more the sacrifice becomes acceptable; for the guilt attendant on all human or animal sacrifice must be exorcized before the sacrifice can achieve salvific power, and there is no more effective way of exorcizing the guilt than to canalize it into a dark figure of evil who is made wholly responsible for the sacrifice.

The Jewish people as a whole is identified with the figure of Judas Iscariot, especially by the myth of the choosing of Barabbas, and Matthew's presentation of the self-curse pronounced at this time: 'His blood be on us, and on our children.'

It is thus the positive salvific value attached to the death of

Jesus, by which it is assimilated to the deaths of gods in Hellenistic
religion, that makes necessary the role of evil attached to the Jews.
The demonization of the Jews inevitably follows, and increases
with every subsequent Christian century. Paul himself merely set
this process in motion; but his combination of the mystery religion
concept of divine sacrifice with the antisemitism inherent in the
Gnostic scheme of radical reinterpretation of the Hebrew Bible
was the seed from which the elaborate antisemitic structures of
later Christianity developed.

In the light of the above remarks, we may now consider more
closely the specific passages relevant to discussion of Paul's
antisemitism. The most obvious case is his outburst in I Thess.
2.14-16:

> You have fared like the congregations in Judaea, God's people
> in Christ Jesus. You have been treated by your countrymen as
> they are treated by the Jews, who killed the Lord Jesus and the
> prophets and drove us out, the Jews who are heedless of God's
> will and enemies of their fellow-men, hindering us from
> speaking to the Gentiles to lead them to salvation. All this time
> they have been making up the full measure of their guilt, and
> now retribution has overtaken them for good and all.

If this passage is the genuine work of Paul, it is the earliest
expression of a fully antisemitic attitude in the New Testament.
The Jews are declared to have been a wicked people throughout
their history. They are compared to the Canaanites by the echo of
Genesis 15.16, 'for the iniquity of the Amorite is not yet full'. Even
more striking is the expression, 'enemies of their fellow-men',
which is the very language of Hellenistic antisemitism as expressed by Manetho, Apion and Tacitus.

So crude and vicious is this attack, that some scholars have
argued that it must be a later interpolation. Certainly, the last
phrase, ' . . . and now retribution has overtaken them for good and
all' is most unlikely to have been written by Paul, for it seems to
imply that the Destruction of the Temple has already taken place.

Moreover, the historical situation implied by this passage does
not seem to fit the time of Paul. The complaint that Christian
communities were being persecuted in Judaea and that the
Thessalonian Pauline community was being persecuted by Jews

seems to belong to the genre of Jewish-persecution fantasies of a
later time, as described by James Parkes.[43] On the whole, this
passage seems to be an expression of a more fully-developed type
of antisemitism than can be ascribed to Paul, and I am now
inclined to regard it as a later interpolation.

The truly Pauline form of antisemitism can be found rather in
his treatment of the Jews in Romans 11, despite the fact that this
epistle is so often quoted to refute the idea that Paul was
antisemitic. The following passages are relevant:

> What follows? What Israel sought, Israel has not achieved, but
> the selected few have achieved it. The rest were made blind to
> the truth, exactly as it stands written: 'God brought upon them
> a numbness of spirit: he gave them blind eyes and deaf ears, and
> so it is still.' (7-8)

> I now ask, did their failure mean complete downfall? Far from
> it! Because they offended, salvation has come to the Gentiles, to
> stir Israel to emulation. But if their offence means the enrich-
> ment of the world, and if their falling-off means the enrichment
> of the Gentiles, how much more their coming to full strength!
> (11-12)

> For there is a deep truth here, my brothers, of which I want you
> to take account, so that you may not be complacent about your
> own discernment: this partial blindness has come upon Israel
> only until the Gentiles have been admitted in full strength;
> when that has happened, the whole of Israel will be saved . . .
> In the spreading of the Gospel they are treated as God's enemies
> for your sake; but God's choice stands, and they are his friends
> for the sake of the patriarchs. (25-28)

In these passages, Paul portrays the Jews as blind and deaf to the
gnosis brought by Christ, who was therefore forced to transfer his
mission of redemption to the Gentiles. So far, this leaves the Jews
merely outside redemption, like the non-pneumatics in the
Gnostic schemes of salvation. But Paul now brings in an insight
derived from mystery religion: that the sin of rejection was itself
part of the pattern of redemption. Paul thus sets up the role of the
Jews in mediaeval Christian society as 'witnesses' to the truth of
Christianity by their sufferings and slavery, by which they expiate

their mysterious and necessary sin until the time of their expiation arrives. This is an attitude that, in itself, does not lead to the worst excesses of antisemitism, but rather gives the Jews an awesome, if unenviable, role as the 'sin-eaters' of society. But this attitude of Paul's is always liable to lead to worse forms of diabolization and to an active antisemitic persecution, such as is foreshadowed indeed by the probably interpolated passage in I Thessalonians, which, even if not written by Paul, was written by some disciple of his who had progressed to a further and more dangerous stage of antisemitism.

There is a curious inability on the part of many commentators to see the antisemitic tendency and potential of Romans 11. The kind of comment that is made is that Paul is chiefly interested here in how Jews can ultimately be included, rather than in their present exclusion; his attitude towards them, therefore, must be regarded as friendly. The hollowness of this approach has been well understood by Rosemary Ruether.[44] Her remarks have been endorsed by Lloyd Gaston, who wrote, ' . . . it is very salutary for Ruether to point out that the interpretations of Romans 9-11 offered to date continue to deny to Israel any positive significance according to its own self-understanding for the period between resurrection and parousia.' Gaston therefore proposes, as a matter of urgency, a new and untraditional exegesis of Romans 11 that, however unconvincing, demonstrates his agonized awareness of the antisemitism of the passage as usually understood.[45] Perhaps the 'friendliness' of Paul's tone here would be better evaluated if, say, a Protestant reader were to imagine his feelings on listening to a Roman Catholic discussion on how Protestants might be brought into salvation at some miraculous time in the future. The kind concern of such a discussion would probably make less impression than its condescension and underlying denial of Protestantism as a valid means of salvation.

Thus, so far from being evidence of Paul's freedom from antisemitism, the passages in Romans were the first step towards the more fully-developed antisemitism of the Gospels and later Christian literature. For further discussion of the level of Paul's responsibility for Christian antisemitism, see ch. 7. The conclusion of the present chapter is that, while Paul's own antisemitism remained on the Gnostic level, it was his isolation of the Jews as divinely-appointed Opposers, together with his introduction of the mystery religion theme of the death of a divine figure by violence, that opened the way to further developments of the Pauline-Christian myth in a more strongly antisemitic direction.

4

Paul and the Eucharist

The purpose of the present chapter is to deepen the thesis of Paul's essential Hellenism from a different angle. I shall argue that Paul, not Jesus, was the originator of the eucharist; and that the eucharist itself is not a Jewish, but an essentially Hellenistic rite, showing principal affinities not with the Jewish *qiddush*, but with the ritual meal of the mystery religions. Since this is a matter of central importance, which has been discussed by many scholars in great detail, the method of the present chapter will have to be somewhat laborious.

The Eucharist in the New Testament

The earliest New Testament account of the institution of the eucharist runs as follows:

> For I have received of the Lord that which also I delivered unto you, that the Lord Jesus the same night in which he was betrayed took bread; and when he had given thanks, he brake it, and said, Take, eat: this is my body, which is broken for you: this do in remembrance of me. After the same manner also he took the cup, when he had supped, saying, This cup is the new testament in my blood: this do ye, as oft as ye drink it, in remembrance of me. For as often as ye eat this bread, and drink this cup, ye do shew the Lord's death till he come. Wherefore whosoever shall eat this bread, and drink this cup of the Lord

unworthily, shall be guilty of the body and blood of the Lord. But let a man examine himself, and so let him eat of that bread, and drink of that cup. For he that eateth and drinketh unworthily, eateth and drinketh damnation to himself, not discerning the Lord's body. For this cause many are weak and sickly among you, and many sleep (I Cor. 11.23-30).

The first important point to consider here is whether Paul is claiming to know about Jesus' eucharistic words through a personal revelation, or through a tradition handed down to him from the leaders of the Jerusalem church. The AV translation quoted above points to a personal revelation: 'For I have received of the Lord ... ', while the NEB translation is remarkably different: 'For the tradition which I handed on to you came to me from the Lord himself.' The latter translation reflects a considerable body of recent scholarly literature. However, I shall argue that the view of earlier scholarship (e.g. Loisy[1] and Lietzmann[2]) that Paul is speaking here of a personal vision has been too easily dismissed.

How is it possible for two such different translations of the same expression to be made? The Greek runs as follows: *ego gar parelabon apo tou kuriou, ho kai paredoka humin.* The argument, then, turns on the meaning of the two words *parelabon apo*. It has been held by some scholars that if direct revelation had been intended, the preposition *para* would have been more suitable than the preposition *apo*, which signifies a remote or ultimate source of information. This contention has given rise to a whole literature, for and against.[3] The upshot seems to be that while *para* is more usual in a context of the direct imparting of information, *apo* is also quite frequently found in such a context (e.g. Matt. 11.29; Col. 1.7). The argument from the 'remote *apo*' is thus inconclusive, and one cannot help feeling that it has been pressed so hard for theological, rather than strictly grammatical, reasons.

Here it is necessary to comment on a fallacious argument of Jeremias.[4] He argues that it is not so much the preposition *apo* that indicates the traditional source of Paul's information as the use of the verb *paralambano*. This verb, Jeremias argues, corresponds to the Hebrew verb *qibel*, which always refers to reception as part of a process of tradition. Thus, merely by his use of the verb *parelabon*,

Paul indicates sufficiently that his account of the institution of the eucharist is derived from the tradition of the church, not from a personal vision (as argued by Loisy, Lietzmann and others). To refute this argument it is sufficient to quote the most memorable passage in rabbinic literature employing the verb *qibel* – the opening of the Mishna tractate Abot. This begins, 'Moses received (*qibel*) the Torah from Sinai'. This shows that even though the verb *qibel* does refer to reception as part of a process of tradition, it can also refer to the first step in that process, the reception from God himself. Thus Paul, saying, 'I received (*parelabon*) from the Lord', may well regard himself as initiating a process of tradition, but does not thereby imply that he has received the information from other human beings, rather than from the heavenly Jesus himself.

Nevertheless, Jeremias also, in his way, takes the 'remote' view of *apo*, in conjunction with the argument about *paralambanein*, on which he places the chief stress. Jeremias' formulation of the 'remote *apo*' argument is as follows. 'If Paul did not construe *paralambanein* (= *kibbel min*, see . . .) with *para*, as elsewhere (Gal. 1.12; I Thess. 2.13; 4.1; II Thess. 3.6), but with *apo*, this was for a good reason. *Para* indicates those who hand on the tradition; *apo*, on the contrary, the originator of the tradition. (Footnote) Examples in Bauer: A. and G., 87 (*apo* V,4). Paul therefore stressed in I Cor. 11:23 with the help of the preposition *apo* that the eucharistic words cited by him out of the tradition go back to Jesus himself.'[5] I would agree with every word of this statement except the words 'go back'. Jeremias appears to leap from the definition of *apo* as referring to the original source to the idea that this source must be remote, relying indeed on his erroneous view of *paralambanein* to supply the missing notion of remoteness.

In any case, the expressions *paralambanein* and *paradidonai* are not necessarily derived from the Hebrew *qibel* and *masar*. As Albert Schweitzer pointed out,[6] these expressions were used in the mystery religions to signify the reception and communication of the revelation received. Schweitzer rejected this derivation only because, in his view, Paul 'did not live in a world of Hellenistic conceptions'. But this is a view that can be seriously questioned.

In addition, however, to the linguistic considerations discussed above, there is a logical consideration which makes it difficult to regard Paul's statement in I Corinthians as referring to the reception of a tradition, rather than to a personal vision. This is that it makes little sense to speak of Jesus as initiating a tradition about what happened at the Last Supper. The only people who could initiate such a tradition were those who were witnesses of Jesus' actions and words at the Last Supper. These witnesses did not receive any tradition from Jesus about what happened: they saw and heard it happening with their own eyes. Jesus may have urged them to 'remember' what happened and to transmit it to later generations; but he did not tell them what happened because they saw this for themselves. If Paul had meant to say that he was presenting a traditional account, he would have said 'I have received this account from those present at the Last Supper', not 'I have received this account (deriving) from Jesus'. On the other hand, it makes perfect logical sense for Paul, who was not present at the Last Supper, to say that he received an account of it 'from' the heavenly Jesus.

Thus the arguments aimed at refuting the *prima facie* likelihood that Paul is claiming to know about the eucharistic words through a personal vision are weak. They have been reinforced, however, by linguistic and textual arguments aimed at showing that the eucharistic style employed by Paul was not of his own composition, but a liturgical formula already current in the early church. The most elaborate argument on these lines, including comparative analysis of the Pauline eucharistic words with those found in the three Synoptic Gospels, is the celebrated essay of Jeremias, which many regard as definitive. Jeremias' conclusion is that, despite the admitted literary priority of the Pauline account, it cannot be regarded as the source of the Gospel accounts. For textual analysis shows that both Paul and the Gospels were drawing on a liturgical tradition already current in the church before the period in which Paul's epistle was written (probably 54 CE).

I shall argue, however, that the composite nature of the Gospel accounts of the Last Supper does not show that their eucharistic aspect stems from any source other than Paul. The considerations used by Jeremias can be given a far more plausible interpretation, in which the composite nature of the Gospel accounts derives from the superimposition of a eucharistic meaning on a narrative of the Last Supper which originally had no eucharistic aspect at all, but a quite different, apocalyptic, message.

Any theory about the eucharistic words of Jesus must take account of the startling fact that the Gospels are by no means unanimous in ascribing eucharistic words or instructions to Jesus at the Last Supper. The Fourth Gospel, in its long account of the Last Supper, ascribes no eucharistic words to Jesus at all (though it gives a eucharistic speech to Jesus elsewhere, in Galilee, John 6.53-8). The Gospel of Luke has two alternative versions, found in different manuscripts, of the Last Supper, called by scholars the Short Text and the Long Text. The Long Text does ascribe eucharistic words to Jesus, and even portrays Jesus as instituting the eucharist as a permanent rite; but the Short Text ascribes only the briefest eucharistic words to Jesus, since all it says is that Jesus referred to the bread as his body. Mark and Matthew (which can be regarded as one account, since Matthew's passage is based so firmly on Mark's) do ascribe eucharistic words to Jesus, but not instructions to institute a rite. Thus the only source that unequivocally ascribes both the words and the instruction to Jesus is the earliest, that of Paul.

This patchy pattern is of the greatest significance. It creates at least the presumption that there was some doubt in the mind of the Gospel writers what to include in their accounts of the Last Supper about the eucharist. If there was, as Jeremias and others argue, a strong tradition in the Jerusalem church, which Paul merely repeated, that Jesus both spoke eucharistic words and instituted the eucharist at the Last Supper, this is not the pattern we would expect to find in the Gospels. We would expect, on the contrary, unanimity in the Gospels that Jesus both spoke eucharistic words at that time and instituted the eucharist. The pattern that we do find suggests strongly that the Gospel writers were faced with the problem that their earliest sources, the traditions of the Jerusalem church, said nothing about any eucharistic aspect of the Last Supper. They were compelled, however, to import such an aspect because of the eucharistic practice of the church in their own period and the belief (whether derived directly from Paul or some intermediate source) that this practice was based on something said by Jesus at the Last Supper. Four different solutions were found for this problem: inclusion of eucharistic words without instruction (Mark/Matthew); inclusion of a bare minimum of eucharistic words without instruction (Luke, Short

Text); inclusion of eucharistic words with instruction (Luke, Long Text); omission of eucharistic material from the Last Supper, and inclusion elsewhere (John). This multiplicity of solutions surely indicates an uneasiness that is not accounted for by the view that the eucharist was firmly founded on early church tradition of a Last Supper origin.

The above presumption receives strong reinforcement from the absence of all reference to the eucharist, as a practice of the early church, in the Book of Acts, where one would most expect to find it.[7] What we do find is that the early followers of Jesus took part in communal meals, in which they 'broke bread' (2.42; 20.7, compare also 27.35). 'Breaking bread' (*bisu'a pat*) is simply the opening of every Jewish meal of a ceremonial character, i.e. at festivals, weddings, etc. Whoever is presiding over the meal (i.e. the head of the household in a family meal, or some respected communal figure in a communal meal), makes a 'blessing' (*berakhah*) over a loaf of bread, thanking God for providing bread, and then divides the loaf, handing a piece to each participant. This is preceded by a *qiddush* over wine only on Sabbaths and festivals, the wine being prescribed as a means of marking the 'rejoicing' of the holy day, in accordance with the association of wine and rejoicing in Ps. 104.15. In this pattern, there is no organic connection between the bread and the wine, each being prescribed for a different purpose, the bread as the formal beginning of the meal, and the wine as acknowledgment of the holiness of the day (it is therefore omitted on a weekday). In the practice of the Jerusalem church, the 'breaking of bread' without use of wine is the normal Jewish practice at weekday communal meals and has no eucharistic significance.

Another important piece of evidence is that of the Didache. This book of observance of the early church does describe a ceremony called a 'eucharist', but this ceremony contains no reference to the body or blood of Jesus, òr to the Last Supper. The ceremony described in chapters ix and x has great affinity to the Jewish *qiddush* on which it is clearly based, and it refers to Jesus throughout in purely human terms as the 'servant' of God, the descendant of 'thy servant David'. The orientation of the ceremony is apocalyptic, looking forward to an ingathering of Israel 'from the ends of the earth in thy kingdom'. Very significant is the

fact that this Didache ceremony, in contrast to Pauline eucharistic
practice, has a wine-bread sequence, like a typical Jewish festival
meal. The prayer of thanksgiving over the bread has clear affinity to
the Jewish *berakhah* over bread, and the whole meal ends with a
thanksgiving prayer based on the Jewish grace after meals. Clearly
the Didache represents the practice of the Jerusalem church, which
probably celebrated a *qiddush* meal of this kind on Sabbaths
(Saturdays) and festivals at the same time as their Jewish brethren
were celebrating the normal Sabbath and festival *qiddush*, bread-
blessing and grace after meals, the difference being merely that the
Nazarene *qiddush* contained mention of the hoped-for return of the
deliverer, Jesus, who would accomplish the deferred ingathering of
Israel. Similarly, in the grace after meals current among Jews
generally after the destruction of the Temple, passages of apocalyptic hope were inserted.[8]

Jeremias argues, however, that chapters ix and x do not describe
the eucharist, but the *agape*, which is the introduction to the
eucharist proper.[9] His arguments are that 'there never was a
Eucharist with the sequence Wine-Bread', and that the closing
words, in ch. x, 'If any is holy, let him come: If any is not holy, let him
repent. Maranatha,' signify an introduction to a eucharist, not the
ending of one. The first argument begs the question. Though the
Pauline eucharist, with its body-and-blood connotation, certainly
had the bread-wine sequence, its precursor in the Jerusalem
church, a close variant of the Jewish *qiddush* meal, but with
apocalyptic overtones, may well have had a wine-bread sequence.
The second is unconvincing in view of the fact that the end of the
eucharist here is apocalyptic. 'Let him come' means 'Let him enter
the kingdom of God', the onset of which is invoked by the expression
'Maranatha'. Uncontrovertible proof of this is that the fully Pauline
eucharistic pattern presented by Justin Martyr still retains this
same apocalyptic formula *at the end*: 'Let grace come, and let this
world pass away. Hosanna to the God of David. If any is holy, let
him come: if any is not holy, let him repent. Maranatha. Amen'
(Apol. I.lxvi). This formula was evidently still the customary
ending to the eucharist in Justin's day, and therefore it must be
regarded as the ending of the Didache ceremony, which, though
called *eucharistia* (here merely an equivalent of the word *qiddush*) was
not a eucharist in the Pauline sense.

Paul and the Eucharist

97

Thus the silence of our sources about Pauline body-and-blood
eucharistic practice in the Jerusalem church reinforces the *prima
facie* reading of I Cor. 11 as meaning that Paul is claiming to derive
his knowledge of the Last Supper from a personal vision, not from
the tradition of the Jerusalem church. If Jesus did really institute
the eucharist at the Last Supper, then those who actually took part
in the Last Supper, i.e. Peter and John, leaders of the Jerusalem
church, would surely have made the eucharist the centre of their
observance. The evidence is that they did not, but simply continued
to practise normal, or almost normal, Jewish observances in
communal meals. This contradiction between the practice of the
Jerusalem church and Paul's claim about what happened at the
Last Supper would not be obvious to Paul's correspondents in
Corinth, who did not have the Jerusalem church before their eyes.

The absence of reference to the eucharist in our sources on the
early church is, of course, known to Jeremias, who has his own way
of dealing with this difficulty. His answer is that the eucharist was
regarded as a mystery, to which it was not permitted to make public
reference. This explains not only the reticence of the book of Acts,[10]
but also that of the Short Text of Luke,[11] and the even more
complete reticence of the Gospel of John,[12] at least in relation to the
Last Supper. This theory of Jeremias requires some discussion.

In Jeremias' view, the expression 'breaking of bread' in Acts
refers to the performance of the eucharist, but in a reticent form.
' . . . he refers to the Lord's Supper exclusively in allusions and
ambiguous phrases: "the breaking of bread" (Acts 2.42), "to break
bread" (Acts 2.46; 20.7,11), perhaps also "food" and "to taste"
(Footnote: *trophe*, Acts 2.46. Cf. Justin, *Apol.* I 66.1,2). It is a
natural conclusion that the intention is that the non-Christian
should not understand the references.'[13] To support the view that
the eucharist was a secret mystery, Jeremias cites comparative
material to show that esoteric topics existed in contemporary
Jewish religion.[14] He also cites Justin Martyr and Hippolytus of
Rome to show that celebration of the eucharist had an esoteric
character.[15]

This argument, however, does not take into account the
distinction between the content of a mystery and the mere naming
of it. All the mysteries of the ancient world strove to conceal their
content from the uninitiated; but none attempted to conceal the

fact of their very existence. That the book of Acts avoids giving the content of the eucharist is understandable, since there was, in any case, no need to give this content in a historical account; but that it should conceal the very fact that the Jerusalem church had a central rite which it celebrated is incredible. What secrets would be divulged by saying, 'They celebrated the Lord's Supper', rather than 'They broke bread'? The parallels adduced by Jeremias from contemporary Jewish esoteric practice are doubly beside the point. First, there was no embargo on naming such mystical topics as *ma'aseh merkabah* or *ma'aseh beresit*, only on divulging their contents to the unsuitably prepared. Secondly, these were not rites, but areas of knowledge. The true parallel to the eucharist is not Jewish mysticism, but the rites of the Temple. These were, in a sense, esoteric, since they could be performed only by the Aaronic priesthood, and others were even forbidden to enter the inner parts of the Temple; but there was nothing esoteric about the details of what went on in the Temple, since all Jews, whether priestly or not, had the right, and even the duty, to study these details as found in the Torah, both written and oral. So there is no parallel in Judaism, or in any other ancient religion, for the concealment of the very existence of a sacramental rite.

Thus Jeremias' attempt to explain the absence of reference to the eucharist in Acts as due to secrecy is unconvincing, and the most natural and obvious explanation of this absence is that the Jerusalem church knew nothing about the eucharist. A further consideration here is the devotion of the Jerusalem church to the rites of the Jewish Temple. We know from many evidences in Acts and elsewhere that the leaders of the Jerusalem church regarded the Temple worship with reverence and even special devotion. Here we may cite not only Luke 24.53; Acts 2.46; 3.1, but also the test of loyalty to the Torah imposed on Paul by the Jerusalem leaders, which involved participation in a Temple rite of purification (Acts 21.23-24). Further, we hear that James, the brother of Jesus and head of the Jerusalem church, was an assiduous follower of the Temple worship (Eusebius *Hist.Eccl.*, ii,23, quoting Hegesippus). This devotion to the Temple is totally incompatible with performance of the eucharist, which replaced, for Christian worshippers, the sacraments of Judaism, and marked the emergence of Christianity as a separate religion from Judaism, not only from the Christian point of view, but also from the Jewish point of view, since the performance of any sacramental act outside the Temple was strictly forbidden by Judaism. Thus any performance of the eucharist by the Jerusalem church would have been an act of secession from Judaism, while all the evidence shows that the Jerusalem church regarded itself as within Judaism. Further, of course, the actual content of the eucharistic rite was repugnant to persons loyal to Judaism, among whom members of the Jerusalem church should be reckoned, since it involved the concept of eating the body and drinking the blood of a divine figure, a concept reminiscent both of primitive rites such as the Dionysian *omophagia* and of their sublimated versions in the Hellenistic cults of Attis and other mystery-religions. That such a concept was repugnant to persons of Jewish upbringing is attested by the Gospel of John, 6.59-67, which describes the Jews as shocked by Jesus' saying, 'Whoever eats my flesh and drinks my blood dwells continually in me and I dwell in him' (6.56). John states that many of Jesus' own disciples objected to this saying (6.60) and as a consequence, ' . . . many of his disciples withdrew and no longer went about with him' (6.66). Jesus even had to seek reassurances from the Twelve, asking 'Do you also want to leave me?', upon which Simon Peter affirmed his loyalty. This incident reflects not any actual incident in the life of Jesus, but the opposition of the Jerusalem church to the Pauline doctrine of the eucharist.[16] It is necessary for John to affirm that Peter, by now regarded, in the church's re-writing of history, as the companion rather than the opponent of Paul, had acquiesced in the institution of the eucharist. The whole episode testifies to the turmoil caused by the introduction of the eucharist, which was regarded by the Jerusalem church as an idolatrous rite.

We can conclude with some confidence, therefore, that the Jerusalem church did not celebrate the eucharist, being unaware of the existence of such a rite in its early years, and continuing to adhere to the sacraments of Judaism. We may also note that devotion to the Temple also implied acceptance of the Aaronic priesthood as the God-ordained performers of sacraments (though not, in Pharisaic Judaism, as having a teaching authority). Once the eucharist was accepted by the Pauline church, this implied not only the supersession of the Jewish Temple, but also of the Aaronic priesthood. The institution of a Christian priesthood arose directly out of the institution of the eucharist, since the administering of the eucharist required a priestly role. This did not happen immediately, since the eucharist was administered at first in the Pauline church by 'prophets', whose priestly qualifications stemmed from charisma, not membership of a priestly establishment. But however administered, the eucharist demanded a priestly function that was quite incompatible with adherence to the Jewish Aaronic priesthood. The loyalty of the Jerusalem church to the Jewish priesthood as valid performers of sacraments (some members of the Jerusalem church were indeed themselves functioning priests in the Temple, Acts 6.7) is a further indication of their non-eucharistic religious practice. It should be remembered, in this connection, that the leaders of the Jerusalem church themselves were not priests. In so far as the word 'church' implies a priesthood, the expression 'Jerusalem church' is a misnomer; a better expression would be the Jerusalem community (it is indeed called a 'synagogue' in James 2.2), which had the same status as other Jewish communities which banded together for some common purpose not incompatible with general loyalty to Judaism, with non-priestly leaders (e.g. the Zealots).

The unawareness of the eucharist shown by the Jerusalem church, led by people who were actually at the Last Supper, is a strong indication that the eucharist was not instituted by Jesus, and that the eucharistic words found in the Gospel accounts of the Last Supper are additions by the redactors of the Gospels, who were forced to make such additions either by their direct awareness of the Pauline account of the Last Supper in I Corinthians, or by the practice of the eucharist in the church of their own time, combined as it was with the belief (stemming ultimately, though not necessarily in the conscious awareness of the redactors, from Paul's vision) that this was instituted by Jesus at the Last Supper. This probable conclusion now needs to be supplemented by more detailed study of the Gospel accounts, showing that, contrary to Jeremias' view, they show signs of editorial tampering particularly in the eucharistic aspects, and that the confusions discernible in these accounts of the Last Supper can best be explained on the hypothesis that the eucharistic aspects are later additions. Particularly interesting in its transitional nature is the version of the Last Supper given by Luke, both in the Short and the Long Text.

The Last Supper in Luke

The Short Text runs as follows (22.14-19a):

14. When the time came he took his place at table, and the apostles with him; and he said to them,
15. 'How I have longed to eat this Passover with you before my death!
16. For I tell you, never again shall I eat it until the time when it finds its fulfilment in the kingdom of God.'
17. Then he took a cup, and after giving thanks he said. 'Take this and share it among yourselves;
18. for I tell you, from this moment I shall drink from the fruit of the vine no more until the time when the kingdom of God comes.'
19a. And he took bread, gave thanks, and broke it; and he gave it to them, with the words: 'This is my body.'

The Long Text adds the following (22.19b-20):

19b. which is given for you; do this in memorial of me.
20. In the same way he took the cup after supper, and said, 'This cup, poured out for you, is the new covenant sealed by my blood.'

One of the controversial aspects of Jeremias' presentation is his attempt to argue that the Long Text is earlier than the Short Text (contrary to his own earlier view). Jeremias himself summarizes the weighty arguments that have led so many other scholars to conclude that the Short Text is the earlier. 'The two basic rules of textual criticism, "The shorter text is the older", and "The more difficult reading is to be preferred", unanimously commend the Short Text.' Jeremias also acknowledges that the Long Text is significantly similar to Paul's formulation in I Cor. 11.24-25, and also that it contains several expressions uncharacteristic of Luke. The conclusion to which these considerations seem to lead is that the extra material was added by some later hand than Luke's, motivated by dissatisfaction with the meagre allowance of eucharistic material afforded by the Short Text (only the words, 'This my body').

Jeremias, however, rejects such a conclusion, arguing that the uncharacteristic style of the eucharistic words in Luke's Long Text derives from the fact that Luke is quoting from a liturgy. Moreover, slight differences between Luke and I Corinthians indicate, Jeremias argues, that Luke is not derived from I Corinthians, but from a liturgical formula underlying both. The way in which the Short Text could be derived from the Long Text (contrary to usual derivation) is that the Short Text quotes only the opening words of the eucharistic portion, relying on the ability of the initiated to supply the rest from their knowledge of the eucharistic liturgy. The Short Text is thus not really shorter than the Long Text, but only appears to be so. Here Jeremias invokes again the concept of secrecy. The Long Text was written by Luke at a time when the need for secrecy was not so strongly felt, and abbreviation of the passage into the Short Text was made by a later hand, when secrecy about the details of the eucharist had developed further.

The above arguments, however, are presented by Jeremias not as his chief reasons for advocating the priority of the Short Text, but merely as obviating the difficulties raised by such a view. The chief reason offered lies in Jeremias' survey of the actual sources in which the Long Text and the Short Text are found. The great majority of sources contain the Long Text, while the Short Text is found in only one Western manuscript (D), in a Syrian translation, and in citations ascribed to Marcion and Tatian. Jeremias is able to prove to his satisfaction that this situation shows an overwhelming probability that the Long Text is prior; other scholars, however, disagree.[17] It is not necessary, however, for our present argument to attempt to settle this matter, which is no doubt destined to undergo further fluctuations of debate. Instead, I propose to show that the Long Text has a composite nature which indicates that it has been built out of *some* shorter text. Whether this building was done by Luke himself or by some later author need not be our concern; nor whether the Short Text as we know it is to be identified (in whole or in part) with the original account of the Last Supper of which the Long Text is a development.

The Long Text of Luke contains certain incoherences and confusions that indicate its composite nature. It may be remarked at once that in all the accounts of the Last Supper in the Gospels (though not in I Cor.) bread and/or wine feature in two quite separate ways: first, in the 'apocalyptic' episode (sometimes, though wrongly, called the 'avowal of abstinence'), in which Jesus says that he will not drink wine (or in one version eat the Passover) until the kingdom of God comes; secondly, in the eucharistic episode, in which Jesus offers bread and wine, saying these are or symbolize his blood and body. The relation between these two separate featurings of bread/food and wine (with the concomitant uncertainty about whether bread precedes wine or vice versa) is a topic that has received insufficient attention, and which may provide the most important clue to the unravelling of the stages through which the Gospel accounts developed.

In Luke we see the following intertwining of these two themes. First, Jesus makes the 'apocalyptic' remark not in relation to the bread, but in relation to the Passover (22.15-16). This attachment of the 'apocalyptic' remark to the Passover has no parallel in Mark/Matthew. Then Jesus makes the 'apocalyptic' remark in relation to the wine (22.17-18). Then he takes bread, distributes it, and makes the 'eucharistic' remark about it. Then (in the Long Text), he takes *another* cup of wine ('the cup after supper'), and makes the 'eucharistic' remark about it. This provision of a second cup as the focus of a separate 'eucharistic' remark has no parallel in Mark/Matthew, in which both the 'apocalyptic' and the 'eucharistic' remarks are made consecutively about the same cup of wine (Mark 14.24-25, Matt. 26.28-29).

These relationships can be shown conveniently in the following table:

	Luke	*Mark/Matthew*	*I Corinthians*
Bread ('apocalyptic')	-	-	-
Passover ('apocalyptic')	22.15-16	-	-
Wine ('apocalyptic')	22.17-18 (first cup)	14.24-25/26.28-29	-
Bread (eucharistic')	22.19	14.11/26.26	17.24
Wine ('eucharistic')	22.20 (second cup)	14.23-24/26.27	27.25

It will be seen that Luke (in the Long Text) is the odd man out. He is the only one to provide an apocalyptic word over food (not the bread, but the Passover, i.e. the paschal lamb), as well as over wine. He is also the only one to provide two separate cups, one for

the apocalyptic word, the other for the eucharistic word. Note
further that while all sources put the eucharistic bread before the
eucharistic wine (a sequence hard to explain in the context of a
Jewish festival meal), Luke is the only one to provide a wine-bread
sequence (though admittedly this is an apocalyptic wine followed
by a eucharistic bread, followed again by a second, eucharistic
wine).

I propose the following theory to explain this strange pattern of
discrepancies. The double use of bread and wine is the result of the
imposition of a eucharistic theme on a narrative that was
originally apocalyptic only. This imposition is seen most clearly in
Luke, where the attempt to provide a eucharistic bread and wine
as well as an apocalyptic wine and bread leads to overlap and
doubling in a strained way that has been smoothed out in the
(superficially) more successful solution found in Mark/Matthew.

The fact that in Luke there is an apocalyptic word over food as
well as over wine indicates that in the original story, the
apocalyptic theme applied to bread as well as to wine; Luke,
however, has displaced the bread-word on to the paschal lamb, in
order to confine the bread-wine sequence to the eucharistic theme,
while Mark/Matthew goes still further by suppressing the apocalyptic theme in relation to food altogether. It did not occur to
Luke, as to Mark/Matthew, to combine the eucharistic and
apocalyptic themes into one sentence over one cup of wine.
Instead he is obliged to distribute the two themes over two cups of
wine. This is awkward, but has the merit of greater logic, for the
conflation of the two themes in Mark/Matthew, as if they were in
fact two aspects of the same theme, lacks sense.

In the original story, which contained only the apocalyptic
theme, the sequence was wine-bread, not bread-wine. Wine-bread
is the natural sequence of a Jewish festival meal, in which the
qiddush is first said over a cup of wine, which is then distributed;
then the 'breaking of bread' takes place, marking the beginning of
the meal. The *qiddush* is not in fact part of the meal but an
introductory and separate ceremony 'sanctifying' the festival day
itself, not the meal. The sequence bread-wine is therefore
impossible, because this would make the *qiddush* part of the meal.[18]
This Jewish sequence can still be seen in Luke's account, since he
shows Jesus beginning with the wine (22.17) and then going on to

the bread (22.19). Since, however, the sequence wine-bread is inappropriate to the eucharistic theme, which demands a bread-wine sequence, he is obliged to change the natural and expected sequel of an apocalyptic word over the bread into a eucharistic word, which then has to be completed by the introduction of a second cup of wine. This second cup does indeed have some justification in Jewish custom, since it was customary (but not obligatory) to have a cup of wine to accompany the saying of grace after the meal; but this grace-cup was of little importance compared with the cup of *qiddush*. Luke is thus forced to attach the eucharistic word not to the prominent and impressive cup of the *qiddush*, but to a secondary and non-obligatory cup which hardly accords with the dignity of the eucharist.[19]

The above explanation of Luke's procedure is based on the assumption that Luke found his own solution to the problem of how to distribute wine and bread between the claims of the two themes, eucharistic and apocalyptic. But it has to be remembered that Paul had already allotted the eucharistic wine to the 'cup after supper' (I Cor. 11.25). Luke therefore may be simply following Paul in this respect, though he had the extra problem not faced by Paul (who simply ignored the apocalyptic theme[20]) of how to fit in the apocalyptic pieces. Paul's allotment of the eucharistic theme to the 'cup after supper' may simply have made Luke's task easier by freeing the earlier *qiddush* cup for apocalyptic use. Paul's own motive in ignoring the *qiddush* cup and assigning the eucharistic words to the 'cup after supper' may be variously explained. It may be that Paul did not regard the Last Supper as a festival meal at all; he makes no mention of the Passover, but simply dates the occasion as the 'night of his arrest'. In this case, there would have been no *qiddush* cup. Or it may be that the sequence bread-wine was so important to Paul because of its mystery-religion associations that he was compelled to find a cup, however, unimportant in Jewish ritual, that followed the bread. Or it may be that the apocalyptic theme was so firmly associated in the tradition of the Jerusalem church with the *qiddush* cup of the Last Supper, that Paul, seeking to add a eucharistic theme to that tradition, had to avoid the *qiddush* cup and fix on some other cup that could have featured in the meal.[21]

In the Mark/Matthew account greater development has taken

place than in Luke in the direction of centralizing the eucharistic theme at the expense of the apocalyptic theme. There is no separate cup of wine for the apocalyptic word, and there is no apocalyptic word at all over food. The effect of this is to suppress the wine-bread sequence altogether. Instead we have a bread-wine sequence only, and this raises serious problems in the context of a Jewish festival meal. This has led some scholars to deny that the Last Supper was a festival meal, citing the account of John, who certainly places the Last Supper on the eve of the festival (13.1), not on the festival itself. Mark/Matthew, however, quite plainly place the Last Supper on the festival, while John's account of the Last Supper contains neither bread nor wine in either a eucharistic or an apocalyptic sense, so can hardly throw light on the very different scenario of Mark/Matthew.

Whether the Mark/Matthew account is later than that of Luke, or represents an independent and more thoroughgoing development in the direction of displacing the apocalyptic theme in favour of the eucharistic theme, we need not attempt to decide.[22] What is chiefly important is to stress the importance of the two conflicting sequences, wine-bread and bread-wine. The wine-bread sequence is Jewish, while the bread-wine sequence is not. This is a far more weighty indication of what parts of the Last Supper narrative are the earliest and most historically authentic than any real or fancied linguistic considerations of 'semitisms', though these will also have to be studied (see below). In the context of a Jewish festival meal, it is the wine-bread sequence that rings historically true, and the bread-wine sequence indicates a superimposed pattern. Therefore, Luke's preservation of the wine-bread sequence is most significant, and this belongs unmistakably to the apocalyptic, not the eucharistic theme, since the opening wine is unequivocally apocalyptic, while the ensuing bread is attached to the eucharistic theme in an equivocal, awkward manner (see below). Thus the close relation between the wine-bread sequence and the apocalyptic theme points to the latter as the central theme of the earliest form of the Last Supper narrative.

If wine-bread is the natural sequence for a Jewish festival meal, where are we to look for the un-Jewish sequence bread-wine? The answer is that this is the natural sequence for a mystery religion communion meal (see note 19). Thus the bread-wine sequence, being natural for a mystical rite of symbolic incorporation of the flesh and blood of a sacrificed god, gives structural indication of the Hellenistic origin of the eucharist, which has been introduced into a narrative which was indeed originally concerned with both bread and wine, but in the reverse order and with a characteristically Jewish apocalyptic theme.

The apocalyptic theme itself has been drastically misunderstood by Christian scholars, reading into it later mythological aspects characteristic of post-Jesus Christianity. Thus when Jesus told his disciples that they would next drink wine together in the kingdom of God, he was not envisaging an interval of long duration, prefaced by his own death and resurrection and finally concluded by his Second Coming. He was envisaging the advent of the kingdom of God (i.e. the earthly messianic age predicted by the Hebrew prophets) in his own lifetime and indeed in the very near future, as a result of his messianic entry into Jerusalem. The purpose of the Last Supper, then, was not to bid farewell to his disciples until some unspecified future time when they would be re-united. Its purpose was to hearten his disciples in preparation for the End-time, the day of the Lord, which Jesus confidently expected to happen the very next day on the Mount of Olives, the site of the miracle predicted by Zechariah.[23] Thus, in the light of historical probabilities, Jesus' apocalyptic word simply had the meaning that he was encouraging his disciples before the fateful day by telling them that all would be well, and their next meal together would be in the messianic kingdom. Before another day was out, the new kingdom of Israel under its divinely-appointed king, the descendant of David and Solomon, would have begun, and they would all celebrate this success by sharing the messianic banquet promised by prophecy.

Thus the common characterization of the apocalyptic word as an 'avowal of abstinence' is misconceived. This characterization depends on the hindsight that the meal to which Jesus looked forward was to be indefinitely delayed by his own unexpected and tragic death. Even on Christian mythological principles, the 'avowal of abstinence' is rather hard to understand. Does it make any sense for the resurrected Jesus, a spiritual being, to abstain from drinking wine? In any case, what would be the purpose of such abstention? Perhaps to mark Jesus' sharing and sympathy with the suffering of his followers on earth, waiting for his Second Coming? The picture of Jesus conscientiously abstaining from drinking wine in heaven lacks even mythological convincingness, and is a product of the perversion of a stirring word of encouragement and declaration of faith from its original meaning.

Scholars, however, try to give some intelligible content to Jesus' alleged avowal of abstinence by the assumption that Jesus began abstaining from wine *at the Last Supper itself*. This at least gives some little period during which the vow could be adhered to, even though it leaves all the remaining period before the Second Coming in a limbo of irrelevance (though perhaps the period between Jesus' arrest and his death should also be regarded as a period of abstinence, though hardly voluntary). To someone familiar with Jewish ritual, however, the picture of Jesus making a *qiddush* blessing over the wine, then distributing it to his disciples, but refraining from drinking from it himself, is incredible. To drink of the *qiddush* wine is a liturgical obligation, not a matter of self-indulgence, and, while it is certainly not unheard of that a person should discharge this obligation for others without partaking himself, this is only on the understanding that he will be discharging the obligation for himself later in the festival proceedings, or has already done so. If we take into account the aspect featured in Luke only, that Jesus made the 'avowal of abstinence' in relation to the paschal lamb also, this would amount to a refusal to take part in the chief rite of Passover, while at the same time attending a full performance of the rite in the company of celebrants. This would not be simply an act of asceticism, but a strange repudiation of the Passover combined illogically with the acceptance implied in his attendance at a rite convened by him and presided over by him.

Such strange behaviour (which could be explained only on the lines that Jesus, as a divine personage, was entitled to ride roughshod not only over Jewish sanctities but over logic itself) is actually not demanded by the text, and even, when it is properly read, contradicted by it. For Jesus is not represented as saying that he abjures the wine before him, but that he will not drink wine 'again' until he drinks it in the kingdom of God. The expression 'not again' or 'no further' (*ouketi*) implies clearly that Jesus is doing something now which he declares that he will not do again or further until the specified time.[24] Only the difficulty of attaching intelligible meaning to the alleged 'avowal of abstinence' has led to the picture of Jesus fasting while his disciples ate and drank.[25] But the concept of an 'avowal of abstinence' itself arose because of the belief that Jesus was miraculously aware of his own coming death – a belief which arose some time after Jesus' death, and which may not even have been associated with the earliest form of the belief in Jesus' resurrection.

Indeed the accounts given of the Last Supper cannot be understood in their relation to historical reality unless it is realized that the chief motivation of the narratives we have is to import the concept that Jesus miraculously knew and accepted what was to happen to him. Even the Gospels retain certain narrative elements showing that Jesus did *not* expect his own death and did not teach his disciples to expect it either. For example, in Luke we find his disciples, after his death, apparently quite oblivious of any teaching that his death was planned, saying, 'We had been hoping that he was the man to liberate Israel' (Luke 24.21), and having to be taught by the resurrected Jesus, apparently for the first time, that this was in accordance with scriptural prophecy. Of course, this can be regarded as part of the theme of 'the stupidity of the disciples' which is a common explanatory device in both the New Testament and later Christian writings; but it is surely more logical to explain this device itself as a way of smoothing over the difficulties of passages which reveal that the disciples were unaware of any intention on Jesus' part to suffer death as a planned part of his mission.

If we take seriously the proposition that Jesus had no miraculous knowledge of his own approaching death, and, like all other Jewish messianic claimants, was acting on the assumption that his claim would prove successful (though, of course, in full awareness of the dangers of such a claim in a country occupied by Rome), then this consideration alone is sufficient to relegate the eucharistic theme in the Last Supper narratives to the status of post-Jesus myth. For the whole eucharistic theme is premised on the notion of Jesus as one about to die as a divine sacrifice. Jesus' injunction, 'Do this in memory of me' (found only in I Corinthians and the Longer Text of Luke) implies his approaching death. Further, to eat the body and blood of Jesus, however symbolically, makes no

sense in relation to a live Jesus. The meaning of such a rite is bound
up with the theme of divine death and resurrection, and the desire of
the initiate to share in this process by incorporation of the divinity.
Thus if Jesus instituted the eucharist, this can only have been in
anticipation of his own death and resurrection, and also in anticipation of a new religion based on this central mystery. But all the
evidence from the practice of the Jerusalem church is that the
earliest followers of Jesus did not regard themselves as having
broken away from Judaism, and this evidence must weigh heavily
in favour of the hypothesis that Jesus himself had no intention of
founding a new religion based on his own death as the supreme
event of his life. Rather he set out to fulfil the prophecies about the
coming of a deliverer who would be faithful to Judaism.

Other aspects of the Last Supper narratives clearly intend to
convey the idea, so necessary to later Christianity, of Jesus'
awareness and acceptance of approaching death. Included in this
category are the following elements:

1. In Luke 22.16, the words 'before my death'.
2. The prophecy of Peter's three-fold denial (Luke 22.31-34;
    Mark 14.30; Matt. 26.34), placed by Luke during the Last
    Supper, but by Mark and Matthew later at the Mount of
    Olives.

A further striking narrative element contributing to the theme of
Jesus' foreknowledge is Jesus' awareness of Judas' intended betrayal (Luke 22.21-23; Mark 14.18-21; Matt. 26.21-23; John
13.21-26). In John, which lacks so many of the Last Supper themes
found in the other Gospels, this theme is very prominent, and the
sub-theme, hinted at in the others, that Jesus actually designated
and appointed Judas (by handing him the sop, 13.26) as his
betrayer, becomes explicit, so that Jesus becomes not only aware of
his approaching death, but the planner and architect of it. The
Judas-theme is likely to be the latest 'foreknowledge' element of all,
since it is entirely lacking in Paul's epistles, which appear to know
nothing of the alleged betrayal by Judas Iscariot (indeed, Paul's
statement that Jesus appeared after his death to 'the Twelve', I Cor.
15.5, is inconsistent with awareness of Judas' alleged defection).

Thus the Gospel narratives as we have them are largely shaped
by the motive of representing Jesus as foreknowing his death. The
only theme that (rightly understood) is not generated by such a

motive is the 'apocalyptic' theme, which is, therefore, the most
genuinely historical element in the whole Last Supper story. The
history of the development of the Last Supper narratives can thus
be reconstructed as follows.

1. *First stage.* It was known to those disciples who attended the
Last Supper that Jesus, at the Last Supper, on distributing the
qiddush wine, said, 'The next wine we shall drink together will be in
the kingdom of God.' Then, when he distributed the bread at the
beginning of the meal, he made a similar speech, meaning, 'The
next bread we shall share together will be at the messianic feast
which will be held to celebrate my victory and ascension to the
Davidic throne in the kingdom of God which is closely at hand.'

2. *Second stage.* Shortly after Jesus' death, Jesus' close disciples,
at first overwhelmed by dismay, became convinced that he was
still alive, having been resurrected by a divine miracle. Jesus
himself had not foreseen his death, but in a post-resurrection
appearance had explained that it was in accordance with biblical
prophecy (Luke 24.25-27). Consequently, the disciples cherished
the memory of the Last Supper as an assurance of ultimate success
and of Jesus' return. They probably celebrated the anniversary of
the Last Supper as part of their observance of Passover (as in the
practice of the Quartidecimani), not as a daily or weekly
observance. Their daily 'breaking of bread', as described in Acts,
was simply a communal meal on the Jewish pattern, and had
neither eucharistic or apocalyptic significance.

3. *Third stage* (first written stage). Paul had a vision (*c.* 50 CE), in
which Jesus told him that at the Last Supper, he distributed bread
and wine (in that order) not in an 'apocalyptic' context, but in
order to institute a mystery rite called 'the Lord's supper'. On the
basis of this vision, Paul instituted the eucharist among his
congregations, though this institution was unknown to the
Jerusalem church, and he refers to his vision in his letter to the
Corinthians (*c.* 54 CE) as validating the rite.

4. *Fourth stage* (Luke, Long Text). Luke (writing *c.* 85 CE)
attempts to combine the 'apocalyptic' theme of wine and bread
with the eucharistic theme of bread and wine in one narrative of
the Last Supper. He derives the details of the eucharistic theme
either directly from Paul's account in I Cor. 11, or mediately from
the liturgy that has grown up in the Pauline church on the basis of

I Cor. 11. The 'apocalyptic' theme (suppressed completely by
Paul) has survived among those traditions of the Jerusalem
church that were transferred to the Pauline church after Paul's
death. Luke interweaves the two themes in a harmonizing
attempt. He transfers the 'apocalyptic' bread to the paschal lamb,
freeing the bread for the eucharistic theme, leaves the *qiddush* cup
as entirely 'apocalyptic', and, like Paul, utilizes the cup 'after
supper' instead as the eucharistic cup. The 'apocalyptic' theme,
however, in his account still remains quite prominent, and his
harmonizing attempt, as a result, is awkward, and indicative of
the disparate nature of his materials, and the difficulty of
combining two separate scenarios, each involving bread and wine,
but in a different order.

Note. The Short Text of Luke may be an earlier, less satisfactory,
attempt to combine the two themes; or it may be, as Jeremias
argues, a truncated version of the Long Text. If the Short Text is
earlier (as the majority of scholars still believe), then it provides us
with an early Last Supper narrative, hardly tampered with
eucharistically, featuring the 'apocalyptic' theme as the central
concern of Jesus at the Last Supper. If, however, the Short Text is
derived from the Long Text, the difficulty of how this can be so is
not best solved by Jeremias' theory that the truncation was
motivated by secrecy about the details of the eucharist. The mere
fact that the eucharist involved eating bread and drinking wine as
symbolic of the body and blood of Jesus was so well known that
secrecy about this would have been pointless. Only the more
esoteric details of the eucharistic ritual could have been subject to
such secrecy. If the Short Text is indeed derived from the Long
Text, some other reason for the truncation must be sought. The
Short Text could have been written by a scribe who was
acquainted with the sources from which Luke and the other
evangelists worked, and was aware that these sources contained
nothing about the eucharistic theme. Feeling some uneasiness
about the freedom with which Luke had incorporated eucharistic
material into the narrative, such a scribe might have decided to
omit nearly all this extraneous material.

5. *Fifth stage* (Mark/Matthew).[26] In this account, the 'apocalyptic' theme has been further subordinated and appears only as an
afterthought in relation to the eucharistic cup. There is no longer

any hesitation between a wine-bread order and a bread-wine order; the bread-wine order is unequivocal, following the order given in I Corinthians, or, mediately, in the liturgy related to I Corinthians. So far, this account represents a stage further than the Long Text of Luke and so might be dated as later. On the other hand, in one important respect, Mark/Matthew has not developed as far as the Long Text: it lacks the words of institution, 'Do this in memory of me', and 'This cup is the new testament in my blood', both being phrases found in I Corinthians. It seems that Mark/Matthew, while being willing to edit the Last Supper account, as found in their sources (whether oral, or written records of the Jerusalem church) to include, and even be dominated by, the eucharistic rather than the 'apocalyptic' theme, balked at altering those sources to such an extent that Jesus was portrayed as actually instituting the rite of the eucharist. It seems better, therefore, to regard the Mark/Matthew account as an independent development of the story, not necessarily later than the Long Text of Luke, showing an alternative reaction to the problem of accommodating the Last Supper narrative to the belief of the church, based on Paul's vision in I Corinthians, that the eucharist had its origin in the Last Supper.

6. *Sixth stage* (John). The latest stage of all, that of John, has surprisingly deleted all reference to both the 'apocalyptic' and the eucharistic themes in its account of the Last Supper. John's account is an elaborate set-piece, having little in common with the Synoptic accounts either in content or in style. John has set himself to imagine how a mystagogal Jesus, in full awareness of his approaching death and its theological meaning, might have devoted himself to addressing his disciples in oratorical style. Only the themes of the betrayals by Judas and Peter are retained from the Synoptic accounts, the latter mentioned very cursorily, the former elaborated to bring out Jesus' lofty foreknowledge and control. John's account of the Last Supper is an imaginative construction, showing its lateness by its acceptance of a protracted absence of Jesus after his death, and by its developed theology. Yet it is still somewhat problematic that John has cast himself so adrift from his sources that he does not even mention the two themes that struggle for place in the Synoptic accounts. Evidently, the eucharistic theme is of great importance to John, because he

devotes another elaborate set-piece to it in a Galilee context (6.47-71), in which he dwells on its most paradoxical and apparently cannibalistic aspects with a special mystical relish. Perhaps the reason for John's omission of the eucharistic theme from the Last Supper is that, as a literary artist, he felt that this was too important a theme to be squeezed into such a narrow compass, competing with the overall Last Supper theme, as he saw it, of Jesus' farewell address on leaving the world, when he gave a panoramic view of the future of the church. He therefore transferred the eucharistic theme to a context in which it could assume central importance. John's omission of the 'apocalyptic' theme is not so hard to understand, since this theme did not have the theological or mystical implications which would qualify it for inclusion in John's concept of the Last Supper.

Nevertheless, John's omission of the eucharistic theme shows that the Last Supper was thinkable without it. The somewhat tentative efforts of the Synoptic evangelists to incorporate the eucharistic theme into their Last Supper narratives had still not eradicated the memory of the original version in which it played no part; consequently, John was not utterly committed to a eucharistic version. The theory of Jeremias that John was seeking to conceal the secret of the eucharist by omitting it in the Last Supper narrative is contradicted by John's open exposition of the most provocative aspects of the eucharistic theme in chapter 6. John, no doubt, took his information about the eucharist from actual experience of the rite and its liturgical practice, not from knowledge of I Corinthians, and was probably not aware of the Pauline account of the Last Supper. Being familiar, however, with the church dogma that Jesus himself instituted the eucharist, he felt free to introduce the theme at any point in the narrative that suited him. The evidence of John, then, is that around 100 CE, there was still some fluidity in the Last Supper story, and the Synoptic remodelling of it to include, or even chiefly feature, the eucharistic theme was not yet fully established.

Summary of the New Testament Evidence

The Gospel accounts of the Last Supper show great uneasiness about fitting in the eucharistic theme. One Gospel, John, omits it altogether. The Short Text of Luke omits it almost entirely. Mark/Matthew gives the eucharistic theme priority over the 'apocalyptic' theme, but omits the words of instruction. Only the Long Text of Luke includes the words of instruction, but this text shows awkwardness in its attempt to integrate the eucharistic with the 'apocalyptic' theme. In strong contrast to this picture of uneasiness is the straightforward pattern of eucharistic words and instructions in I Corinthians, where the 'apocalyptic' aspect is totally ignored. The best explanation of the relationship between I Corinthians and the Gospels is thus that the latter are trying, with difficulty, to incorporate into their Last Supper narratives the eucharistic material which they find either in I Corinthians itself, or in some source related to I Corinthians, such as the eucharistic liturgy. The original source or sources used by the Gospels for their Last Supper narratives, however, did not contain eucharistic material at all, but centred on the 'apocalyptic' theme. The historical conclusion to which this argument leads is that Jesus did not institute the eucharist, the fundamental concepts of which were alien to him as a Jew. The creator of the eucharist was Paul, whose immediate source was a vision in which Jesus gave him eucharistic information about the Last Supper. Paul's less immediate source for the eucharist, however, was the Hellenistic institution of the communion meal, found especially in the mystery-religions (see below), with which Paul was acquainted in Tarsus, a centre of mystery-religion.

Linguistic Considerations

It is now time to consider the linguistic arguments which Jeremias, in particular, has put forward to combat the view that the Gospel eucharistic material is derived from Paul's account in I Cor. 11. Jeremias argues:

1. That the account of the Last Supper in I Cor. 11 contains semitisms that are untypical of Paul's style, showing that he derived this account from church tradition.

2. That the Gospel accounts, particularly that of Mark, contain further semitisms, showing that they are partly derived from some source other than I Corinthians.

3. That even the Long Text of Luke, which appears to be heavily

dependent on I Corinthians, contains semitisms which show it to be derived from a liturgical source from which I Corinthians is also derived.

In reply to these contentions, the following may be urged.

1. *General Considerations*

The fact that Paul's eucharistic language is not typical of his style certainly does not prove that this language was derived from church tradition, itself deriving from Jesus' own words. It is at least as likely that Paul is using language derived from the terminology of the mystery-cults. One very probable example of this is Paul's use of the expression, 'the Lord's supper' (*kuriakon deipnon*). This expression is likely to have been associated with mystery religion communion meals.[27] Consequently, the expression 'eucharist', derived from Hellenistic Jewish sources, and associated with the *qiddush*-type festival meals of the Jewish-Christian church (see above), was substituted for Paul's expression 'the Lord's supper' which became totally obsolete. Another expression used by Paul that is most probably derived from mystery-religion is the word 'body', used in relation to the bread. As many scholars have pointed out, the coupling of 'body' and 'blood' is foreign to Semitic usage (which employs the coupling of 'flesh' and 'blood', *basar ve-dam*). Here then we have two key expressions, used by Paul, which point to a mystery religion rather than a Jewish origin.

The above two examples raised an important methodological consideration. This is that it is by no means always helpful to look for the existence of 'semitisms' as an indication of temporal priority. Sometimes a 'semitism' is an attempt to give a Jewish colouring to something that is basically Hellenistic. Thus the re-naming of the 'Lord's supper' as the 'eucharist' is a move from a Hellenistic expression to a Jewish one; and it is indisputable that the Hellenistic expression came first, since it is used by Paul and is the only designation of the ceremony found in the New Testament. We can even see the same movement of 're-Judaization' in our second example above, that of body/blood. In the Gospel of John, we see that the body/blood dichotomy has been changed to a flesh/blood dichotomy (John 6.51-57). This passage is undoubtedly later than I Cor. 11.24, which speaks of a body/blood

dichotomy, and the change in John is no doubt motivated by a
desire to give a more Jewish colouring to the topic. While the
notion of 're-Judaization' is a familiar one in twentieth-century
New Testament scholarship, it is doubtful whether the term has
been employed in the most relevant contexts.

A further point is that 'semitisms', even when genuinely prior in
time, are not necessarily a proof of Jewish provenance. This point
applies especially when the 'semitism' in question is an Aramaism.
The Aramaic language was used in the first century by many
peoples other than the Jews. In Tarsus, for example, where Paul
was born and spent his youth, Aramaic was the common language
of the people, Greek being used mainly for more formal or public
occasions. Thus an Aramaism in the language of eucharistic
material does not necessarily point to a Jewish origin. It may
equally point to an origin in the formulae of mystery-religion
centres where Aramaic was spoken. Far more reliable as an
indication of Jewish origin is a Hebraism, since Hebrew was
spoken almost entirely by Jews. Often it is difficult to distinguish
in a Greek text between a Hebraism and an Aramaism, but in our
Last Supper narratives there is indeed one outstanding Hebraism
which tells us much (see below). Hebraisms, where discernible,
are all the more important in view of recent research which has
shown that the use of Hebrew in the time of Jesus was much more
widespread than was previously supposed.[28]

A further important general point in approaching the 'semitisms' in the accounts of the Last Supper is that commentators,
including Jeremias, have failed to appreciate fully the distinction
between the two themes discussed above: the eucharistic theme
and the 'apocalyptic' theme. That these two themes exist in the
accounts is, of course, understood; but the question is not even
considered whether both themes are original to the story, or in fact
one of them has been superimposed unhistorically on the other. If
it is accepted, on the basis of the arguments given above, that the
eucharistic theme is a later addition, and that the 'apocalyptic'
theme is the sole constituent of the original story, all the
'semitisms' that have been observed in the basic framework of the
story (i.e. in the breaking of the bread, the taking of the cup, the
offering of thanks) will be seen to belong to the 'apocalyptic'
theme, not the eucharistic theme for which they have been

claimed. At the very least, such a possibility should be considered, in preference to the unreflective assumption that all these 'semitisms' testify to the earliness of both themes equally. Or, to put the point in another way, the existence of such a possibility means that evidence of 'semitisms' in the framework of the accounts cannot be taken to prove the earliness of the eucharistic material, which may have been added to a framework which served originally for the 'apocalyptic' material only.

2. *Paul's account*

A corollary of the last point is that the presence of 'Grecisms' in Paul's account in I Cor. 11 cannot necessarily be taken to prove that this account is later than that of Mark. Jeremias argues that, while Paul's epistle is undoubtedly the earliest literary source for the Last Supper, it is actually later than the source used by Mark, since the latter contains 'semitisms' which are corrected into 'Grecisms' by Paul. This argument, if valid at all, can apply only to the explicitly eucharistic material, not to the framework material, which did indeed exist before Paul's account was written, but, at least possibly, for a non-eucharistic purpose. In the course of re-writing the story he 'Grecized' certain 'semitisms' which he found in the framework; but this does nothing to prove that the eucharistic material was not his own addition to an originally 'apocalyptic' story.

The only 'Grecisms' that are relevant, then, are those found in the actual eucharistic words over the bread and the wine. Here Jeremias does indeed find some 'Grecisms' as against Mark and Luke. These are:

> v. 24. Paul has *humon* (in relation to the bread), whereas Mark has *pollon* (14.24) (in similar relation to the wine). Moreover, the whole expression, *to huper humon*, 'has a form not possible in a Semitic language', and this whole expression is lacking in Mark.
>
> v. 25. Paul includes the copula *estin*, which is omitted in Luke 22.20.
>
> vv. 24 and 25. Paul places the possessive pronoun before the noun, whereas Mark (14.22 and 24) places it after the noun in

semitic fashion. Luke also has this semitic word order (22.19 and 20).

This is the total relevant evidence from which Jeremias concludes, 'The account of Paul presents therefore linguistically a transformation of the old semitizing tradition . . . '[29] We may consider now whether this evidence justifies such a sweeping conclusion, and his further conclusion that Paul's version of the eucharistic words is later than those found in Mark and Luke.

It must be said that the above evidence is very flimsy. Mark could easily have changed *humon* to *pollon* for some reason other than that he found this 'semitism' in a source earlier than Paul. *humon* must have seemed puzzling and imprecise, since it could mean that Jesus' self-sacrifice was on behalf of his disciples only, not for humanity in general. It may well be that Mark was not the originator of this change, but that the change had already been made in the liturgy of the eucharist; a liturgical development, on the present argument, subsequent to Paul's eucharistic manifesto in I Corinthians. If *pollon* came first, why would Paul have changed it to *humon*? Such a change could not be motivated merely by a desire to make the matter more intelligible to Greek-readers, for it is an actual change of meaning, not merely of expression. General principles of criticism demand that the more difficult and less precise expression should be regarded as earlier than the smoother and more exact expression. As for the semitic character of *pollon* (derived, as Jeremias argues, from the Hebrew *rabbim*, meaning not just 'many', but 'the community at large'), this may be due to a desire to 're-judaize' a concept felt correctly to be alien to Jewish tradition, i.e. the idea of salvation achieved through the sacrifice and incorporation (whether symbolic or real) of a human figure. An uneasiness about a new concept could be allayed by assigning it a phrase with a Jewish air, just as the 'Lords's supper' was made more respectable and less obviously pagan-derived by giving it the name 'eucharist'. Clearly, on Jeremias' method, we would have to conclude that 'eucharist' came first, since it is a 'semitism', but we know that this is not the case. Jeremias' method is therefore suspect, being mechanically linguistic, and lacking in due regard for the religio-social circumstances in which a reversion to 'semitism' might be a helpful psychological device.

Another important consideration in assessing *pollon* as a 'semitism' is that Mark may well have derived this word not directly from a Semitic language but from the Septuagint, where it appears in a relevant context in Isaiah 53.12. Mark, wishing to give a Jewish colouring to the eucharistic concept, did not even have to draw on a knowledge of Hebrew or Aramaic.

Paul's whole sentence in relation to the bread, 'This is my body for your sake' (*touto mou estin to soma to huper humon*) is cryptic to the point of unintelligibility. It is therefore natural and easy to see the variants in the Gospels as attempts to add intelligibility, rather than as earlier versions prior to Paul. Thus Mark solves the problem by omitting the cryptic *huper humon* altogether in relation to the bread, and adding it in an expanded and more intelligible form to the saying over the wine, which thus throws light on the bread-saying too. Luke, on the other hand, adds the word *didomenon* to the bread-word. This is much smoother Greek than Paul's, and this change shows that a difficulty was certainly felt about Paul's expression (contrary to Jeremias' attempt to argue that Paul's expression is not only characteristically Greek, but unproblematic[30]).

Jeremias' argument in this context (that Paul's *estin* is a Grecism and thus constitutes a later version than Luke's) is hardly convincing in view of the haphazard use of *estin* in the Gospel accounts. While Luke omits *estin* in 22.20, he includes it in 22.19, while Mark includes it both times, though his account is, according to Jeremias' own argument, the most semitic. It must be concluded that the use of *estin* is hardly a reliable indication of a Grecism, but that the word is inserted or omitted for stylistic reasons only.

Similarly, the weight that Jeremias puts on the word-order of possessive pronoun and noun is hardly justified. Mark's expressions *to soma mou* and *to haima mou* are just as good Greek as Paul's *mou esti to soma* and *toi emoi haimati*. Others who have investigated possible Aramaisms in the Gospels (e.g. Matthew Black) have not seen fit to include this aspect. It is surely essential to the definition of a 'semitism' that it should read awkwardly in Greek. Why should Paul alter a good Greek phrase just because it happened to coincide with a semitic idiom? We must conclude, then, that the difference between Paul's and Mark's word-order is merely a matter of stylistic preference.

Thus Jeremias' contention that Paul's 'Grecisms' point to the lateness of his account of the eucharistic words is not persuasive. I now turn to the other side of Jeremias' argument on Paul, which is on the opposite tack – that some of Paul's expressions are untypical of him, and can only come from some liturgical version of the eucharistic words which he is quoting.

One of the relevant examples of this given by Jeremias (relevant because contained in the eucharistic words themselves, not in the framework, which, as argued above could just as well have an apocalyptic context) is Paul's use of the word *huper* in 11.24. For though Jeremias argues that the following word *humon* is a Grecism, he argues that the word *huper* itself, followed by a genitive, is a semitism, as found in both Mark 14.24 and I Cor. 11.24.[31] One may simply ask whether Paul is using semitisms in the non-eucharistic contexts of II Cor. 7.12 and 9.3, which Jeremias himself points out as typical of Paul's Greek style.

Jeremias' chief argument here, however, is based not on any residual semitisms in Paul's account, but on certain 'liturgical' phrases which do not seem typical of Paul's style, and which Jeremias therefore thinks have been taken by Paul from an already existent liturgy. Thus there is Paul's 'sonorous introduction': ' . . . the Lord Jesus, on the night of his arrest, took bread . . . ' Jeremias even argues that Paul changed Mark's 'for many' into 'for you' because he had in mind the actual liturgical formula in which the priest was offering the eucharist to the congregation, addressing them as 'you'. This hardly seems to square with the explanation given by Jeremias elsewhere that Paul made this change as a 'Grecism' in order to render the phrase more intelligible to a Greek-speaking readership.

The main general point, however, that it is necessary to make is that if Paul was in fact creating a new rite, then he would naturally adopt a style suitable for such a solemn occasion and this might involve some departure from his usual epistolary style. Indeed Paul may be quoting from a liturgy which he had previously composed himself. He is reminding the Corinthians of an account of the Lord's Supper which he has already transmitted to them previously, and it may well be that he also gave them a liturgy for the rite. Moreover, even if Paul's liturgy contained some material derived from earlier liturgical rites, it was not necessarily derived from the Jerusalem church but might easily be from some mystery-religion liturgy that was known to him. This might well explain the 'sonorous' obscurity of the phrase *to huper humon*, which certainly sounds liturgical, but has nothing to do with any Jewish liturgy. A prominent example of non-Jewish liturgical style is the very name that Paul gave to the rite – the 'Lord's supper'.

We may conclude this section on the linguistic aspects of the Last Supper narratives by turning to the important point (see above) that genuine Hebraisms, if available, are far more important indicators of authentic derivation from the historical Jesus than 'semitisms' which may be derived from either Hebrew or Aramaic (since Aramaisms may arise from a variety of sources, some of them not Jewish). An undoubted Hebraism to be found in the Last Supper narratives is the expression 'the fruit of the vine', which is clearly derived from *peri ha-gaphen*, the familiar phrase which figures in the 'blessing' (*berakhah*) over wine. Another phrase that is undoubtedly Jewish, though it may be either a Hebraism or an Aramaism, is 'the kingdom of God'. An undoubted Hebraism is the expression 'Amen'. All three of these phrases occur in the 'apocalyptic' part of the narratives, and they support the thesis that the earliest material is apocalyptic.

My conclusion is that linguistic investigation is far from proving that the eucharistic material is earlier than Paul, as Jeremias argues. The 'semitisms' adduced belong overwhelmingly to the framework of the story and to the 'apocalyptic' section, and the latter contains the most authentically Jewish material of all. The few 'semitisms' that have been observed in the eucharistic material itself can be explained quite easily without recourse to the theory that they derive either from Jesus or from a liturgy earlier than Paul, while Paul's own eucharistic account, where it shows an unusual style, is best understood as deriving this from the subject-matter, and from Paul's intention, unusual in his letters, to create ritual, or rather to validate a ritual which he had already created. Indeed, if Paul was in fact quoting from a liturgy, it was from one that he had himself composed at a time earlier, but not much earlier, than the composition of his first epistle to the Corinthians; for it is clear from his account that he is referring to a rite, and a validation of it, with which his readers were already familiar, and that he is repeating a story which he has already communicated to them orally.

The Eucharist and the Mystery religions

Some remarks have already been made above about the similarities between the eucharist and the communion-meals of the various Hellenistic cults usually called 'mystery religions', though this term does not apply fully to all of them. We may now survey these similarities in more detail, and also consider the points of radical dissimilarity that distinguish the eucharist from Jewish ceremonies of communal eating, especially the *qiddush*.

1. *The name 'the Lord's supper'*. Paul does not use the term 'eucharist', but 'the Lord's supper' (*kuriakon deipnon*), a term which he uses as the regular designation for the ceremony. Yet in the second century we find Justin Martyr using the term 'eucharist' (*Apol.* I. lxvi) and the term 'Lord's supper' has evidently dropped out of use. It seems probable that this was because the expression *kuriakon deipnon* was in use in other cults which centred on a salvific figure addressed and designated by devotees as 'Lord' (*kurios*). Paul himself refers to these other sacramental meals, calling them 'the table of devils' (I Cor. 10.21). For the change by the Pauline church to the use of the term 'eucharist', which was already in use by Jewish-Christians for the very different ceremony described in the Didache, see above.[32]

2. *The emphasis on the bread*. Paul inverts the natural order wine-bread, for a festival meal, giving the wine what is an insignificant place in a Jewish meal. In the Eleusinian mysteries, the central place was occupied by an ear of corn, while in the rites of Attis (which are likely to have been Paul's immediate inspiration), the communion-meal comprised eating followed by drinking.[33] The eucharist, therefore, is in the tradition of the agriculture-based mysteries in which bread was central. In the practice of the eucharist, in early times, bread was so primary that the wine could be omitted, or water could be substituted. This fact has been used by some scholars to explain the vexing problem of the missing eucharist in Acts, where we have merely the assertion that the members of the Jerusalem church 'broke bread' together. Since, however, this expression was used of every Jewish communal meal, it hardly functions as an adequate expression for a eucharistic rite.

The evidence is that in early times, the eucharist took place as the culmination of an actual communal meal. Only later was the eucharist separated from the meal (or *agape*) as an isolated rite. Paul himself seems to recommend such an isolation in I Cor. 11.22. That a special ceremony should take place over bread at the end of a meal, rather than at its beginning, is quite alien to Jewish custom; and this too points to the non-Jewish origin of the eucharist. One might point in this connection to the Jewish ceremony of the eating of the *aphiqoman* (a piece of the unleavened bread) at the end of the Passover meal. But, as Jeremias remarks, this detail of the Seder was added at a late period.[34]

3. *The expression 'after supper'*. Paul uses the expression *meta to deipnesai*, in connection with the cup of wine, and this expression is repeated by Luke, but not by Mark/Matthew. The expression thus did not figure in the original 'apocalyptic' account of the Last Supper, in which the wine preceded the bread. We might be content to explain that Paul, wishing to adhere to the mystery religion sequence of bread-wine, added this phrase to explain the departure from the usual Jewish festival sequence of wine-bread by adducing the cup associated with the grace after meals. But there is the further consideration that the cup of wine 'after supper' is found in pagan practice in celebration of the ancient pre-Olympic deity the *agathos daimon*, who lies in the background of several mystery religion deities. The phrase 'after supper' may thus be further indication of pagan influence on Paul's eucharistic rite, especially as the Jewish designation of the final cup is not 'the cup after supper' but 'the cup of grace' (*kos shel birkat hamazon*), and it is drunk not immediately after supper but after the reciting of grace.[35]

4. *Bread as 'body' and wine as 'blood'*. The most weighty evidence, however, for the non-Jewish origin of the eucharist remains the concept of the bread and wine as the body and blood of Jesus, with the concomitant notion that, by partaking in the eucharist, a believer is ingesting the deity, and thereby entering into mystic communion with him and gaining a share in his immortality. This concept is characteristic of mystery-religion, and totally foreign to Judaism.

It has been argued that Paul himself does not express the idea of eating the body or drinking the blood of Jesus, but that this is found first in the Gospel of John. But the very idea that the bread is

Jesus' body and the wine his blood, plainly expressed in Paul's account of the eucharistic words implies very directly that those who eat the bread and drink the wine are ingesting Jesus himself. Further, Paul refers to the sacrament as 'spiritual food' and 'spiritual drink' (I Cor. 10.3), when he says that the supernatural water drunk by the Israelites in the desert was Christ. So the notion of ingestion of the deity, whether meant literally or symbolically, was certainly very much in Paul's mind.

In the Eleusinian mysteries, the initiated became deified (*entheoi*) by partaking in a meal which represented the body of Dionysus.[36] In the mysteries of Attis, a meal of bread and liquid, representing the body of the god, enabled the initiate to participate in his passion and resurrection. The use of the term 'body' (*soma*) in this connection in Paul's eucharistic account is very revealing, for this word has very rich Greek associations, but no Jewish ones, for the Hebrew word *guph* could never be used in a context of eating, and would never be used in counterpoise with 'blood' rather than *basar*. The whole notion of 'eating the god' is familiar in a Hellenistic setting, but bizarre in a Jewish one. In Latin poetry, it is a commonplace to speak of eating Ceres (meaning bread) or drinking Bacchus (wine), and this is not just a poetical trope, but the poetical residue of sacraments in which these foodstuffs were regarded as divine. It is possible, of course, to trace these concepts back to prehistoric origins of totemistic or cannibalistic feasts, in which the divine animal or a human victim was eaten in tribal communion-feasts. In the time of Paul, such literal versions were long outmoded and existed only in the form of surviving primitive myths, such as that of the dismemberment and eating of Dionysus, though indeed the savage ceremony of the Dionysian *omophagia* was well-known from references in the Greek poets and was still practised in a tamer form. But on a sublimated level, on which foodstuffs were regarded as symbolic of the actual god (or, in a more magical mode, as becoming transubstantiated into the god), these ideas were pervasive in the pagan world.

In Judaism such ideas not only did not exist, but were outlawed as characteristically idolatrous. Even in the Jewish sacrifices, most of which were at least partly eaten, either by the priest or by the offerer or by both, there was never any suggestion that what was being eaten was God. On the contrary, the strict requirement that

the blood of the animal should never be eaten, whether when
sacrificed or slaughtered for ordinary eating, seems to be actu-
ated by a prohibition against imbibing *mana*. For the Bible says
that 'the blood is the life' (Gen. 9.4; Lev. 17.14); and this means
that when one eats meat, one must not eat the life with it. All life
is divine, and this is therefore a ban on eating God. Only God
can eat life, and therefore, in sacrifice, the blood of the animal
must be poured on the altar. Man may eat meat, but not the holy
life that is in the animal. These ideas are ingrained in Judaism
and were much pondered over in the intertestamental period, as
the Book of Jubilees shows (though rabbinic law, unlike that
book, permitted the eating of blood by Gentiles, considering that
the blood only became consecrated, and therefore forbidden as
'life', if the animal has been consecrated by *shehitah*, which is not
required of Gentiles). Thus the eucharistic saying that enjoins or
implies the eating of divine life and blood touches a nodal point
of Judaism, coming with the force of blasphemy and idolatry,
and contradicting the essential humanism of Judaism, which
enjoins the acceptance of a valid human role and the illegitimacy
of attempts to escape from humanity by recipes for acquiring
godhead. Such an idea is totally at variance with Judaism, and
this is essentially what makes the eucharist underivable from the
qiddush or any other Jewish rite.[37]

Conclusion

An analysis of the Gospel accounts of the Last Supper shows
them to be composite, in the sense that they consist of a core
narrative with an 'apocalyptic' theme, overlaid with the eucharistic theme, which has been introduced from an external source.
The obvious choice for this source is Paul's account in I Corinthians, or some derivative from this. The objections raised to this
prima facie solution on structural and linguistic grounds are
unpersuasive, since they fail to recognise the basic conflict in the
Gospel narratives between the underlying 'apocalyptic' theme
and the imposed eucharistic theme, and allot evidential weight,
in favour of the earliness of the eucharistic theme, to 'semitisms'
which mostly belong to the framework or to the 'apocalyptic'
theme.

The un-Jewish nature of the eucharistic theme (particularly the ingestion of divine body and blood, with the implication of a divine sacrifice in which the worshipper partakes) remains the chief factor militating against a Jewish derivation of the rite.

The argument thus reinforces the thesis of this book, which sees Paul's thought as deriving chiefly from Hellenistic religion, and as constituting a radical departure from the standpoint of Jesus.

Postscript on Baptism

The subject of baptism is relevant, because here too we have a rite which is derived outwardly from Judaism, but is remodelled in Pauline thought in such a way that its aims become non-Jewish and Hellenistic. The eucharist is derived outwardly from Judaism in that its starting-point is the celebration by Jesus of a festival meal preceded by a *qiddush*. Paul, however, imports into the eucharist an idea that was alien to Jesus: the mystical ingestion by initiates of divine substance. The result is that the eucharist can no longer be called a *qiddush*, but must be regarded as a mystery religion communion meal. Similarly, Paul's thinking on baptism transforms it into a non-Jewish rite.

Baptism in the first century was a ceremony of entry to Judaism by converts, and was combined with the offering of a sacrifice in the Temple, and, in the case of males, with circumcision. There was some discussion in the second century by rabbis as to whether baptism was necessary for males (b. Yebamot, 46a). It was not regarded as a mystical initiation, but merely as a rite of passage from the status of Gentile to that of Jew. Baptism also featured within Judaism as a means of cleansing oneself from ritual impurity (incurred by touching the corpse of a 'creeping thing', for example) before entering the Temple or eating holy food. The baptism offered by John the Baptist, however, evidently was not for ritual purity purposes, but acted as a symbol of entering upon a new life of repentance; thus it had much in common with the baptism of converts, who were also entering upon a new life. Other messianic campaigns of repentance in Jewish history (e.g. that of Shabbetai Zevi) were also marked by wholesale baptism.

Paul's concept of baptism, however, ignores repentance and contains a radically new idea: that through baptism, the convert shares in the crucifixion and resurrection of Jesus (Rom. 6.1-4).

A full discussion of Pauline baptism is not undertaken in this book. Here it is only noted that Pauline baptism, like the Pauline eucharist, is a mystical and even magical sacrament by which the passion and resurrection of Christ is appropriated by the believer for his own salvation. This aim differentiates these rites from the Jewish *qiddush* and immersion. While the eucharist corresponds to the regular communion meal of the mystery cults, Pauline baptism is the analogue of the *taurobolion* in the cults of Mithras and Attis, and is essentially a once-for-all rite of initiation into a mystery.

5

Paul and Pharisaism

The arguments pursued above have aimed to show the affinity between Paul's religious concepts and those of Hellenism. The question may be asked, however, 'What about the manifold similarities that have been detected by scholars between Paul's style of expression and thought and those of Pharisaic and rabbinic Judaism?' Scholars have had different motives in pointing out these alleged similarities: an older, Romantic school of thought, of whom Renan may be taken as typical, did so in order to contrast the beautiful simplicity of Jesus with the contorted Pharisee-derived intellectuality of the theologian Paul; while a newer, more positive and ecumenic, school does so in order to stress the alleged continuity between Jewish and Pauline thought. Yet another school, that of feminism, returns to the negative image of Paul as a Pharisee, in order to blame Christian denigration of women on the alleged residual Pharisaism of Paul.

We must distinguish here between three aspects of the enquiry into Paul's relationship to Pharisaism:

1. The alleged affinity of Paul's theological ideas to those of Pharisaism (e.g. the deification of Jesus as a development of Jewish angelology); this aspect has been dealt with in Chapters 2 and 3.

2. The transformation of Pharisaic concepts by Paul where, though the result is new, it is couched in a Pharisaic or at least Jewish terminology; this aspect entered into the discussion of the eucharist in Chapter 4. Here it was noted that there is an element

of Judaization of what are basically non-Jewish ideas. This is part of Paul's endeavour to give a Jewish clothing to his scheme of salvation, which roots itself in the Old Testament and enrols the whole succession of prophets in its behalf. But this is not in any way a proof of Paul's Jewish or Pharisaic background, any more than the meditations of the Gnostics on Genesis, or of Muhammad on the Hebrew Bible, prove them to be Jews. When we find in Paul, as we frequently do, a Jewish expression ('Christ', for example) being used in a way that is alien to Jewish thought (as in the expression 'in Christ', for which no-one has ever even claimed to have found a Jewish parallel), it is perverse to carry away as one's chief conclusion, 'Ah, that shows how Jewish Paul was!' Yet this is one of the chief methods of argument of, for example, W. D. Davies. It should also be noted that these 'Judaized' ideas do not require any specialized knowledge of Judaism. One did not have to be a trained Pharisee, for example, to be aware of the existence of the word 'Messiah' (Greek 'Christ') in Judaism. The use of such words by Paul, as Judaism-derived nomenclature for his own special concepts, does not argue anything more than a superficial acquaintance with Judaism.

3. The alleged use by Paul of idioms, methods of argument and midrashic themes characteristic of Pharisaism. This is the nub of the question, and will occupy the remainder of this chapter. It would be a powerful reinforcement of the view that Paul's thought stems from Judaism, and not from Hellenism, if it could be shown that the fabric of his literary style and habit of argument is characteristically Pharisaic. If it could be shown that there is something indelibly and unconsciously Jewish and Pharisaic about the way in which Paul develops his arguments, illustrates them and drops incidental comments about them, this would be the very best proof that he himself came from a Pharisaic background, as he claimed; and that his thinking was a natural development of that background, rather than deriving from Hellenistic influences, as argued in this book. This might be called the 'fingerprint' method of proof, based not on the content of Paul's writings but on those elements which he did not consciously intend and could not avoid.

There are certain questions which we must ask, however, before embarking on such an enquiry. What is the meaning of the expression, 'characteristically Pharisaic'? What were the Pharisees like in Paul's time? At one time, this was thought to be an easy question to answer: the Pharisaic style of thought and expression was to be found in the rabbinic writings. It was on this basis that Strack and Billerbeck wrote their work on rabbinic parallels to the New Testament. In more recent times, however, great doubt has been thrown on the alleged continuity between the first-century Pharisees and the 'rabbinic movement' of the post-Destruction period. The earliest substantial literary work of the rabbinic movement, the Mishnah, was redacted at about 200 CE. The Pharisees themselves left no literature, though the opinions of prominent Pharisees, including Hillel, Shammai, Gamaliel I (mentioned in the New Testament) and Johanan ben Zakkai, are quoted in the Mishnah and other rabbinic works. The leaders most often quoted in the Mishnah, however, are not Pharisees but 'rabbis' who came to prominence after the Destruction of the Temple (70 CE): among the earliest of these are Gamaliel II, Eliezer ben Hyrcanus, Joshua ben Hananiah, Akiba ben Joseph and Ishmael ben Elisha, who, though all born before the Destruction, pursued their adult activities after it. Another complication is that the Mishnah is largely a legal work, containing only a small proportion of exegetical or theological material. Though such material is abundant outside the Mishnah in other rabbinic works, these are of even later redaction, viz. the Midrashim, the earliest of which (the Tannaitic Midrashim) were redacted in the third and fourth centuries. Thus much of the material that has been adduced to throw light on the thinking and style of the Pharisees was first committed to writing in the third century, at the earliest; a good deal, indeed, belongs to compilations made even later, the Talmudim and the Homiletic Midrashim, redacted from about 400 CE to as late as 1000 CE.

If we adopt a very strict attitude towards dating (i.e. that material cannot be considered earlier than the date of its redaction), then nothing in the rabbinic literature can be regarded as serviceable in throwing light on the Pharisees. This very strict attitude has been adopted by certain New Testament scholars. There has been a tendency in New Testament scholarship to switch from one extreme approach to another – from an uncritical assumption that all the rabbinic writings are relevant, to an equally uncritical assumption that they are entirely irrelevant. If the rabbinic writings are indeed irrelevant, we cannot quote from them either to prove that Paul was a typical Pharisee or that he was not. For information about the Pharisees, we have to turn to literature earlier than the rabbinic writings: that is to say, to Josephus and to the Gospels and Acts. Other first-century writings that hitherto were regarded as being non-Pharisaic (pseudepigrapha and Qumran Scrolls) now begin to be taken into account, on the ground that Pharisaism, being an unknown quantity, may have been more like them than was previously realized. Some would say that the best evidence of what a Pharisee was like is actually to be found in the writings of Paul; for, since he says most categorically that he was brought up as a Pharisee, and since it is unthinkable that he was not telling the truth, then we must define the Pharisees in terms of this fortunately available first-hand evidence.[1]

Most scholars, however, do not find this simple, if circular, argument satisfactory, and try to find some outside evidence to corroborate Paul's Pharisee credentials. Neither the evidence from the Gospels and Acts nor that from Josephus gives us much of the flavour of Pharisee expression or style of thinking, though both sources do provide some valuable information about the general standpoint and status of the Pharisees. We learn from the Gospels that the Pharisees were held in high esteem as authorities on the laws, though the Gospels also accuse them of hypocrisy and cruelty. From Acts we learn that Gamaliel, the leader of the Pharisees (though we are not told here that he was their leader; this we know from rabbinic sources) was widely respected and loved. From Josephus, we learn that the Pharisees, as opposed to the Sadducees, believed in respecting extra-biblical 'traditions'; that they were frequently in collision with secular authorities; that they were more lenient in their interpretation of the laws than the Sadducees; and that they were popular with the people, who regarded their views as authoritative. We also learn from Josephus some of the doctrines of the Pharisees, such as their belief in both free-will and fate, and from both Josephus and the New Testament we learn that they believed in the resurrection of the dead.

This rather sparse information provides few if any points of contact with Paul's writings, though we do gain from these sources the valuable point that their general characterization of the

Pharisees is in accord with rabbinic Judaism; the emphasis on legal expertise, on leniency of judgment, on transmission of traditions, on popular authority, all accord well with the movement described in the rabbinic writings. The sparse information found in the New Testament and Josephus, therefore, should lead us towards rather than away from the rabbinic sources as evidence for the detailed thought and manner of expression of the Pharisees.

As for the Pseudepigrapha and the Qumran writings, these should certainly not be discounted as sources for certain aspects of Pharisaic thought, not because there is any vacuum of information elsewhere, but precisely because study of the rabbinic literature (e.g. by Gershom Scholem) confirms that there was a mystical and apocalyptic aspect to rabbinic thought. Thus in assessing Paul's type of mystical and apocalyptic expression, it is certainly relevant to compare it (and contrast it) with that of the intertestamental literature, as Schweitzer did, but this should be part of a general recourse to rabbinic literature, not an exclusion of it. At the same time, we should be alert to *differences* between the mysticism and apocalypticism of the Pseudepigraph and Qumran writings and those of Pharisaism, especially as regards the place and importance allotted to these aspects.

We do not, in fact, have to confine ourselves to the New Testament, Josephus, and the intertestamental literature, since the extreme view that the rabbinic writings are irrelevant is untenable. Several scholars have protested recently at the attempt to exclude the rabbinic writings from discussion of the New Testament. The alleged discontinuity between the Pharisees and the rabbinic movement has been challenged. The late redaction of the Mishnah and Midrashim does not argue their irrelevance, as they are compilations of oral material much of which dates from a time far earlier than their date of redaction. Moreover, the Targums have to be taken into account; and some at least of their content must be regarded as deriving from the first century. To regard the founders of the Mishnah, the generation of Gamaliel II, Eliezer, Joshua and Akiba, all of whom experienced Temple times in their youth, as belonging to a different thought-world from that of the Pharisees, is becoming more and more implausible. While it is important to be selective in the use of rabbinic material, guarding against the use of late or pseudepigraphic passages, much of it is of the greatest service in reconstructing the style and modes of expression of the Pharisees.[2]

Thus, with greater caution in using rabbinic material, and with wider discretion in using extra-rabbinic material, the project of assessing Paul's writings as to their affinity or non-affinity to Pharisaism, remains what it originally was: does Paul write and think like a rabbi?[3]

In order to give us some bearings in this matter, it may be a good idea to ask, 'Are there any passages in the New Testament that do breathe the atmosphere of Pharisaism, as judged by the style of the rabbinic writings?' We have already noted that the direct references to the Pharisees in the New Testament, while useful in some ways (despite their hostile bias), do not give us this atmosphere, since they contain no example of Pharisee teaching or preaching. (Exceptions are the speech of Gamaliel in Acts 5, defending Peter and his companions, and the speech of the 'scribe' on love of God and neighbour in Mark 12.22-23.) But there are in fact many passages which are indeed redolent of rabbinic style. These passages do not explicitly refer themselves to the Pharisee milieu, for they are represented as the sayings of an opponent of Pharisaism; they are the sayings of Jesus himself, the style and vocabulary of which show close similarities to those of the rabbinic writings.

Jesus' use of parables is a case in point. We do not find parables in the Pseudepigrapha or in the Qumran writings, but we do find them in profusion in the Midrashim. It should be noted that in the New Testament, it is only in the Synoptic Gospels that we find Jesus preaching in parables; the Fourth Gospel contains none, an indication of its lateness and its removal of Jewish traits from Jesus' character. In Paul's writings we do not find a single parable. Some scholars have endeavoured to argue that the Pharisees did not use parables at all, since the rabbinic parables are late, being found in works of late redaction. According to this view, Jesus was the inventor of this mode of preaching, otherwise unknown in his period. Later, some rabbis, for some reason, decided to take up the use of parables in their preaching, apparently modelling them closely on the parables in the New Testament, a work which they regarded as heretical.[4] This unlikely hypothesis derives from the extreme view, rejected above, on the dating of rabbinic material, and on the alleged discontinuity between Pharisaic and rabbinic Judaism. The most likely view is that parables were part of Pharisee preaching, which accounts for their existence in the rabbinic Judaism that consistently represents itself as the continuation of Pharisaism. Since we do not have any Pharisee writings, but only a reasonable presumption that there was a good deal in common between the Pharisees and the rabbis, evidence that one Jew, Jesus, preached in a manner that would have been instantly recognizable to the rabbis of the second century creates a presumption that Jesus too had something in common with these later rabbis; and the link can only be Pharisaism, which connects the rabbis to the first century. Indeed the existence of a rabbinic style of preaching in the first century, as seen in the sayings of Jesus, is itself evidence that the Pharisee movement is not necessarily divided by a gulf from the later rabbinic movement simply because of the interval of time between them.[5]

Quite apart from the parables, there are many turns of phrase in Jesus' sayings that are typical of rabbinic style. For example, when he says that it is easier for a camel to go through the eye of a needle than for a rich man to enter heaven (Matt. 19.24), this extravagant turn of phrase is typically rabbinic (though the parallel rabbinic phrase expressing impossibility is even more extravagant, involving an elephant and a needle, see b. Ber. 55b, b.BM 38b; in b. Yeb. 45a, however, the animal is indeed a camel, but instead of going through the eye of a needle, it dances in a tiny area, a *qab*). When Jesus speaks of the hypocrite as criticizing the mote in his neighbour's eye while having a beam, or plank, in his own (Matt. 7.4), he is using an expression current in rabbinic parlance (b. Arakh. 16b, b. BB 15b). Such fingerprints of style place a person better than anything else.[6] If we could find such idioms in Paul's writings, we would certainly be justified in arguing that they corroborate his Pharisee background.

It will of course be said that the rabbinic-style sayings of Jesus in the Synoptic Gospels (but not in the Fourth Gospel) do not prove that Jesus really preached in this way, since they could be part of the 're-judaization' process which has been discerned, especially in the Gospel of Matthew. Some scholars, following Norman Perrin's 'criterion of dissimilarity', would even say that any sayings of Jesus that can be duplicated in rabbinic writings are *ipso*

facto disqualified from authenticity, or at least thrown into doubt –
a principle that Samuel Sandmel rightly called 'antisemitic'. But
we do not need to consider this point here, since the Gospel of
Matthew itself is quite early enough (about 80 CE) to establish the
fact that rabinic-style thinking existed many years before the
redaction of the Mishnah. Even if the Gospel of Matthew is a
Jewish-Christian production (a proposition with which I personally disagree, being of the view that the Jesus sayings are
authentic) then a Pharisaic-rabbinic type of Judaism lies behind
it, and this establishes the existence of a Pharisaism strongly
related to rabbinic Judaism less than twenty years after Paul's
epistles. This alone would justify an enquiry into Paul's affinity or
non-affinity to Pharisaism in terms of the rabbinic Judaism known
from the Mishnah and associated literature. Thus the sayings of
Jesus, if authentic, attest to Pharisaism-rabbinism shortly before
the time of Paul; if arising from 're-judaization', they attest to
Pharisaism-rabbinism, on a community scale, shortly after the
time of Paul's main activity. In either case, they make rabbinic
Judaism relevant to our enquiry. In fact, the 're-judaization'
theory would make this result easier to reach, since it postulates
behind the Jesus-sayings a Pharisaic-rabbinic community, not
just an individual whose connection to a community would have
to be argued.

We now return to discussion of the Jesus sayings, using 'Jesus'
as shorthand for 'either Jesus or a re-judaized Jewish-Christian
community'. Jesus is typically rabbinic not only in his idioms but
also in his style of argument. An example is his argument for
healing on the Sabbath, based on the analogy of circumcision.
This argument is recorded by John, not by the Synoptics, and is a
rare touch of rabbinism in this Gospel; it may be a genuine Jesuan
tradition or a reflection of Jewish practice in John's day (around
90 CE), which of course did not come into being suddenly at that
time, and would certainly have stemmed from Temple times,
especially as John quotes it as something well known and familiar.
In this saying (John 7.22-23), Jesus refers to the ruling that
circumcision overrules the Sabbath law: i.e. though incisions are
usually forbidden on the Sabbath, an exception is made when a
child's circumcision day (the eighth from birth) coincides with the
Sabbath. Now this particular legal ruling (*halakhah*) features in the

rabbinic literature and is unknown from any other source. Nothing is said about it in the Bible, which does not raise the question of what to do if the circumcision day coincides with the Sabbath. This is thus a typical piece of rabbinic decision-making, and, as it happens, the first reference found to it is in a Gospel, which thus testifies to the existence of rabbinism at an early period, when Pharisaism flourished. Even more interesting is that the inference that Jesus then makes (that healing too should be allowed on the Sabbath) is also to be found in the rabbinic literature (Mekhilta Shabbeta on Ex. 31.13), where this same reason is given for the rabbinic ruling that healing is permitted on the Sabbath, even when the method of healing constitutes a breach of the Sabbath laws.[7] Thus we have here a passage redolent of rabbinic-type thinking at a time long before the redaction of the Mishnah.[8] This confirms that it is not anachronistic to speak of rabbinism in the first century, and that it is just such rabbinisms that we should be looking for in our enquiry about Paul.

Paul himself specifically claims that he had a Pharisee training: 'Circumcised the eighth day, of the stock of Israel, of the tribe of Benjamin, an Hebrew of the Hebrews; as touching the law (or: in my attitude to the law), a Pharisee' (Phil. 3.5). In Galatians he stresses his proficiency in Pharisee learning: 'And profited in the Jews' religion above many my equals (contemporaries) in mine own religion, being more exceedingly zealous of the traditions of my father' (Gal. 1.14). In Acts, we are given further details: 'I am verily a man which am a Jew, born in Tarsus, a city in Cilicia, yet brought up in this city at the feet of Gamaliel, and taught according to the perfect manner of the law of the fathers (NEB: thoroughly trained in every point of our ancestral law), and was zealous toward God, as ye all are this day' (Acts 22.3). This is reinforced by Paul's speech before Agrippa: 'My manner of life from my youth, which was at first among mine own nation at Jerusalem, know all the Jews; which knew me from the beginning, if they would testify, that after the most straitest sect of our religion I lived a Pharisee' (Acts 26.4-5). It is in Acts too that Paul claims that he is 'a Pharisee, the son of a Pharisee' (Acts 23.6).

Some of the statements in Acts go beyond what Paul himself claims in his writings, but his assertion of his possession of

Pharisee learning and prominence is clear. We have to consider, therefore, whether anything in his writings gives support to this claim.

In *The Mythmaker* (Chapter 7), I gave an introduction to this line of enquiry. I pointed out that it is precisely where Paul seems to come closest to rabbinic style and method that he can be shown to be far removed from it. For example, Paul is fond of using the *a fortiori* argument, known to the rabbis (who regarded this argument as their chief logical instrument) as the *qal va-homer* argument. But Paul does not observe the rabbinical rules in using this argument. He uses it in the imprecise, rhetorical style characteristic of Hellenistic literature. Someone trained in rabbinic methods would not use an invalid *qal va-homer* argument, any more than someone trained in Aristotelian logic would use an invalid syllogism, however far he had travelled from adherence to Aristotelian philosophy.

Yet Paul does use the *a fortiori* argument rather more frequently than one would expect from a Hellenistic author. This suggests the possibility that he at least knew that this type of argument was expected of someone who claimed to be a Pharisee. The possibility arises that Paul, while not actually a trained Pharisee, sometimes tried, by his style of argument, to give the impression that he was one. I tested this possibility in a detailed examination of an argument of Paul that purports to be halakhic in character: this is the argument in Romans 7.1-6 about freedom from the law. The argument is introduced very consciously as that of a legal expert: 'I am speaking to those who have some knowledge of law.' Yet on examination it turns out to be muddled and incompetent from a halakhic standpoint. Paul is unable to distinguish between two quite different legal topics: (1) that a woman, after the death of her husband, is free to marry someone else; (2) that a person becomes free of legal obligations after his own death. Paul thinks that these two topics are equivalent, and slips from one to the other in a confused manner in elaborating his analogy to the abrogation of the law for Christians. Such confusion is unthinkable in a trained rabbi, as anyone acquainted with the clear and logical style of rabbinic legal thinking can testify. It is certainly within the scope of rabbinic style to elaborate a legal analogy for something that is essentially non-legal, such as the relationship between God and

Israel, but in such an analogy the terms are never confused; while Paul, in his attempt, is unable even to keep clear in his mind what corresponds to what – whether it is the wife or the husband who corresponds to the church or to the Torah or to Christ.

Thus it is Paul's very attempt to sound like a Pharisee that reveals him as a non-Pharisee. Of course it is true that even the muddled argument discussed above shows that Paul knew certain things about Judaism. He knew that a widow, in Jewish law, is free to re-marry. He also knew, what was not quite so obvious, that a dead person is free from legal obligations, a topic discussed in the Talmud, in the context of regulations about shrouds.[9] Such knowledge, on the part of Paul, is often taken to prove conclusively that he was an expert Pharisee. It does not prove that he had more than a smattering, such as could be picked up from attending sermons in the synagogue. It is the ability to handle such knowledge in a context of legal argument that would prove expertise, and Paul fails this test.

As a further contribution to the thesis that Paul, even when he attempted a rabbinic style, was a would-be Pharisee rather than a Pharisee, I offer the following comments on arguments used by Paul in his most intellectually ambitious work, the Epistle to the Romans, especially those in which he offers proofs from scripture, since it is in scriptural exegesis that Pharisee characteristics might well be expected to appear.

An interesting argument is the following:

Then what advantage has the Jew? What is the value of circumcision? Great in every way. In the first place, the Jews were entrusted with the oracles of God. What if some of them were unfaithful? Will their faithlessness cancel the faithfulness of God? Certainly not! God must be true though every man living were a liar; for we read in scripture, 'When thou speakest thou shall be vindicated, and win the verdict when thou art on trial.'

Another question: if our injustice serves to bring out God's justice, what are we to say? Is it unjust of God (I speak of him in human terms) to bring retribution upon us? Certainly not! If God were unjust, how could he judge the world? Again, if the

truth of God brings him all the greater honour because of my
falsehood, why should I any longer be condemned as a sinner?
Why not indeed 'do evil that good may come', as some
libellously report me as saying? To condemn such men as these
is surely no injustice.
                                                (Rom. 3.1-8)

We are concerned here not with the argument, but with the style
or method. It is important to note that the scriptural quotation,
from Psalms 51.4, is not from the Hebrew Bible, but from the
Septuagint (the difference is that the Hebrew Bible says, not 'win
the verdict when thou art on trial', but 'be cleared (or just) (*tizkeh*)
in passing sentence'. There is quite a difference in meaning, for in
the Septuagint, it is God who is on trial, while in the Hebrew Bible,
God is the judge. Yet it is the Septuagint that he quotes, and this is
true throughout Paul's writings; whenever Paul quotes scripture,
and there is some difference in import between Hebrew and
Greek, it can be seen that he is quoting the Greek. This fact has
proved uncomfortable for the image of Paul as a Pharisee; so the
theory has arisen that some editor, coming after Paul, has altered
all his scriptural quotations, originally from the Hebrew, into
Septuagint readings, for the benefit of Greek readers. However,
there is no shadow of manuscript support for this theory, as one
would expect if it were true.

It might be argued, in this particular case, however, that the
Hebrew reading fits Paul's argument better, since he goes on
to speak about God as judge. But this is to misconstrue the
continuation, which is indeed about a possible trial of God on the
charge of injustice (Paul is constrained to apologise for this daring
concept, but no doubt feels himself supported by his quotation
which has already raised the image of God on trial). It is thus the
Septuagint reading that fits better, and we have here a case of Paul
basing his argument on a text that a Pharisee would have rejected
as unauthoritative.

Paul's apology ('I speak of him in human terms') has been
claimed by Daube as a Pharisee idiom.[10] He admits, however, that
the rabbinic expression he has in mind, 'The Torah speaks in the
language of men',[11] does not carry the same meaning as Paul's
expression here and elsewhere.[12] Daube exaggerates the similarity
of the two expressions; to translate the one as 'I speak after the

manner of men' and the other as 'The Torah speaks after the manner of men' is to conceal the differences between *kata anthropon* and *kilshon benei adam*. The rabbinic saying refers to expressions in the Torah which may seem redundant, but which, it is being asserted, do not require any special exegesis since they are natural Hebrew idioms. Paul, on the other hand, is using his expression to apologise for a statement which, taken too literally, might seem irreverent. The rabbinic way of expressing such an apology for seeming irreverence is 'as it were' (*kibeyakhol*), which is very different from Paul's phrase. Daube, however, takes into account that at a far later period, in mediaeval times, the rabbinic expression, 'The Torah speaks in the language of men', came to mean something rather similar to Paul's expression (not actually an apology for irreverence, but an explanation of biblical anthropomorphisms). On this slim basis, Daube constructs a theory that its original rabbinic meaning in the time of Paul was an apology for irreverence; this meaning changed between Paul and the second-century rabbis, and then changed back to something like its original meaning in the Middle Ages. On shaky theories such as this the belief of scholars in Paul's rabbinic idioms has been built.

The chain of argument in the Pauline passage quoted as a whole shows no sign of rabbinic style. It is based on a Hellenistic dialogue form known as the 'diatribe', which derives ultimately from the Platonic dialogue.[13] Here Paul conducts an argument with an imaginary opponent, who raises theological objections to his standpoint on God's justice. The imaginary opponent has often been identified by commentators as a Pharisee. There is some doubt about the sequence of thought; many explanations have been offered about how Paul moves from his discussion of the Jews to his consideration of theodicy. The argument that might indeed make sense in the mouth of a Pharisee is the accusation that Paul's viewpoint was tantamount to saying, 'Do evil that good may come.' Certainly a belief in the efficacy of faith that discounts all human moral effort as worthless is open to the objection that this gives *carte blanche* to evil-doing, which will only enhance God's glory by giving him an opportunity for infinite forgivingness. Such an objection is not found in the rabbinic literature, which never finds it necessary to take cognizance of a

doctrine of human moral worthlessness in order to combat it; but
Paul may have encountered this argument in controversy with a
Pharisee opponent. If so, this argument cannot be adduced as
evidence of Paul's own Pharisaic background, since it cannot have
arisen until Pharisaism came into conflict with the Pauline
theology.

We now continue our study with the passage immediately
following:

> 9. What then? Are we Jews any better off? (AV: Are
> we (Christians) better than they?) No, not at all! For we
> have already drawn up the accusation that Jews and Greeks
> alike are all under the power of sin. 10. This has scriptural
> warrant:
> 'There is no just man, not one;
> 11. no one who understands, no one who seeks God.
> 12. All have swerved aside, all alike have become debased;
> there is no one to show kindness; no, not one.
> 13. Their throat is an open grave, they use their tongues for
> treachery, adders' venom is on their lips,
> 14. and their mouth is full of bitter curses.
> 15. Their feet hasten to shed blood,
> 16. ruin and misery lie along their paths,
> 17. they are strangers to the high-road of peace,
> 18. and reverence for God does not enter their thoughts.'
> 19. Now all the words of the law are addressed, as we know, to
> those who are within the pale of the law, so that no one may
> have anything to say in self-defence, but the whole world may
> be exposed to the judgment of God. 20. For (again from
> scripture) 'no human being can be justified in the sight of God'
> for having kept the law: law brings only the consciousness of
> sin.
> (Rom. 3.9-20)

Paul here resorts to extended quotation from scripture, to show
that all, Jews and Gentiles alike, are helplessly in the grip of sin,
and equally in need of salvation through faith. This is in fact a
catena of quotations, taken from Psalm 14.1-3, Psalm 5.9,
Psalm 10.7, Proverbs 1.16 (Isa. 59.7-8), Psalm 36.1, Job 5.16
(Psalm 107.42), Psalms 143.2.

The mere fact that Paul makes such extensive use of scripture is often taken to prove his Pharisee background. The above catena certainly shows a wide acquaintance with scripture. But commentators have found great difficulty with this string of quotations, since they are far from proving Paul's point, being so obviously taken out of context. Most of the psalms quoted make a clear distinction between the righteous and the unrighteous. Consequently, it has been argued that part at least of this section of quotations has been added by a later editor.

O'Neill[14] argues that only the first quotation (contained in verses 10 and 11 above), taken from Psalm 14, was cited by Paul, while the quotations in verses 12 to 18 are editorial additions. In corroboration of this, he argues that the quotations in verses 12 to 18 are all taken 'word for word' from the Septuagint, while the quotation in verses 10 and 11 is closer to the Hebrew version ('a free translation from the original Hebrew'). This is in accordance with O'Neill's view, mentioned above, that 'Paul himself used the Hebrew of the Old Testament direct, and the later glossators and commentators the standard Greek translation'.

When one looks carefully through this catena of quotations, however (and this is also true of all the other examples given in O'Neill's book on Romans of Paul's alleged use of the Hebrew Bible), one finds that things are not quite as O'Neill says. The first quotation, allegedly translated from the original Hebrew, contains a feature found only in the Septuagint, namely the addition of the expression 'not one' to verse 1 of the Psalm, as well as to verse 3. In the Hebrew, this expression is added in verse 3, but not in verse 1. Paul, however, adds it to both verse 1 and verse 3.[15] It is thus more likely that Paul is quoting inexactly (probably by heart) from the Septuagint than that he is translating, however freely, from the Hebrew. It is true that Paul's Greek for 'not one' (*oude heis*) is not the same as the Septuagint's (*ouk estin heos henos*). He also substitutes *dikaios* for the Septuagint's *poion chrestoteta*. But the addition of a phrase found only in the Septuagint is surely more significant than the inexactness of the quotation. It is significant too that Paul, where he departs from the Septuagint, also departs from the Hebrew; in other words, the Septuagint is translating the Hebrew more faithfully than Paul is. This again suggests inexactness of memory in quoting from the Septuagint, rather than 'free' recourse to the Hebrew original.

The second half of O'Neill's thesis is that there is an exact correspondence between the quotations in verses 12 to 18 to the Septuagint. This turns out to be incorrect too. The quotation from Isaiah 59.7, for example, differs from the Septuagint in several ways, but not in any way that suggests translation from the Hebrew. In other cases it is impossible to tell whether the 'editor' is using the Septuagint rather than the Hebrew since they do not show any difference. O'Neill's whole thesis is therefore wrong; the alleged contrast between free translation from the Hebrew (by Paul) and exact quotation from the Greek (by an editor) does not exist, and the conclusion is that Paul himself is responsible for all the quotations, which he is quoting with some inexactness from the Greek. Further, the contrast that O'Neill makes between the quotation from Psalm 14, which he does ascribe to Paul and regards as 'telling', and the other quotations, which he regards as inappropriate, is also incorrect; for Psalm 14 too makes a distinction between the unrighteous and the righteous (see verse 5 for the righteous). In any case, the fact that quotations are not appropriate, because taken out of context, does not prove that they were inserted by a later editor, as it is quite in character for Paul to quote out of context. Some scholars, indeed, have argued, on the contrary, that Paul's propensity to quote out of context shows him to have the true midrashic style of the rabbis. It would be hard, however, to find a rabbinic parallel for such monumentally inappropriate quotations as we find here, where texts that stress the distinction between the righteous and the unrighteous are used in an attempt to prove that the righteous do not and cannot exist.

The only one of Paul's quotations from the Hebrew Bible that does have some appropriateness is the last one, from Psalms 143.2, ' . . . for in thy sight shall no man living be justified'. This is indeed from a psalm in which the point is not the distinction between the righteous and the unrighteous, but the impossibility of perfect righteousness. But of course Paul takes this point far beyond its meaning in the psalm, which is that none of us is perfect, and that we need therefore God's mercy in judgment. This is one of the cardinal points of rabbinic theology, which dwells on God's attribute of mercy, by which his attribute of justice is tempered. Paul's point, on the contrary, is that there is no such thing as righteousness at all, and this viewpoint, which abandons the moral struggle as utterly hopeless, is alien to all rabbinic thinking, which regards the admission of the impossibility of moral perfection as an *encouragement* to moral struggle, not as the negation of it (since the individual is being encouraged to do his best, not to aim at an impossible perfection). Paul makes clear in the subsequent verses that the law exists only to convict us of moral failure; it is only in this sense that he does not 'make void the law'. But as a guide to moral progress, Paul asserts, the law has no function, since only 'faith' can bring justification, either to Jews or Gentiles.

I now turn to chapters 4 and 5 of Romans, which have often been described as the supreme example of sustained rabbinic thinking by Paul. A typical example of this kind of description of these chapters is the following: ' . . . he reverted to arguments of the type which were admired in rabbinical circles, to verbal quibbles, to the use of Old Testament quotations forced into meanings which their writers did not intend. It was artificial pleading of a kind which had delighted Paul when he was a pupil of Gamaliel. Naturally enough, he had never quite freed himself from that early Pharisaic influence, while he felt that reasoning of this kind would make a quite special appeal to the educated Jewish readers of his letter. From any other point of view this type of argument, based upon perversions of the Old Testament scriptures, is almost worthless. (A sustained example of it will be found in the fourth chapter of the Epistle.) . . . Judged from the modern standpoint, such passages in this Roman letter show Paul at his worst.'[16] This is an interesting and typical, if not very distinguished, example of an approach to Paul's alleged rabbinism that has now become out of date as being 'polemical' and unnecessarily disrespectful to rabbinic Judaism. Nowadays, in the ecumenical approach, Paul's rabbinism would be equally stressed, but in a more appreciative fashion. Whether polemically or ecumenically expressed, however, the view that Paul's style is genuinely rabbinic is mistaken.

In chapter 4, Paul argues that Abraham is the chief biblical example of faith, as opposed to works. He quotes the verse in which Abraham's faith was 'counted to him as righteousness' (Gen. 15.6) as proof that good works do not come into the reckoning. This is an ingenious use of a biblical verse in a sense contrary to both the biblical context and to rabbinic exegesis: giving someone credit for faith would not be regarded by either biblical or rabbinic authors as ruling out credit for good deeds too, since they did not regard faith as the antithesis of good deeds, but rather as complementing them. The mere fact that Paul is here twisting a biblical verse in an ingenious way does not make him rabbinic, for such ingeniousness is found in the gnostic authors. Indeed, Paul's whole procedure here, as pointed out above, p. 51, is reminiscent of the Gnostic exegetes of Genesis. He enrols Abraham on his side much as the Gnostics enrolled such non-Jewish figures as Seth or Melchizedek, seizing on what they conceived to be an alternative, non-Jewish line of teaching in the Hebrew Bible. Paul goes even beyond the Gnostics, however, by enrolling the very ancestor of the Jews, Abraham (*before* his circumcision), in his support as a non-Jew, using also to this end the fact that Abraham was the ancestor of non-Jewish nations as well as of the Jews.

I conclude that there is nothing in chapter 4, in the style of argument or of biblical exegesis that is rabbinic.

Chapter 5 contains the *a fortiori* arguments that have been held to show rabbinic influence, since the *a fortiori* argument (*qal vahomer*) was the chief logical instrument of rabbinic legal reasoning. As pointed out above, however, Paul does not observe the rabbinic rules in his use of this type of argument, especially the all-important rule of *dayo*, which lays down that no term should appear in the conclusion of the argument unless it has first appeared in the premises.

An example is the following:

> For if by the wrongdoing of that one man death established its reign, through a single sinner, much more shall those who receive in far greater measure God's grace, and his gift of righteousness, live and reign through the one man, Jesus Christ (verse 17).

This is a most untidy argument by rabbinic standards. It might be paraphrased, 'If one man's sin could produce death, how much more could one man produce immortality for those who are sinless.' The term 'immortality' does not appear in the premises at all, and should therefore not appear in the conclusion, by rabbinic analysis of the conditions for the validity of a *qal va-homer* argument. It is like saying, 'If a bad cook can burn the dinner, how much more can a good cook produce an excellent *coq au vin*.' The conclusion does not follow at all from the premises, though it may be true in itself. (A valid argument would be, 'If a good cook can burn the dinner, how much more can a bad cook burn the dinner'.)

But Paul's argument is faulty on other grounds too, for the parallelism is lame. The reader thinks that the 'one man' who is a sinner is going to be contrasted with the 'one man' who is sinless; instead it is the people who are saved who are sinless, and nothing is said about the qualifications of the saviour. This means that the argument, so far from being a valid *qal va-homer*, is not even a soundly-constructed analogy. If the parallelism were (1) Adam – sinful – death (2) Christ – sinless – life, one could at least say that Paul, though failing in his attempted *qal va-homer*, has discerned a pattern of opposition between the beginning and the end. But he cannot even do that correctly. Altogether, one could hardly think of a more broken-backed argument, and no trained rabbi would perpetrate it. That Paul was trying to sound like a rabbi in using this type of argument may well be true, and to an untrained audience, he may well have seemed very rabbinic; but his very attempt to sound rabbinic proves very effectively that he was no rabbi.[17]

Chapter 6 contains no argument or expression that has been claimed as rabbinic, except the expression 'the wages of sin' (verse 23), which is similar to the rabbinic expression *sekhar 'averah*, as found for example in the well-known saying, 'The reward of a sin is another sin, and the reward of a good deed is another good deed' (Abot 4.2). The phrase, however, was probably used frequently in sermons, and Paul's use of it does not argue anything more than a certain amount of synagogue attendance on his part.

Chapter 7 begins with Paul's most strenuous attempt to sound like a rabbi, his analogy about legal obligation ceasing after death, criticized above. From the standpoint of rabbinic legal logic, it is a pitiful effort. In the rest of the chapter, Paul expresses the dilemma of one who finds the law an unhelpful burden. Earlier scholars argued that this was a typically Pharisaic dilemma; but increased knowledge of rabbinic literature has rendered this untenable. Few scholars today would argue that there is anything Pharisaic about Paul's despairing assessment of the viability or helpfulness of the Torah. Neither in style nor content does this passage strengthen the thesis of Paul's rabbinism.

Chapter 8 is pure Gnosticism, with its contrast between the body and the spirit. Paul's statement that 'the life-giving law of the Spirit has set you free from the law of sin and death' might have come straight out of a Gnostic treatise. Expressions like 'those who are according to the flesh' (verse 5) arise from a dualism that has no parallel in Pharisaism or any other kind of Judaism. There is considerable eloquence in the peroration of the chapter, but it is a Gnostic, not a Jewish, eloquence, expressing a yearning for divinization and escape from the trammels of the body.

Here we touch on the vexed question of Paul's 'apocalypticism', which also has some relevance to the question of Paul's alleged Pharisaism. The excellent work of Glasson (1980) has shown that all Jewish apocalypticism, whether in the Hebrew Bible or the intertestamental literature, relates to a messianic kingdom *on earth*, and not to a translation of the elect as divine or semi-divine beings to a higher spiritual realm. Since the work of Schweitzer, it has become usual to see Paul as considerably, or even chiefly, influenced by Judaism in the apocalyptic sense; and because the earlier view of scholars that Pharisaism was non-apocalyptic has been abundantly disproved, Paul's 'apocalypticism' has been taken as further evidence of his Pharisaic roots. This, however, has been to ignore the difference between Jewish and Gnostic apocalyptic. It was the Gnostics, and not the Jews, who aspired to escape from the human condition and become gods; and this is the kind of apocalypticism that Paul displays. Such an aspiration arises from acosmism; it regards the world as essentially evil and irredeemable. Judaism, however, in all its forms, including Pharisaism, regarded the redemption of this world as the final aim of history; a messianic age of peace, justice and prosperity was to round off the tribulations of human history and give them significance. After that final stage of human fulfilment, there might indeed come a further stage, called sometimes in the rabbinic writings 'the World to Come', when human limitations would be sloughed off, and the righteous would bask in the 'radiance of the Shekhinah' (though even this came far short of divinization). But this was not the subject of apocalyptic expectations or yearnings, being regarded as something beyond all history and extraneous to it, and in a way gratuitous. All the prophets of the Hebrew Bible, says the Talmud, prophesied about the messianic age, not the World to Come (b. Sanh. 99a). Paul, it might be said, simply omitted the messianic age and skipped to the World to Come; and thus his apocalypticism was an individual variant on a Jewish theme. But this interpretation does not fit the facts. A human, earthly resolution of the historical process was essential to Judaism; anyone who rejected it was rejecting Judaism in favour of acosmism. Nowhere does Paul give any hope of a redeemed earth. Further, Paul's picture of the divinization of the faithful is strongly reminiscent of Gnostic aspirations both in content and phraseology, and not at all reminiscent of the expressions associated with the rabbinic idea of the World to Come.[18]

The question of Paul's apocalypticism raises also that of Paul's mysticism, which has been held recently to show strong affinities to Jewish mysticism in general, and Pharisaic/rabbinic mysticism in particular.[19] The main Pauline passage under discussion in this context is his account of his journey to the third heaven (II Cor. 12.1-9). But heavenly journeys were common in Graeco-Roman as well as in Jewish mysticism. There is nothing specifically Jewish about Paul's brief description. For example, Paul says nothing about travelling through 'palaces' (*heikhalot*), or about seeing the 'throne' (*merkabah*) of God, or about encountering angels such as Metatron. Nothing can be concluded from this account, unless Paul's silence about characteristically Jewish aspects of mysticism can be held to show that his mystical journey was of a Hellenistic kind. An argument from silence is not strong, but certainly Paul's account does not strengthen the case for Paul's Pharisaic background either.[20]

Chapters 9, 10 and 11 deal with Paul's view of the Jewish people: why have they, or most of them, rejected Christ, and what is to happen to them? I shall discuss the content of these chapters

later, in connection with the Gaston-Gager-Stendahl thesis that
Paul never intended his Gospel for the Jews, but only for the
Gentiles. Here we are concerned only with style. Paul makes
lavish use of scriptural quotation, and this alone has been
sufficient to make his style seem typically Pharisaic to many
commentators, especially when the exegesis is particularly far-
fetched.

In chapter 10, there is an argument that has been much
advertised as rabbinic in character:

> Of legal righteousness Moses writes, 'The man who does this
> shall gain life by it.' But the righteousness that comes by faith
> says, 'Do not say to yourself, "Who can go up to heaven?"' (that
> is to bring Christ down), 'or, "Who can go down to the abyss?"'
> (to bring Christ up from the dead). But what does it say? 'The
> word is near you: it is upon your lips and in your heart.' This
> means the word of faith which we proclaim. If on your lips is the
> confession, 'Jesus is Lord', and in your heart the faith that God
> raised him from the dead, then you will find salvation. For the
> faith that leads to righteousness is in the heart, and the
> confession that leads to salvation is upon the lips. Scripture
> says, 'Everyone who has faith in him will be saved from shame.'
> (Rom. 10.5-10)

On this passage, Joseph Klausner comments as follows: 'Paul here
changes one part of a passage from the Pentateuch to suit his
needs, and in place of "Who shall go over the sea for us?" he
substitutes another Scriptural phrase, "Who shall descend into
the abyss?"; then he interprets this garbled passage arbitrarily,
drawing from it conclusions desired and needed by him, although
there is no hint of them in the passage itself; continuing, he
supports his interpretation with a supposed verse from the
Prophets, although even in the Septuagint this verse lacks the
words "in him", while in the place of the reading "shall not be put
to shame" of the Septuagint, the Hebrew has "shall not make
haste".'[21]

Yet Klausner's general conclusion is that this is a typically
rabbinic piece of reasoning! He uses this passage among others to
substantiate his statement, 'It would be difficult to find more
typically Talmudic expositions of Scripture than those in the

Epistles of Paul.' One may well ask, 'Where, in the whole rabbinic literature, does one find a garbled quotation from Scripture? What rabbi quotes from the Septuagint, and even garbles that?' Klausner comes very close to saying that anything lamely or absurdly argued in Paul's Epistles is *ipso facto* rabbinic in style.

A rabbi might depart far from the plain meaning of a biblical text in his interpretation. He might even resort to an outrageous pun on a word in a text, in order to extract a meaning that is not there. But what he would never do is to misquote the text deliberately in the first place. Also there is always the principle underlying all far-fetched midrashic interpretations, 'A biblical text never loses its plain meaning' (b. Sanhedrin 34a and elsewhere): in other words, the fanciful interpretation does not supplant the plain meaning, but supplements it. Paul's interpretation of Deut. 30.12-14, however, leaves no room for the restitution of the plain meaning, since by interpreting the passage as being about Christ, he explicitly excludes and contradicts the plain meaning, which concerns the Torah. This procedure is non-rabbinic, not simply because it substitutes Christ for the Torah, but because it ignores every canon of rabbinic interpretation.

Chapters 12 to 15 consist of moral exhortation and prescriptions, and one might expect to find rabbinic influence here if anywhere, since the area covered is similar to that of the *halakhah*. Indeed, Daube has seen in these 'haustafeln' of Paul's a special feature of rabbinic style, namely the use of participles for injunctions. Daube points out that in the Mishnah and other rabbinic writings, rules are not stated in the imperative, but in the form of participles, which are the Hebrew way of expressing the customary present tense (since in Hebrew the verb 'to be' is not used as an auxiliary but simply omitted). For example, 'On the first days of the month women are singing (may sing) dirges, but are not wailing (may not wail)' (Daube's example, but the usage is pervasive). Daube points out correctly that this mild way of laying down rules, by which a rule is described rather than prescribed, expresses the status of the rabbinic writings as non-canonical works that do not claim divine inspiration but merely note the way things are done.

Daube thinks that Paul is employing the same usage in his string of participles in Romans 12. Daube points also to similar

usages in I Peter, where the use of participles is even more
uniform than in Romans (where an occasional imperative or
infinitive creeps in).

Most significantly of all, however, Daube points to similar
usages in the hortatory parts of the Didache. Daube is thus
not really arguing that these participles derive from Paul's
personal rabbinic background and training, but that all these
texts have drawn their material from 'Hebrew codes of the
primitive Christian community'. I Peter, he argues, is not dependent on Paul, but draws directly from these codes of the
early church.

At the same time, Daube notes correctly that in the rabbinic
material, participles are used for matters of detailed practice
(i.e. *halakhah*, whether ritual or societal) not for matters of general moral exhortation, where the imperative is used as in the
Bible. Thus where the subject-matter corresponds most closely
to the New Testament haustafeln (i.e. in the tractates Abot and
Derekh Eretz), rabbinic style differs. The closest parallel, as
Daube again points out, is in the Manual of Discipline of the
Qumran sect, where participles are used for exhortatory
material similar to that found in the New Testament.

The conclusion for our purposes here is that Paul's haustafeln
do not derive their style from Paul's individual rabbinic training
and experience since they are not his original composition. Paul
was here simply transcribing material from a manual of discipline of the Jerusalem church which he had to hand, though no
doubt with some additions and adjustments of his own, including the intrusion of imperatives and infinitives at times. The
Jerusalem church used the haustafeln style of participles in
common with other Jewish groups of the time, of whom the
Pharisees may or may not have been one (the non-participial
style of Abot suggests not). In any case, these participial injunctions cannot be used to support the case for Paul's rabbinic
background, though they might possibly be used to argue the
Pharisaic background of the Jerusalem church and, consequently, of Jesus.

The actual content of the moral precepts urged by Paul
in these chapters again proves nothing about his background,
since they were to be found in his source, the manual of the

Jerusalem church. Where Paul does insert material of his own, this is manifestly not of Pharisaic inspiration, since it concerns a very un-Pharisaic problem: namely, the need for tolerance of those 'weaker' brethren who were unable to wean themselves from Jewish dietary practices and the observance of Jewish festivals.

Our survey of Romans, then, has not revealed any sign of genuine rabbinic style or method in Paul's writing. It does reveal at times an ambition on Paul's part to give the impression of rabbinic learning, and it is these very efforts that prove most clearly that he did not possess such learning. There *are* genuine instances of Pharisaic style in the New Testament, but these are all embedded in the teaching of Jesus. Thus stylistic study confirms that the traditional teaching of the church about Jesus and Paul should be reversed: it was Jesus who was the Pharisee, and Paul the non-Pharisee.

Finally, something should be said about Paul's alleged use of Midrashic legends; a point often stressed in arguments supporting Paul's Pharisaism. An instance often mentioned is Paul's reference to the miraculous well that followed the children of Israel in the wilderness (I Cor. 10.4). But, as I pointed out in *The Mythmaker*, this legend is found in Pseudo-Philo, which was available in Paul's time in Greek. No Pharisaic training or learning was required to know this legend, which in any case was probably told in sermons in the synagogues. Knowledge of legends, in general, is no proof of Pharisaic learning, since they were told to children, were known to the illiterate, and can be found in non-Pharisaic sources. Thus Paul's reference to the legend that the serpent seduced Eve (II Cor. 11.3) might be used with more justification to argue Paul's affiliation to the Gnostics, to whom this legend was more important than to the Pharisees.

Once the illusion of Paul's rabbinic style has been abandoned, it will be possible to discern more fully the genuine elements of Paul's literary style, which stem from Hellenistic models. Some excellent work has been done recently on this topic by S. K. Stowers, J. L. White, Helen Elsom, and others.[22] Such work ought to be regarded as central in the literary study of Paul's epistles, instead of being relegated to the side-lines. Paul wrote in Greek, and his epistles are part of Greek literature. The acknowledgment of this simple fact is far more important than the pursuit of influences from Pharisaic/rabbinic style, which are at most superficial.

6

The Gaston–Gager–Stendahl Thesis

In recent years a view about Paul that has gained much ground is that associated with the names of Lloyd Gaston, John G. Gager and Krister Stendahl.[1] This is the view that Paul never forsook Judaism or intended to found a new religion taking the place of Judaism. His mission was not to the Jews, whom he regarded as being in no need of salvation, since they had their own covenant with God which remained valid for all time. He was solely an apostle to the Gentiles, for whom Judaism had previously not made adequate provision. Paul's scheme of salvation through identification with Jesus Christ was meant only for Gentiles, and he did not expect or require Jews to resort to this kind of salvation. Jews, in other words, were not required to seek salvation through Jesus Christ, but through their own traditional method of adherence to the Torah and observance of its moral and ritual precepts in a spirit of love of God and man.

This is a picture which, one can see, has its attractions for many people seeking to solve the problem of Christian antisemitism. The question here, however, is whether it represents accurately the teaching of Paul as found in his writings. Unfortunately, the Gaston-Gager-Stendahl view is reached only by ignoring obvious features of Paul's thought – so obvious, indeed, that one wonders how they could possibly be overlooked.

Whatever plausibility the Gaston-Gager-Stendahl (GGS) view has derives from the conviction that Paul was rooted in Pharisaic Judaism and that all his categories of thought were Jewish. It is this basic conviction that carries these authors through the initial improbabilities of their thesis, and leads them to construe familiar passages of Pauline hostility against Judaism into a milder sense, or as directed only against certain forms of Jewish Christianity, or against certain forms of Gentile attachment to Judaism. The thesis of the present book, therefore, in so far as it has established the essential Hellenism of Paul's thought – its derivation from Gnosticism and mystery religion rather than from Jewish sources – enables us to look at Paul's views on Jews and Judaism from a more objective standpoint, without the need to manipulate them into a meaning opposite to the obvious one. I shall confine myself here to commenting on the arguments of Gaston, since he shows, in his writings, a deeper acquaintance with the Jewish sources than the other two authors.

We may begin by looking at an important passage in which Paul expresses his attitude towards Judaism and his own mission:

> The qualification we have comes from God; it is he who has qualified us to dispense his new covenant – a covenant expressed not in a written document, but in a spiritual bond; for the written law condemns to death, but the Spirit gives life. The law, then, engraved letter by letter upon stone, dispensed death, and yet it was inaugurated with divine splendour. That splendour, though it was soon to fade, made the face of Moses so bright that the Israelites could not gaze steadily at him. But if so, must not even greater splendour rest upon the divine dispensation of the Spirit? If splendour accompanied the dispensation under which we are condemned, how much richer in splendour must that one be under which we are acquitted! Indeed, the splendour that once was is now no splendour at all; it is outshone by a splendour greater still. For if that which was soon to fade had its moment of splendour, how much greater is the splendour of that which endures! With such a hope as this we speak out boldly; it is not for us to do as Moses did; he put a veil over his face to keep the Israelites from gazing on that fading splendour until it was gone. But in any case their minds had been made insensitive, for that same veil is there to this very day when the lesson is read from the old covenant; and it is never lifted, because only in Christ is the old covenant

abrogated. But to this very day, every time the Law of Moses is read, a veil lies over the minds of the hearers. However, as scripture says of Moses, 'whenever he turns to the Lord the veil is removed'. Now the Lord of whom this passage speaks is the Spirit; and where the Spirit of the Lord is, there is liberty. And because for us there is no veil over the face, we all reflect as in a mirror the splendour of the Lord; thus we are transfigured into his likeness, from splendour to splendour; such is the influence of the Lord who is Spirit. (II Cor. 3.6-18)

It certainly requires an ingenious interpretation to construe the above passage in any sense other than the traditional one: that Judaism, while having a limited validity for a time, has been abrogated by a new dispensation which is one of the Spirit and not of the letter. Surely the people criticized in this passage are not Jewish-Christians, but Jews, who, it is alleged, fail to understand their own scripture, which foretells its own supersession, and fail to achieve the true liberty which comes with the new covenant. This passage breathes a sense of the superiority of Paul's message, for which he claims divine inspiration (verse 6), to the message delivered by Moses, now superseded; not the delivery of a message of salvation intended for Gentiles only, which is to exist in parallel with the Mosaic dispensation.

Gaston, however, manages to find an exegesis of the passage that does not involve any derogatory view of Judaism. His exegesis depends on the following notions:

1. That Paul's polemic is not against Jews but against his rivals in missionary activity in Corinth;

2. That this rival group consisted of charismatics who claimed special spiritual gifts, including having shining faces when in ecstasy;

3. That this rival group had some special writings (not the Torah) which they claimed to have received from a divine source.

Thus Gaston's understanding of the passage is that Paul is contrasting his own mission, which depends on rational argument, with that of his rivals, who support their claims by charismatic displays; Paul is also defending his lack of special heaven-sent writings to back his authority. This explains Paul's references to Moses's shining face and to the written word that kills; these references do not concern Moses himself or the written text of the Torah. Paul is not contrasting himself with Moses at all, but only with his rivals in Corinth.

Gaston supports this schema with translations of his own that differ considerably from the NEB version quoted above. For example, he translates verses 12-14 as follows:

> 12. Having such hope, therefore, we speak freely and openly; 13. and not like [they say:] 'Moses used to put a veil on his face' in order that the Israelites might not gaze on the goal of the transitory. 14. But their thoughts have been dulled. For up to this day that same veil remains during [their] reading of the ancient covenant, and it has not been revealed to them that in Christ it is done away with.

By the simple device of inserting the words '[they say]' into the text of verse 13, Gaston transfers the offending thoughts and lack of understanding from the Jews to Paul's opponents in Corinth. Thus the word 'their' in verse 14, which by proximity relates to the Israelites, now relates instead to these opponents, whose characteristics and views Gaston has conjured up specially for the purpose of fitting the needs of his exegesis. Gaston justifies this apparently arbitrary procedure by saying that otherwise there is a non sequitur between verse 12 and verse 13, and also there is a 'strange transfer' of the veil from Moses to the Israelites. As for the alleged non sequitur, it has as much logic as one can usually expect from Paul: he is saying that there is no need for him to veil his own words in the way Moses veiled his face. The 'strange transfer' of the veil from Moses to the Israelites is typical of Paul's inability to follow through an analogy consistently, as we saw repeatedly in the last chapter. Any method of exegesis that bases itself on the assumption that Paul never commits errors of logical sequence is misconceived.

But in any case, who are these opponents of Paul, who have shining faces, carry heaven-sent writings and misread scripture? Paul's opponents in Corinth, as in Galatians, are none other than the emissaries of the Jerusalem church, who oppose Paul's teaching from the standpoint of Christians who adhere to the Torah. It is only on the slenderest of evidence that Gaston alleges that these emissaries claimed authority on the basis of charismatic gifts or heaven-sent writings. The most obvious explanation of their claim to authority superior to that of Paul is that they were emissaries of the Jerusalem apostles, who, unlike Paul, were the direct disciples of Jesus during his lifetime. The writings which Gaston preposterously likens to those which Enoch received from heaven, were simply letters of introduction proving them to be genuine emissaries from Jerusalem. Moreover, to represent Paul as disclaiming charismatic gifts and urging his own rationality in contrast to charismatic opponents is a travesty of Paul's actual standpoint, which was that it was precisely by virtue of his own continual colloquy with the heavenly Jesus that his own ministry was superior to that of the Jerusalem apostles.

The true explanation of the passage, then, is the accepted one: Paul declares that, contrary to his opponents, he does not need letters of introduction, since the Spirit is his authority; this leads to general remarks on the inferiority of the written Torah to the new covenant of the Spirit. In bringing in his 'midrash' about Moses's veil, Paul falls into the confusions of sequence that are usual with him whenever he attempts a rabbinical style. Gaston's re-interpretation and re-translation of the passage form a truly desperate effort to remove Paul's meaning, which is derogatory to the Torah and to Judaism, while allowing them a limited and temporary authority.

After this example of the GGS style of exegesis, we may turn to more general examination of the thesis itself. It consists of the following propositions, all of which, I shall argue, are mistaken:

(1) Paul regarded the Torah as eternally valid for Jews.

(2) Paul regarded the worship of Jesus as intended only for Gentiles as their special mode of salvation.

(3) The provision of this mode of salvation was necessary, since Judaism itself provided salvation only for Jews, not for Gentiles. The fault or 'mis-step' of the Jews upbraided by Paul was not that they rejected his Gospel (which was not for them) but that they objected to his providing salvation for the Gentiles.

I now discuss these propositions individually.

1. *Paul regarded the Torah as eternally valid for Jews*

For a full discussion of Paul's attitude to the Torah, see pp. 48 to 53, where I argued that Paul regarded the Torah as having a limited validity, having been 'promulgated' by angels, not by God. I also drew attention to texts such as Galatians 4.21-27 (the allegorization of Sarah and Hagar as types of the new covenant of Christ, which brings freedom, and the old covenant of Sinai, which brings slavery), which echo the phraseology of the Gnostic literature on the topic of the Torah. If Paul indeed regarded the Torah as slavery and as limited in authority, he was not upholding its validity even for the Jews after the advent of Christ.

Further, when inveighing against the emissaries of the Jerusalem church who persuade Gentile Christians to adhere to the Torah, it seems abundantly clear that Paul is attacking the Torah in absolute terms, not merely as unnecessary for Gentiles; and, if so, he must be denying its necessity for Jews too.

In Galatians 4, Paul appears to say very clearly that the Jewish observances ('special days and months and seasons and years') comprise a form of slavery to the lower powers (*ta stoicheia tou kosmou*). When he opposes the need for circumcision for Gentile converts to Christianity, he does not say that this is an obligation only for Jews; he vilifies the rite in an unrestrainedly hostile way, calling it a 'mutilation' (Phil. 3.2-3), and wishing that its practitioners would go the whole way and castrate themselves (Gal. 5.2-12).

How does the GGS school deal with the above awkward texts? As the passages pile up that need to be explained away, each demanding its ingenious and tortuous re-reading and re-translation, the persuasiveness of the GGS case becomes more and more attenuated. Gaston says, indeed, 'Given the history of Christian bias so well documented by Ruether, perhaps in every case of doubt the positive interpretation should be favoured. This is true with respect to textual criticism, translation, and the many decisions that have to be made on exegetical options.'[2] Is this a matter of giving the Jews the benefit of the doubt, or Paul? If Christian exegesis of Paul has been anti-Jewish, and if this is regrettable, does it follow that the solution is to exonerate Paul by claiming by hook or crook that he has been wrongly interpreted?

Gaston does not think that there was any Jewish doctrine that the Torah was given to Israel by angels, not by God. His criticism of this hoary misconception is trenchant and salutary, and much to be welcomed.[3] But this makes Gal. 3.19, where Paul appears to say that the Torah *was* given by angels, a great problem for him; for he cannot accept that Paul is thereby demoting the Torah in a Gnostic manner. His solution involves the idea that Paul is speaking here not about the Jews, but about the Gentiles, and he is referring to an alleged Jewish doctrine that while the Jews received their Torah directly from God, the commandments given to the Gentiles were mediated by angels. Thus, once more, Paul is concerned with the spiritual dilemma of the Gentiles, left in an unsatisfactory state by Jewish theological concepts, and requiring a new scheme of salvation which Paul is supplying, by which they would achieve a direct relationship with God, instead of being administered by national guardian angels. This concept, by means of which Gaston interprets Gal. 3 and 4, will be treated more fully under (3). Here it should be noted that the Bible describes God as giving commandments directly both to Adam and Noah (Gen. 1.28, 9.1-7), not through angels. Thus the Gentiles, no less than the Jews, received their commandments from God. Gaston, however, translates Paul's expression *diatageis* as 'administered', rather than 'promulgated', though the examples of the use of this verb by Hesiod (which he quotes) contradict this rendering. In general, Gaston's interpretation of Gal. 3 and 4 as concerned with Gentiles, not Jews, and with Gentile laws, not the Torah, is very strained. For example, Gal. 3.10 reads, 'On the other hand, those who rely on obedience to the law are under a curse; for Scripture says, "A curse is on all who do not persevere in doing everything that is written in the Book of the Law."' This clearly, as the text quoted shows, refers to the Torah. Is it plausible that when the word 'law' reappears, a few verses on, as having been promulgated by angels, it now means something very different, namely commandments given to the Gentiles? Further, to support his thesis, Gaston has to argue that the 'special days and months and seasons and years' of Gal. 4.10 are not the festivals of the Jewish religious year but some observances of a Gentile Christian sect, against which Paul's whole diatribe is directed. This kind of misreading is a return to a thesis that has been abandoned by most scholars, who agree that Paul is attacking here the Jewish Christians and their advocacy of Jewish observances (see above. p. 46).

Gaston's exegesis of the Sarah-Hagar passage (Gal. 4.21-31) is

even less convincing. The nub of this exegesis is that when Hagar
is identified with the covenant of Sinai, this does not mean that
Hagar is being identified with the Jews, because Sinai can also
signify Gentiles! Here Gaston relies on a midrash on Deut. 32.2
('The Lord came from Sinai and shone forth from Seir. He showed
himself from Mount Paran') that explains that Seir and Paran are
references to the Edomites and the Ishmaelites; before God offered
the Torah to Israel, he offered it first to them, but they refused,
upon which they were put in the charge of angels. Gaston now
points out that both Seir and Paran are in Arabia, and thus the
Torah was offered to Gentiles in Arabia. Gaston can now say that
the whole contrast between Sarah and Hagar is not between
Christians and Jews, but between Israel (including both Jews and
Christians) and Gentiles, who received a law in the Arabian
desert, but not a covenant, and thus find this law a curse rather
than a blessing.

Gaston has to admit that there is some difficulty in that Paul is
addressing this argument to Gentiles who probably did not know
the above midrash, which Paul unaccountably does not explain to
them. Gaston's answer is that his exegesis 'presupposes a prior
knowledge by the Galatians of the traditions connecting Gentiles
with Sinai and the angels of the nations . . . But then, nearly every
interpretation of this passage presupposes some prior knowledge
on the part of the readers.'

An even stronger objection, however, is that the midrash quoted
connects the Gentiles to Arabia, but not to Sinai, or even the Sinai
Desert. Mount Seir and Mount Paran, where the midrash says
that God appeared respectively to the Edomites and the Ishmaelites, are different and distant mountains from Mount Sinai, and it
is with Mount Sinai that Paul connects Hagar. So, with some
admiration, or at least stupefaction, for Gaston's ingenuity, one
must conclude that Paul, as commentators hitherto have all
thought, did indeed mean to identify Hagar with the Jews and
their Sinai covenant and slavery, in contrast to Christians whose
spiritual mother, he alleged, was Sarah, a symbol of freedom. If
this familiar interpretation means (as Gaston realizes with
commendable revulsion) that Paul is expressing thoughts that are
hostile to Judaism, then this is a fact about Paul that has to be
accepted, not conjured away. The idea that a reference to the

covenant of Sinai denotes Gentiles and not Jews is bizarre. Gaston does say that his exegesis of this passage, as of other passages, is 'experimental'. An experiment that fails can be useful, provided only that its failure is acknowledged.

We now turn to Romans 9, 10 and 11, where Paul discusses the Jews explicitly. These chapters have always been understood to mean that, in Paul's view, and to his great sorrow, the Jews have failed to acknowledge Christ, but this failure came about through the mysterious purpose of God, and eventually the Jews' blindness would be removed and they would become converted to Christianity, so finally receiving the blessing promised to them through Abraham. This interpretation has sometimes been represented as a very positive attitude towards the Jews, but Gaston quite rightly denies this, pointing out that such an attitude denies all validity to post-Jesus Judaism, excludes the Jews from salvation until the Last Days, and defines the salvation of the Jews entirely in terms of conversion to Christianity. Such an attitude towards Judaism is thoroughly unacceptable to Gaston and his colleagues, who therefore seek a new interpretation of Paul's position in these chapters.

Gaston's exegesis of these three chapters is as follows. Paul is saying, not that the Jews have failed to acknowledge Christ as universal saviour, but that they have failed to realize that Christ has come to save the Gentiles. 'Israel was faithful to Torah as it relates to Israel, but with respect to the goal of that Torah as it relates to Gentiles, they stumbled and were unfaithful.' Gaston argues that the Jews did not expect the Gentiles to be saved until the End-time; they were therefore hostile to Paul's mission, which was to set up a Gentile church which would exist alongside the Jewish church and form together with it the saved body of Israel, both awaiting the End-time together.

An important element in Gaston's exegesis is his new translation of 11.28. Gaston's version is, 'With respect to the gospel, to be sure, they are hostile for your sake, but with respect to the election they are beloved for the sake of the fathers.' The word *echthroi* is translated by AV as 'enemies', and by NEB as 'God's enemies' ('God's' being an explanatory addition). Gaston's change assists his explanation that Paul's complaint against the Jews is that they were hostile to his mission to the Gentiles, not that they refused salvation through Christ (which was not meant for them). Gaston argues, in support of his translation, '*Echthros* in the NT is always active and never passive (hated, i.e. by God).' This is a very doubtful statement. Like the English word 'enemy', *echthros* can signify the recipient of hostility or the active purveyor of it, or both. In Romans 5.10, for example, the passive meaning is more likely. Here, we have to decide from the context. The obvious pointer is the symmetry of the two balancing phrases in this verse, 'enemies for your sake' and 'beloved (*agapetoi*) for the sake of the patriarchs'; just as in the second phrase, the Jews are the recipients of God's love, so in the first phrase they are the recipients of his displeasure, not the dispensers of displeasure of their own to something other than God. Gaston is aware of this difficulty, conceding that his translation 'breaks a certain parallelism in the two halves of the verse', but answers, ' . . . but so do the two different senses of *dia* ("for your benefit" and "because of").' But why should not *dia* be translated 'because of' in both cases? This makes perfect sense, but Gaston's 'hostile for your sake' is a very awkward, perhaps impossible, construction. Further, the parallelism of *kata men to euaggelion* and *kata de ten eklogen* is very strained in Gaston's translation, but perfectly natural in the usual translation. So this new translation of 11.28 cannot be judged a success, and the exegesis of it must return to the old concept that the Jews are temporarily (i.e. until the *parousia*) under the displeasure of God.

On the other hand, Gaston's exegesis of chapter 9 of Romans is a partial success. Here he does demonstrate, I believe, that the accepted exegesis of verses 6-21 is wrong. Gaston shows that all that Paul is saying in these verses is that the Jews have received election because of their descent from Abraham and Sarah. The later interpretation, which makes these verses disinherit the Jews in favour of the Christian church is a misunderstanding. The passage about Jacob and Esau (10-13) does *not* identify the Jews with Esau, and should not be interpreted as similar to the Hagar-Sarah opposition in Gal. 4. If Gaston has succeeded in rescuing only these verses from antisemitic exegesis his effort has not been without result.

The conclusion of this chapter, however, resists Gaston's attempts to give it a milder meaning. Here Paul says that the Jews, despite their election, failed because of relying on works instead of faith. This is the plain meaning of verses 30-33. Gaston argues that this is not the meaning: the Jews are being criticized only for their failure to accept Paul's mission to the Gentiles, by which the Gentiles, through faith, will join the election together with the Jews. Thus Gaston translates verse 31 as follows: 'Israel, on the other hand, in pursuing the Torah of righteousness [for Israel alone] did not attain to [the goal of] the Torah.' By inserting phrases in brackets, one can always change the meaning of a sentence as one likes. Again, in verse 32 Gaston interpolates ideas that are not there: 'Israel did not reach the goal of the race because it stumbled on a rock, and it stumbled because of lack of trust or faithfulness, because it was distracted, as it were, by works. Not that Paul has anything against works, but in themselves they do not lead to the goal. To be faithful to the goal of the law means to acknowledge that the righteousness of God is there also for the Gentiles.' All this is not in the text; it is eisegesis, not exegesis. The plain meaning of these verses is that Israel has failed by preferring works to faith; thus the Gentiles, not the Jews have achieved justification. This is the accepted exegesis, and it is correct. The fact that Paul begins this chapter by defending the election of the Jews does not mean that their election, in Paul's view, continues to be valid (except in the sense, as he explains later, that it ensures their inclusion at the time of the *parousia*). On the contrary, Paul uses the election of the Jews, which, he argues, was an arbitrary decision on the part of God, to explain how God can now make an equally arbitrary decision to elect the Gentiles instead (verses 22-23). It is true that there is a certain inconsistency in Paul's argument, since it is based at first on God's power of arbitrary decision, but finally on the superiority of faith to works; but this kind of inconsistency is quite usual in Paul's writings.

Nowhere, indeed, does Paul state explicitly what Gaston understands to be his main criticism of the Jews: that they opposed his mission to the Gentiles. Where is the evidence that the Jews in the time of Paul opposed missionary activity? As we shall see in section (3), the evidence is all to the contrary. The opposition of the Jews to Paul was not because he believed in the salvation of the Gentiles, but because he wished to abolish the covenant of Sinai and the Torah as the way of salvation for the Jews, and substitute, for Jews as well as for Gentiles, the worship of Jesus.

2. Paul intended the worship of Jesus as a means of salvation for Gentiles only, not for Jews

This is the most baffling contention of the GGS school, since proofs are not hard to find that Paul, on the contrary, regarded the worship of Jesus as essential for all. Yet the GGS school cannot do without this proposition, however unlikely it may be, since without it, their whole allegedly Pauline conception of Judaism as a parallel branch of Israel to that of Gentile Christianity cannot be sustained; instead, there is only one religion and one salvation, 'in Christ', leaving no room for the survival of the Torah in Paul's thought.

Questions that arise about the GGS position are these: (1) Why did the Gentiles have to have such a different mode of salvation from the Jews? (2) What is the position of Paul himself, and his Jewish helpers and followers? Do they belong to the Jewish or to the Gentile scheme of salvation? (3) What is the role of Jesus' violent death on the cross in the Gentile scheme of salvation? (4) How does Paul's doctrine of the divinity of Jesus affect his expectation of Jewish acceptance of his scheme of salvation for Gentiles? (5) What is the position of the Jerusalem church in Paul's alleged double scheme of salvation? (6) Is the Christ-salvation definitely for Gentiles only, and not for Jews, or is it just not *necessarily* for Jews?

These questions do not receive the same answers from all members of the GGS school (that is when they receive answers at all). As before, I shall examine Gaston's writings as the deepest and most detailed expression of this standpoint.

Gaston's answers to the above questions, as far as I have been able to discover them, are as follows: (1) Paul thought that the Gentiles could not be saved by repentance within a law-type covenant, like the Jews, since they were too far gone in sin, and needed a more drastic remedy. (2) Paul himself and possibly his Jewish followers in the Gentile mission detached themselves from observance of the Torah, not out of disapproval of such observance by Jews, but because they wished to share the lot and manner of salvation of their Gentile flock.[4] Gaston thus does not share the view of some scholars (e.g. W.D. Davies) that Paul remained an observant Jew. (3) The violent death of Jesus had no atoning role in Paul's theology. 'For Paul . . . Christ died not so much for our sins as to give life to the dead, and in Paul's "pattern of religion", Christ occupies almost exactly the same place as Sinai does within Judaism'.[5] It is not surprising that Gaston omits the aspect of atonement, since it is hard to see how the death of Christ, if an atonement for the sins of mankind, could have this effect only for Gentiles. (4) Paul expected that most Jews would be reluctant to accept the divinity of Jesus, but hoped that some of them would. (5) The Jerusalem church were Jews who accepted the divinity of Jesus together with observance of the Torah. Paul accepted this as a valid position for them, since they were not involved in missionary activity to the Gentiles. On the other hand, he opposed violently some Jewish-Christians (not official emissaries of the Jerusalem church) who combined the stance of the Jerusalem church with a mission to the Gentiles, and insisted on observance of the Torah by Gentile converts to Christianity. (6) Worship of Christ, in Paul's view, was essential for Gentiles; desirable but not essential for Jews. It is not clear whether Gaston thinks that, for Paul, Christ has a salvificatory role for Jews who both believe in his divinity and observe the Torah. Which is it that saves such Jews, Christ or the Sinai covenant? Or both? Gaston remarks tentatively that perhaps the Jewish Christians of the Jerusalem church divided up the task of salvation between the Torah and Christ, relying on the former for covenant and the latter for atonement; a division of function that Paul tolerated, but did not expect to be a lasting compromise: eventually the Jerusalem church would fade away, and there would only be Gentile Christians, on the one hand, and Torah-Jews on the other.[6] But is it an option for a Jew, not engaged in the mission to the Gentiles, to abandon the Torah and rely on Christ entirely for salvation instead? Paul, Gaston asserts, having undertaken at the Jerusalem Council not to preach such a position to Jews, kept this promise thereafter; but I am not sure whether Gaston thinks that Paul ruled out such a position as untenable in itself.

We thus have before us the full Gaston position (including some significantly cloudy areas) on the Christ-salvation for Jews and Gentiles in Paul, and we may now enquire whether there is any reason to suppose that this is anything like what Paul really thought.

A key passage bearing on whether Paul thought that Christ's salvation was for Jews as well as for Gentiles is Gal. 2.15-21:

> We ourselves are Jews by birth, not Gentiles and sinners. But we know that no man is ever justified by doing what the law demands, but only through faith in Christ Jesus; so we too have put our faith in Jesus Christ, in order that we might be justified through this faith, and not through deeds dictated by law; for by such deeds, scripture says, no mortal man shall be justified. If now, in seeking to be justified in Christ, we ourselves no less than the Gentiles turn out to be sinners against the law (or: no less than the Gentiles have accepted the position of sinners against the law), does that mean that Christ is an abettor of sin? No, never! No, if I start building up again a system which I have pulled down, then it is that I show myself up as a transgressor of the law. For through the law I died to law – to live for God. I have been crucified with Christ: the life I now live is not my life, but the life which Christ lives in me; and my present bodily life is lived by faith in the Son of God, who loved me and gave himself up for me. I will not nullify the grace of God; if righteousness comes by law, then Christ died for nothing. (NEB translation)

These words follow the incident in which Paul rebuked Peter for vacillating in the matter of Torah-observance. Some commentators regard this passage as part of Paul's rebuke, others do not. The statement, as translated above, seems to be a straightforward statement of the position that the Christ-sacrifice takes the place of the Torah for Jews as well as for Gentiles. Such a statement would destroy the Gaston position about Paul, since it allows no place for a Torah-community of Jews pursuing their salvation in their own way, with no obligation to seek salvation through Christ. Consequently, Gaston has to resort again to extensive re-translation.

His most drastic re-translation is of the last sentence (verse 21), as follows: 'I do not set at nought the grace of God; for since through law is [the] righteousness [of God], consequently Christ has died as a free gift.' Gaston argues that *dorean* cannot be translated 'in vain', but at most as 'needlessly', and that it sometimes means 'as a free gift', e.g. Rom. 3.24, which he suggests is the meaning here. The meaning of the whole sentence would therefore be that Paul is denying that his defection from the observance of Judaism is a denial of God's grace in revealing the law, since this very law predicted that Christ would offer his death as a gift for the redemption of the Gentiles. The unlikeliness of this translation derives not only from the use of added matter in square brackets, and the translation of *ei* as 'since', but mainly from the sheer clumsiness of expression (if this is what is meant) as contrasted with the naturalness and fluency of the sentence if it bears its generally accepted meaning. If the meaning of *dorean* should be 'needlessly' ('without sufficient cause') rather than 'in vain' ('without sufficient result'), this meaning is quite adequate for the accepted interpretation of the passage.

In this sentence, Gaston takes 'law' to have a good sense, namely the revelation of God in the Hebrew Bible foretelling the coming of Christ. But elsewhere in the passage, and in the continuation in chapters 3 and 4, Gaston takes 'law' to have a bad sense, relating to Gentiles not to Jews. Thus the 'law' promulgated by angels (3.19) is not the Torah, but the law of the Gentiles, administered by national guardian angels (see above and section 3), and it is from this that the Gentiles, not the Jews, are being emancipated. Gaston has to argue that Paul continually switches without warning from one sense of 'law' to the other.

One has to conclude, then, that Gaston's exegesis of Gal. 2 and 3 is too strained to be credible, and that the accepted understanding of these chapters is correct: Paul is rejecting the Torah as a means of salvation, since it has been rendered obsolete by the death of Christ.

One remark of Gaston's in the course of his exegesis, however, must be welcomed. He points out, in arguing that the passage just quoted cannot be a continuation of Paul's rebuke of Peter, that it does not make sense to say that Peter was regarded as abandoning Jewish observance simply because he ate with Gentiles, for Judaism did not forbid this (Gaston quotes here Mishnah, Ber. 7.1 which presupposes that eating with Gentiles is permitted). This is quite true, and here Gaston once more shows his acquaintance with Jewish sources and his freedom from many of the usual misapprehensions about them. Nevertheless, even if our passage, as Gaston argues, is not a continuation of the Peter (Cephas) incident, but a general disquisition on Paul's reasons for giving up

observance of Jewish law, this does not remove difficulty from the
sentence which definitely does belong to Paul's rebuke of Cephas
(2.14), or, in the light of Jewish law, from the Cephas story as a
whole, which Gaston indeed finds puzzling.[7] Nor does his
detachment of our passage from the Cephas incident make
Gaston's interpretation of these verses appreciably more plausible.

3. Judaism provided salvation only for Jews, not for Gentiles

It is an indispensable pillar of the GGS position that Judaism,
in the time of Paul, did not make adequate provision for Gentiles.
Whereas Gaston and his colleagues repudiate the whole stance of
the Gospels and Acts as to the alleged defects in Judaism itself
(especially 'works-righteousness'), they, in a sense, reinstate these
charges in another area of Judaism, namely its provision for the
spiritual needs of Gentiles. According to GGS, Judaism, while
providing 'commandments' for Gentiles (the so-called 'Seven
Noachic Laws'), did not provide any sense of covenant to
accompany these laws. The relationship to God allotted to
Gentiles by these laws was exactly that wrongly alleged by the
Gospels and Acts and later Christianity as prevailing among the
Jews themselves: an anxious commitment to piling up credit
marks by the observance of commandments, combined with a fear
of exclusion from salvation if any of them were transgressed. Thus
Paul was allegedly filling a real gap in Judaism by providing a
sense of covenant for Gentiles 'in Christ'. Unfortunately, the same
kind of selectiveness and misinterpretation that went into the old
picture of intra-Jewish Judaism (as elaborated by Ferdinand
Weber, Emil Schürer, Franz Billerbeck, Rudolf Bultmann and
others, and refuted by Travers Herford, James Parkes, George
Foot Moore and E.P. Sanders) has gone into this more recent
reconstruction of first-century Jewish attitudes to Gentiles. I
confine myself, as before, to Gaston's treatment of this subject,
which has provided the guidelines for the whole school of thought.

First, it has to be said that Gaston allows far too little weight to
the simple fact that Judaism allowed and encouraged full
conversion of Gentiles to Judaism. Even allowing (for the
moment) the contention that there was no form of covenant for
Gentiles outside Judaism in the first century (and Gaston admits

that there was such provision at a later date), there was full provision for the entry of Gentiles into the Jewish covenant by baptism, and, in the case of males, circumcision. So, even supposing that first-century Judaism thought that all Gentiles outside the Jewish covenant were lost souls, the position of Judaism would not be worse than that which prevailed later in Christianity. When Paul said, 'For there is no difference between the Jew and the Greek' (Rom. 10.12), he was referring to believers (see previous verse), and he was by no means saying that there was no difference between Christians and heathens. The Christian church, in deciding *nulla salus extra ecclesiam*, was not reversing any decision of Paul's. Similarly in Judaism all converts became full Jews, and the rabbinic writings, basing themselves on scriptural texts about loving the stranger, stress the duty to welcome proselytes as equals. Moreover, as the New Testament itself testifies (Matt. 23.15), the Jews were active missionaries in the first century. Paul's own epistles testify to this, since he complains so bitterly about Jews who seek to convert his flock to observance of the Torah. So it cannot be said that conversion to Judaism was too infrequent to be taken seriously as a mode of providing covenant status to Gentiles. In the first century, the nation of Adiabene, the remnant of the ancient Assyrian Empire, was converted to Judaism. Over a century before, the Idumaeans, the reputed descendants of Esau, were converted to Judaism, and became pious, even fanatical, Jews. (Modern research has disproved Josephus's statement that they were converted by force. This statement was motivated by Josephus's desire to placate his Roman masters by discounting the extent of Jewish missionary activity). So, in so far as there was a stream of thought in first-century Judaism denying the possibility of salvation outside the Jewish covenant, this was the exact analogue of the attitude of the church in relation to Christian *salus*. Even if one takes the GGS view of Paul as assigning validity simultaneously to two covenants, that of Sinai for Jews and that of Christ for Gentiles, this still leaves the great majority of mankind in an uncovenanted condition. So can one really say that Paul was filling a gap in Judaism, or that he was, for the first time, providing an opportunity for Gentiles to enter the covenantal condition?

But, it will be replied, Paul, on the GGS theory, was now offering a two-covenant pattern, both of which provide a covenant condition. True, he was now closing the Jewish option to Gentiles, but the new option for Gentiles was more attractive, for it did not require observance of a difficult Torah, and it also did not require change of nationality and a commitment to marry only within the Jewish fold. Yet, without these difficult commitments, it still offered a covenant condition not inferior to that contained in Judaism, having the same guarantee of salvation not dependent on fulfilment of commandments.

We tend, however, to think of the matter in terms of a situation which did not exist at this time. Conversion to Christianity did not mean joining a majority community, as it did later; it meant joining a tiny minority sect, and usually meant the abandonment of family and societal ties. So Paul's new option for Gentiles hardly presented a less difficult choice than conversion to Judaism. Marriage, too, was forbidden outside the Christian community.

It should be noted that, even according to the GGS theory, Paul was not offering a wider field of options to Gentiles; he was angrily insistent that Gentiles must not any longer become converted to Judaism, but must accept only the option of salvation through Christ. Why this should be so, on GGS principles, is difficult to understand. If the two methods of salvation were equally efficacious, why should a Gentile be forbidden to choose Judaism, rather than Christ-salvation, if he so wished? On the accepted view, there is no difficulty here: Paul did *not* have a two-covenant theory at all. Since salvation could come only through Christ, whether for Jews or for Gentiles, he was understandably furious that Gentiles should choose the obsolete Judaism. While he was prepared to be tolerant of Jewish-Christians who, through inertia, found it hard to give up Torah-practices all at once, he had no patience with any Gentile who took up Jewish practices *ab initio*, for this amounted to a spurning of the validity of the Christ-salvation. This makes perfect sense, but the GGS view has no explanation of Paul's anger.

So far, I have been arguing on the basis that Judaism offered only one covenant: even on this basis, salvation was offered to all Gentiles who entered the Jewish covenant by conversion, and thus there was no gap in Judaism to make a Pauline provision of salvation necessary. But in fact Judaism did not offer one covenant, but two, and, unlike GGS Paulinism, Judaism offered Gentiles a genuine choice between the two. The second covenant was the Noachic covenant, by which a Gentile could achieve salvation without becoming converted to full Judaism. It is true that the Noachic covenant was a second-best: only by full conversion could a Gentile achieve not only salvation but membership of the priest-nation, the Jews. But this was not a limitation to salvation, any more than a Roman Catholic who decides that he does not have a vocation for the priesthood, thereby gives up his hopes of heaven. Paulinism, on the other hand (according to the GGS theory), offered a Gentile covenant that made the Gentiles entirely equal to the Jews, though achieving salvation by a different route. But Judaism already offered Gentiles a way to become entirely equal to the Jews: by full conversion to Judaism. In addition, it offered, as a complete bonus, a way of achieving salvation without such great sacrifice, but also without such high rank in the universal Jewish church. In practice, this second route often acted as an interim stage towards full conversion, either of the Gentile himself, or of his children.

Gaston, however, argues that this second route (i.e. entry to the Noachic covenant) did not, in the first century, offer salvation of any kind to Gentiles, and it is in this area of discussion (as well as in his failure to appreciate the importance of the option of full conversion), that Gaston adopts the selectiveness and prejudice in the use of Jewish sources that he deplores in the area of Torah-Judaism itself. He argues, in effect, that the Noachic Laws were just a way of keeping Gentiles in order, not a way of salvation for them.

Gaston agrees that at a later date, Judaism did develop a doctrine of salvation for Gentiles, summed up in the rabbinic saying, 'The righteous of the Gentiles have a share in the World to Come'. But even then, there was little definition of what constituted righteousness in a Gentile; and (according to Gaston) it was not until the Middle Ages, in the writings of Maimonides, that a connection was made between the Noachic Laws and the 'righteousness' by which a Gentile achieved the World to Come. It was Maimonides, on this view, who finally said that this 'righteousness' was achieved specifically by observance of the

Seven Laws, provided that this observance was regarded as stemming from Divine revelation, not just from rational considerations. 'Before Maimonides, the concept of the Noachic commandments really has nothing to do with the point under consideration for "the righteous among the nations" are never mentioned in connection with them. As they are discussed in the Talmud (Sanh 56-60a), the context is of actual (if at times theoretical) court decisions concerning Gentiles living in an independent land of Israel (resident aliens). There is no reference to a covenant of grace or the possibility of repentance and atonement, and the penalty of violation is (theoretically) death . . . The point is to keep the land from being polluted, and such stipulations have nothing to do with the "righteous among the nations of the world." Of the commandments chosen, one comes from Gen. 9.4 and the other six are ingeniously derived from Gen. 2.16, "And the Lord God commanded Adam." This is an important verse because it shows that from the beginning God related to his creatures through commandments and that Adam is an appropriate figure to use when thinking about the relationship between God and the Gentile world.'

This statement is puzzlingly self-contradictory. If the Noachic laws are only about 'resident aliens' and about 'polluting the land', what have they to do with Adam? Or Noah for that matter? If these laws were given first to Adam, the first man, and then to Noah, the first man in the post-Diluvian era, surely this gives them universality as a *lex gentium*? And surely a *lex gentium* given by God in direct revelation, first to Adam, and then to Noah has some spiritual significance for mankind as a whole? The Talmud makes clear that these were the laws by which mankind lived during the whole period before the giving of the Torah on Mount Sinai; and all the figures counted 'righteous' in this pre-Sinai period (e.g. Enoch, Methuselah, Noah, Shem, Eber, Abraham, Isaac, Jacob, Joseph) were so because of their adherence to this code of laws. It is true that the rabbinic writings sometimes say that some pre-Sinai figure 'kept the whole Torah'; but this is regarded as supererogatory virtue on their part, since they had no obligation to keep Sinaitic laws in advance of their promulgation; and the same rabbinic writings also excuse pre-Sinai figures for conduct in contradiction to the Sinaitic laws (e.g. Jacob's marriage to two sisters, in contravention of Lev. 18.18) on the ground that they were bound only by the Noachic laws.

Thus it is totally wrong to say that the Noachic laws were regarded as concerning only 'resident aliens', since they concerned the most revered figures of early biblical history, including the Patriarchs themselves. Quite apart from this, Gaston is wrong in saying that the Talmud does not connect the Noachic laws with Gentile 'righteousness'. For example, in the very Talmudic passage quoted by Gaston there is the saying of Rabbi Meir, 'Whence do we know that a Gentile who studies the Torah is as a High Priest? From the verse, "Ye shall therefore keep my statutes and my judgments which, if a man (*adam*, i.e. any human being) do, he shall live in them" (Lev. 18.5). Priests, Levites and Israelites are not mentioned, but *men*: hence thou mayest learn that a Gentile who studies the Torah is as a High Priest.' The Talmud, finding Rabbi Meir's view contradicted by a saying of Rabbi Johanan forbidding a Gentile to study the Torah, reconciles the two views by saying that Rabbi Meir's saying refers to the study by a Gentile of the Seven Noachic Laws. Thus the Seven Laws, in this Talmudic passage, are regarded as giving life to Gentiles, just as the Jewish Torah does to Jews, and 'life' in this scriptural verse is always taken to mean spiritual as well as physical life, i.e. salvation.

Another important Talmudic text showing how the rabbis regarded the Noachic Laws is the query (Sanh 74b) whether a Gentile is obliged to suffer martyrdom rather than transgress the Noachic Laws. This query does not really apply to all the Seven Laws, but only to the three which are identical with the three laws (prohibitions against murder, idolatry and incest) for which a Jew must suffer martyrdom. The verbal similarity between the formulation of these three laws in the rubric of the Seven Laws and in the rubric of the Martyrdom Laws shows that there is a strong affinity between these two codes: one the basic law of humanity, and the other the basic principles of Torah Judaism, for which a Jew must sacrifice his life. In this context of martyrdom, can one uphold the idea that the Seven Laws relate only to possible pollution of the Land by 'resident aliens'?

In fact, the only aspect of Maimonides's statement that adds anything to the Talmud is his assertion that the Seven Laws save Gentiles only if they acknowledge the origin of these laws in the

Divine revelation of the Torah. I do not know of any Talmudic
source for this statement, and the Midrashic stories of Abraham's conversion to monotheism through the use of his own
reason surely contradict Maimonides's formulation.

Gaston further seeks to demote the salvific character of the
Noachic Laws by connecting them to intertestamental and rabbinic ideas about the rule of angels over the Gentiles. This topic
really has nothing to do with the subject. There are Talmudic
and Midrashic passages which say that after the Gentiles refused
the Torah, they were put under the rule of angels, while Israel is
ruled by God alone. But nowhere is the rule of angels connected
in any way to the observance by Gentiles of the Noachic laws.
These laws are everywhere regarded as addressed to Gentiles by
God himself through his revelation to Adam and Noah. The rule
of angels over Gentiles relates not to matters of morality, but to
political events; when one nation fights with another, it is
conceived that their guardian angels also take sides. The passages that say that the Gentile nations refused the Torah do not
mean that they thereby removed themselves from the sphere of
salvation; only that they failed to achieve special status as the
priest-nation of God.

There are certainly some anti-Gentile passages in the rabbinic
literature. For example, there are passages saying that even
though the Gentiles were given the Noachic Laws, their sinful-
ness led God to cancel this revelation. The question is then
asked, 'Does this mean that a Gentile who, nevertheless, observes
the Noachic Laws, receives no reward from God?'; and the
answer is given, 'No, he does receive reward, but only on a lower
level than if the revelation were still in force.' This illiberal
statement obviously arises from anti-Gentile prejudice, which
doubted the earlier belief that Gentiles could be saved; even so,
the salvation is not entirely cancelled, and of course no one
doubted that Gentiles could still be saved by conversion to
Judaism, so this late attitude is roughly, but not quite, on the
same level as Christian pronouncements about *salus*. In the first
century, when Jewish-Gentile relations in the Graeco-Roman
world had not yet been affected by disaster, the efficacy of the
Noachic Laws was not yet doubted. So the situation is the
opposite to what Gaston says: a belief in Gentile salvation

became attenuated later by bitter Jewish experiences from Gentiles.

Thus Gaston's whole picture of Jewish attitudes towards the salvation of Gentiles is mistaken. Further, his picture of 'works-righteousness' on the part of Gentiles is based on misconceptions. He points out that some Gentiles who were 'God-fearers' were not satisfied with the Noachic Laws, but still did not wish to embark on full conversion to Judaism. Consequently, they supplemented the Noachic Laws by observing some of the specifically Jewish Torah laws, such as the Sabbath, or dietary laws. Gaston sees this as an anxious process of gaining extra marks towards salvation; and this anxiety of 'God-fearers' about adding commandments to one's credit is, he conceives, the object of Paul's diatribes against legalism, not the practice of the Jews themselves. Study of the Talmud on this question, however, leads to a different conclusion. Observance of commandments other than those of obligation was not regarded as an anxious scramble for salvation by gaining extra credits. It was regarded as a supererogatory exercise of piety, by which one might attain extra saintliness, but which had nothing to do with salvation. Salvation was achieved, whether by Jew or Gentile, within the covenant of obligation, where the operation of repentance and atonement compensated for the inevitable sins or omissions.[9]

But again, Gaston denies that Gentiles, under the Noachic dispensation, were ever regarded as having the option of repenting for their sins. Instead, he says, they were to be punished by death for their sins, without any opportunity for repentance. This is an astounding statement. A whole biblical work, the book of Jonah, which the rabbis knew as well as the rest of scripture, is concerned with Gentile repentance. The repentance of the inhabitants of Nineveh must have been within the Noachic Covenant, for neither in the biblical narrative nor in Jewish tradition did they become converted to Judaism. The topic of Gentile repentance is mentioned frequently in the rabbinic literature;[8] indeed it is often said that God is much more forbearing in awaiting Gentile repentance than in relation to Israel, whose sins are punished immediately. In a comment on Jonah, the Mekhilta (Pisha, Bo,1) says that Gentiles are more inclined to repent than Israel. Another saying is, 'God is on the watch for the nations of the world to repent, so that He may bring them under His wings' (Num. R. Naso, x,1). This last saying may or may not refer to conversion to Judaism; in either case, the concept of Gentile repentance was by no means strange to the rabbis.

Gaston notes that Paul has nothing to say about repentance in his scheme of salvation for Gentiles, but does not explain why this is so, if Paul wishes to provide a parallel form of salvation to that of Judaism. Why should a person of Jewish Pharisaic background provide a form of salvation for Gentiles that promises immortality without repentance? Why indeed have two covenants of such very different kinds? If Paul, however, is building his scheme of salvation not on Jewish models, but on Hellenistic recipes for immortality, then the omission of repentance is easy to understand, and if he is offering just one scheme of salvation, for both Jews and Gentiles, the whole difficulty disappears.

It is also a difficulty in Gaston's scheme that the Jewish opposition of which Paul complains relates to his mission to the Gentiles, not, as in accepted interpretation, to his abrogation of Jewish law for Jews as well as for Gentiles. It is hard to see how Paul's activities with Gentiles could have come to the attention of Jewish authorities, or why they should have cared about such activities, since Gentiles were not required to adopt the Torah. If it was known that Paul was converting Gentiles to a non-Torah form of monotheism, this was perfectly in accordance with Jewish doctrine about the Noachic laws, and would have aroused no opposition. Gaston suggests that Paul might have been criticized because he thought that the time had already come for the conversion of the Gentiles, while Jewish authorities thought this would take place only in the Last Days. But millennial movements were common in Judaism, and behaviour appropriate to the Last Days would be met with tolerance, as by Gamaliel in Acts 5. The complaint against Paul that he attempted to induce *Jews* to forsake the Torah would indeed have aroused strong opposition from Jewish authorities, and this is the only convincing explanation of their attitude of opposition towards him.

Altogether, Gaston's attempt to make a space for Paulinism by denigrating first-century Judaism's provision for Gentile salvation is a failure. It is one of those side-steps, familiar from the history of New Testament exegesis, by which a form of denigration of

Judaism dislodged from one area is reinstated in another, so that antisemitic diatribes can be given some meaning or application after all. The plain fact is that Paul's diatribes against 'law' are directed not against some non-existent Gentile form of law, but against Torah-Judaism itself. Gaston and his school are aware that such denigration cannot be substantiated against Torah-Judaism, and that in the Gospels and Acts, it is indeed Judaism that is the target. But they hoped to find a New Testament enclave free from anti-Judaism in the writings of Paul, who, they realize, has always been quoted by Christian anti-Judaism as its chief fount of authority. Their contention is that this understanding of Paul was a mistake, which began with his first interpreters. Paul himself, they argue, meant no such thing. He worked out a two-covenant system which died with him, but which could be resuscitated for the benefit of twentieth-century ecumenism. This 'experiment' in exegesis has been carried out with great ingenuity by Gaston, so that its failure may be considered definitive.

7

Paul, Hellenism and Antisemitism

In the earliest form of Hellenistic antisemitism, that of Manetho, Chaeremon, Apion, there was a simple uninvolved hatred of the Jews. In so far as these antisemites used the Hebrew Bible, they did so merely to obtain an outline of Jewish history which they could caricature and invert: thus they derived from the Bible the story of the Exodus from Egypt, and inverted it into an ignominious expulsion.

With the Gnostics, however, a new form of antisemitism arose that was much more involved in Judaism. It was no longer a simple hatred, but an ambivalent relationship. The Hebrew Bible (or at least the early chapters of Genesis which reflected the Gnostics' cosmological concerns) was read with great attention and subjected to deep and startling exegesis, by which the God of Judaism was given a place in a cosmological scheme, the Torah was explained as his flawed production, and the Jews were represented as his acolytes and dupes. The Jews and their Bible were thus regarded as religious data of importance which had to be accounted for in cosmic terms. Chapter 1 considered what kind of people would have taken this attitude to Judaism, and concluded that they were not renegade Jews (as much present-day opinion holds), but Hellenist intellectuals hovering on the fringes of Judaism, i.e. lapsed converts or prospective converts who turned away at the brink of conversion in revulsion against the presumptuous Jewish religious claims, which conflicted with the high claim of Hellenism to provide the deepest wisdom. On this

reading, the antisemitism of the Gnostics derives ultimately from
the same source as that of the outright dismissive antisemites such
as Apion – from the cultural rivalry between Hellenism and
Judaism; a rivalry much exacerbated by Jewish attempts, by Philo
and many others, to appropriate Hellenism as an adumbration of
Judaism, and especially to equate the High God of Plato and
Aristotle with the God of the Hebrew Bible.

Gnostic antisemitism, however, remained on a relatively mild
level. The chief animus of the Gnostics was not against the Jews
as a people but against the God of the Hebrew Bible, and the
Jews were despised as his dupes rather than hated as evildoers.
Our problem, in this book, has been to chart the process by
which Gnostic antisemitism developed into the much more viru-
lent Christian antisemitism, in which the Jews were hated as the
killers of Christ and as active and dangerous evildoers in the
service of Satan. This picture of the Jews can be found in certain
passages of the New Testament, such as Stephen's diatribe in
Acts 7.52-53, and Matthew 23.33-36, and was developed further
in the writings of the church Fathers and in later mediaeval
diabolization.

The writings of Paul, I have argued, act as a link between
Gnostic and Christian antisemitism. While his thought was
predominantly Gnostic, he added the element that was necessary
for Christian antisemitism – the conception that the pitiable,
violent and agonized death of Jesus was the indispensable means
of atonement and divinization for mankind. This element was
derived not from Gnosticism (which despised bodily death as a
trivial incident in the biography of the spirit), but from the
mystery religions, where the violent death of Dionysus and other
man-god deities was regarded as the means of achieving salvation
and immortality.

To what extent, then, was Paul responsible for Christian
antisemitism? It is not the contention of this book that Paul
himself created Christian antisemitism in its full-blown form. In
his epistles, Paul does not refer to the Jews as the killers of Christ
(except in I Thess. 2.14-16, which, we concluded, is of very
doubtful authenticity), but as the rejecters of Christ's message of
salvation. On the other hand, Paul does not quite follow the
Gnostic path of dismissing the Jews as insignificant people who

have completely missed the boat through their incomprehension. Paul is much concerned that the Jews should eventually partake in the full pattern of salvation. He therefore develops the idea that the 'blindness' of the Jews is only temporary. Even more important, he conceives that this temporary blindness is itself a necessary element in the total pattern of salvation. It is this conception of the necessary evil that provides the fatal link with later Christian antisemitism. For it very soon became clear to Christian thinkers that if the 'blindness' of the Jews led them to reject the salvific message of Christ, this same 'blindness' also led them to bring about his death; and if their rejection of Christ was fated and necessary, so was their alleged crucifixion of him. Thus the Jews soon made the transition into the full figure of the Judas-nation, whose appalling crime was fated and even designated by God as the means to salvation for mankind in general.

Thus, paradoxically, it is Paul's concern for the Jews and refusal to dismiss them from history that brings about their position in Christianity as the 'sin-eaters' who produce salvation for others through their guilt. One could put this, however, in another way. Paul, like the Gnostics, is engaged in an ambivalent relationship with Judaism, but his engagement with Judaism is deeper than theirs. He engages with the Hebrew Bible, not to dismiss it eventually as the flawed work of the Demiurge, but in order to enlist it in his scheme of salvation. His personal aim is not to be a bearer of *gnosis* outside the mainstream of the biblical succession, but to be the last and greatest of the Hebrew prophets, to whom the religious leaders of the Jews must eventually bow down in reverence. Consequently, he must provide a means for the return of the Jews and the nullification of their present rejection of his ideas. In order to return eventually, they must play some interim role within the Pauline myth, and this is provided by the theory of their necessary 'blindness'. This retention of the Jews as continuing to play a role among the *dramatis personae* of Christianity is the germ of their position in later Christianity as the wretched 'witnesses' to the truth of Christianity by their continuing misery and long expiation of their fated crime.

This is not to absolve Paul of antisemitism altogether. His antisemitism, however, is of an intermediate kind, somewhere between that of Gnosticism and that of later Christianity. The Jews, in Paul's scheme as in Gnosticism, are an uncomprehending and matter-bound people, locked in slavery to obsolete laws and observances. On the other hand, they still have a role and a destiny. If Paul could have dismissed the Jews, in the Gnostic manner, as merely contemptible, the antisemitism of his successors might have remained at the Gnostic level. But he prepared the Jews for the negative election by which they became the communal Sacred Executioner for Christianity, a role corresponding to that of the accursed sacrificers in Greek religion.

What kind of person, then, was Paul himself, if his religious stance was mainly derived from Hellenistic sources, Gnosticism and mystery religion, yet he aspired to a role of dominance within Judaism? In *The Mythmaker*, I argued that Paul's particular mixture of Hellenistic and Jewish influences is best explained by the hypothesis that he was an uneasy convert to Judaism, as the Ebionites testified, and not a born Jew and Pharisee, as he himself asserted. In the present book, I have attempted to show that the central elements of Paul's thought are derived from Hellenistic religion: that his acosmism and moral pessimism are derived from Gnosticism, and his concept of salvation through the violently-dying god from mystery religion. On the other hand, his determination to graft these alien elements on to Judaism show both a tenacious attachment to the Jewish tradition and milieu, and his ambition to make his mark on them.

Earlier scholarship was willing to acknowledge the Hellenistic derivation of Pauline Christianity; Rudolf Bultmann even gloried in it. The resultant gap between Jesus and Paul, however, was too hard to bear; and thus more recent scholarship has concentrated on asserting the Jewishness of Paul. This has resulted in a mass of analogizing material in which superficial similarities between Pauline ideas and those found in the Pseudepigrapha, Qumran literature, and rabbinic literature have been pressed hard, and fundamental dissimilarities have been ignored. In particular, the central Pauline notion of salvation through a descending and violently-dying god has received little attention, since it cannot be found in any Jewish source.

The present book attempts to right the balance by pointing to the Hellenistic elements in Pauline religion and refuting attempts to align these with Judaism. The result is inevitably to widen the gap once more between Jesus and Paul. The affinity of Jesus is with the Jerusalem church and its practice of Judaism, not with the Pauline church and its abandonment of Judaism.

Notes

1. Gnostic Antisemitism

1. See Dan (1987) for a defence of Scholem's definition of Gnosticism.
2. See Mansfield (1981)
3. For Solomon, see, for example, Pesikta Rabbati, 15 (preamble), commenting on I Chron. 29.23. For Hezekiah, see b. Sanh. 98b, view of R. Hillel.
4. See Maccoby, *Mythmaker*, p.220, discussing Deut. 4.12 and 36; 33.2; Isa. 63.9; Josephus *Ant.* xv.136; Canticles Rabbah I.2, and criticizing W.D. Davies (1984), pp 85-6. It may be added that Paul, in Col. 2.18, is probably not opposing Gnostic 'angel-worshippers', as modern theory has it, but referring to Jews and Jewish-Christians who, by observing dietary laws (v.16), show reverence to the angels who allegedly gave them the Torah. The juxtaposition of 'dietary laws' and 'angels', in a context of criticism of Judaism, in our present passage, gives further confirmation of this interpretation.
5. There is also the strong possibility that there were Gnostic sects that arose neither out of Christianity nor out of Judaism. For example, the tractate *Eugnostos the Blessed* appears to present a Gnostic scheme unaffected by either Jewish or Christian influences. For the relationship between this work and the Christianized *Sophia Jesu Christi*, see Jaques E. Ménard (1980). For the view that even *Eugnostos* has a Jewish background, see Parrot (1975).
6. Pearson (1980).
7. Stroumsa (1985). Methodologically important are the following remarks by Stroumsa (pp. 48-49): 'The parallelisms in the texts quoted above thus reveal the existence of definite links between the Jewish and Gnostic versions of Eve's adultery and/or seduction. As to the direction of this influence, the linguistic arguments support a Jewish influence on the Gnostic texts. Such a hypothesis does not, of course, imply that the redactor of *Hyp. Arch.* knew the pun in its original context. It does suggest,

however, that in the Gnostic milieu where *Hyp. Arch.* originated, there
was some knowledge of rabbinic exegesis – knowledge which could have
hardly reached these milieus through non-Jews. Moreover, the myth of
Eve's sexual relations with the serpent does not seem to have been widely
known in early Christian literature, a fact which strengthens the
hypothesis of Jewish influence on the Gnostic mythologoumena. Although the rabbinic texts were probably redacted at a later date than the
Greek or Aramaic *Vorlage* of the Gnostic texts, a previous oral tradition
may be assumed. The evidence of the Targum – and of the Gospel of John
– reflects the early date of the original Jewish exegetical traditions.
Moreover, it is easier to understand Gnostics attributing previously
known legends about the serpent to the demiurge, than to imagine rabbis
integrating scandalous Gnostic sayings about God the Creator into their
own thought simply transferring them to Satan or the serpent. It is thus
reasonable to see in the Gnostic texts the radicalization of Jewish
conceptions.'

8. Actually, Solomon was not begotten in adultery, according to the
Bible; the child begotten in adultery died at birth (II Sam. 12.18), and
Solomon was later begotten in wedlock. However, the Torah forbade
marriage between partners previously guilty of adultery, so David's
marriage to Bathsheba could be regarded as illegitimate.

9. Pearson, 'Jewish Elements', p. 157. Pearson, however, seems to
overestimate the degree of similarity between Philo's concept of 'the seed
of Seth' and that of the Gnostics.

10. Stroumsa (1984, p.53, n. 70) attempts to find a rabbinic source for
the notion that Seth was the ancestor exclusively of the righteous in a
passage in *Pirqei de-R.Eliezer* 22, after emendation. It is doubtful,
however, whether this passage, even after emendation, bears the
meaning suggested. Certainly Seth was the ancestor of 'all generations of
the righteous', as were Adam and Noah; but he was ancestor of all
generations of the unrighteous too. The Midrash merely wishes to dwell
on the positive side of Seth's place in history; or alternatively the Midrash
wishes to say that only the righteous can be regarded as spiritual
descendants of Seth (a concept similar to that of Philo, and not wholly
different from that of the Gnostics, except that the latter gave a mystical
meaning to spiritual descent that made it more ontologically real than
physical descent). In view of the genealogical tables in Gen.10 and I
Chron.1, showing that all the nations of the earth were descended from
Noah, the descendant of Seth, it is hard to see how any rabbinic support
could be given to the idea that only the righteous are physically
descended from Seth. The only (possibly) Cainite survivor of the Flood,
according to rabbinic legend, was Og, the gigantic king of Bashan (see

Gen.R. on Gen. 14.13), but he cannot take over the role of ancestor of all the wicked, since all the most villainous figures of the Hebrew Bible are clearly descended from Noah, and therefore from Seth.

11. On the other hand some Gnostics attempted to explain the descent of the righteous from Seth by the hypothesis that at the time of the Flood, some of the righteous were snatched to safety by the higher powers (Apocalypse of Adam, 69). It is also necessary for this hypothesis that Noah was descended not from Seth but from some other son of Adam, contrary to the biblical genealogy (Gen. 5).

12. The exception is the Apocalypse of Moses, and its expansion, the Life of Adam and Eve, in which Seth receives revelations from Adam, but does not himself play a salvific role.

13. Stroumsa's intricate and enlightening study of the Sethian theme in Gnostic, Jewish and Manichaean sources tends to obscure the fact that there is a great disproportion, in that the Jewish sources very rarely mention Seth.

14. The notion that the Gnostic Seth might be related to the Egyptian god Seth has been refuted in Pearson, 'The Egyptian Seth and the Gnostic Seth', 1977.

15. See Scholem (1974). Scholem's view is that Yaldabaoth means 'progenitor of Sabaoth'. For argument against Scholem, see Fallon (1978), pp. 32-34. Dan, however, argues plausibly that Yaldabaoth is an abbreviation of the formula *Yah 'Elohim 'Adonai Zeva'oth*, often found in the Hebrew Hekhalot texts as a compound name of the Creator God (Dan, 1983).

16. See Irenaeus, *Adversus Haereses*, 31.1-2.

17. See b. Shabb. 145b-146a; b. Yeb. 103b; b. Ab. Zar. 22b; Gen.Rab. 19.13. For Sammael as the father of Cain, see Targum Ps. Jonathan on Gen. 4.1. See Bowker (1969), p. 132, and Stroumsa (1984), p. 47-9.

18. See Layton, 1980-81, Vol. 1: The School of Valentinus. Valentinianism, however, proved unviable, despite its attempt to provide for the laity, because of its peculiar notion that sex relations were allowed only to the 'perfect', who alone were able to achieve the mystery of a sexual union free from lust.

19. This was a view proposed by Robert M. Grant, but later abandoned by him. See Grant (1959), pp. 27-38.

20. Green (1985).

21. See Patai (1967).

22. This is basically the view of Jonas, who says, 'Gnosticism originated in *close vicinity* and in partial reaction to Judaism' (Bianchi, 1967, p. 102).

23. See Lewis (1986), p. 128, 'In the Qur'an and the sacred biography, the important thing about the Jews of Medina is not so much that they opposed the Prophet, as that they were defeated and humbled.'

2. Paul and Gnosticism

1. Bultmann (1952), vol. 1, p.173.
2. MacRae (1980), pp. 130-1.
3. W.D. Davies (1984), pp. 85-6. See also Morton Smith, *JBL*, Sept. 1953, p. 192; Strack-Billerbeck on Gal. 3.19; Grundmann, *TWNT* (3), Walter Bauer, *Wörterbuch*, 4th ed, 1952; Kittel, *TWNT*, p. 82.
4. See Matt. 11.1; Luke 3.13; 8.55; Acts 7.44; 18.2; 20.13; 24.33; I Cor. 7.17.
5. Some have cited Deut. 33.2 and Isa. 63.9, which only say that God was accompanied by angels when he gave the Torah, not that the angels gave it.
6. Deane (1942), p. 212.
7. For the contrary view of the Gaston-Gager-Stendahl school, see below n.1 and chapter 6.
8. See Maccoby (1986), pp. 191-92.
9. On the other hand, I consider that Lloyd Gaston has succeeded in establishing that the contrasted pair Esau and Jacob (Rom. 9.13) was not intended by Paul to symbolize the rejection of the Jews, as assumed by later Christian exegesis. See p. 164.

3. Paul and the Mystery Religions

1. A recent school of thought argues that Paul intended his scheme of salvation through the death of Christ for non-Jews only, and regarded Jews as sufficiently covered by their own scheme of salvation through the Covenant and the Torah. (See Gaston, (1970), Stendahl, (1976), Gaston, (1979), Gaston, (1987), Gager, (1983).) For criticism of this view, see Maccoby (1986), pp. 93-95 and p. 216, pointing out that Judaism already provided a way of salvation for Gentiles without requiring them to become converted to Judaism, though full conversion to Judaism was regarded as the *via optima*, and as also freely available to all Gentiles. Here it may be added that Paul's own practice (I Cor. 9.21) showed that he regarded the Torah as non-obligatory for Jews. It is clear that Paul, while he did not insist that Jews should abandon the practice of the Torah if they felt more comfortable with it (I Cor. 7.18-20), regarded the Torah as no longer obligatory for Jews (as in the case of Peter, Gal. 2.11-14), and as actually forbidden to non-Jews (Gal. 5.2). The relegation of the Torah to the status of an optional extra or indulgence for Jews amounts to its complete abrogation as a scheme of salvation. Moreover, the contention of Gaston and others that Paul did not seek the conversion of Jews to Christ, regarding his mission as to Gentiles only, is contradicted by many

passages, including I Cor. 9.20, and by Paul's continual practice of preaching in synagogues. Thus the traditional view that Paul intended the supersession of Judaism and the substitution of a new way of salvation for all, whether Gentiles or Jews, is correct. For detailed criticism of Gaston's re-interpretation of Pauline texts, see chapter 6.

2. See, for example, Wellhausen (1885), p. 425, and, especially, Weber (1897), passim.

3. See especially Sanders (1977).

4. Davies (1965), p. 25.

5. Davies (1965), p. 32.

6. The doctrine of Original Sin is explicitly denied in both II Baruch (54.15-19) and IV Ezra (7.127-31), the two most pessimistic pre-rabbinic Jewish works.

7. For example, in I Enoch, the figure of the Elect One has sometimes been identified as a Messiah-figure. This is an error, for the Messiah is mentioned elsewhere in the same work as a human personage quite distinct from the Elect One. The Elect One is an angel, whose status is carefully subordinated to God. There is no suggestion that he is destined to undergo death as an atoning figure.

8. *Ap. John* 24.34-25.7. See MacRae (1977).

9. For Eve and Norea, see Stroumsa (1984), pp. 42-61. For Sophia, see Irenaeus, *Adversus Haereses*, 30.

10. Davies (1955), pp. 154-62, commenting on H. Windisch.

11. See Driver, S.R. and Neubauer, A., (1877); Maccoby, (1988), pp. 198-203.

12. The Greek Olympic official cult did indeed oppose the idea of the death of gods, insisting that the gods were 'immortal', as in Homer. This made the cult of Dionysus, the archetypal violently-dying and rising god, unofficial and, in a sense, disreputable. Yet, as shown by Jane Harrison and Walter Burkert, Dionysian religion was in fact the deepest element in Greek religion, underlying and informing the whole corpus of myth.

13. An example of this attitude is the midrash that represents the angels as objecting to God's plan to create man. God replies, 'They will fulfil my Law', and when the angels say, '*We* will fulfil it', God replies, 'You cannot', explaining that angels cannot fulfil the commandments about birth, death and food, since they are not born, do not die and do not eat (Tanhuma B. Behukkotai, 56b). In general, the frequent midrashic theme of the jealousy of angels towards man testifies to the rabbinic view that, in some important respects, man is superior to the angels.

14. Cambridge University Library MS Or. 1080, Box I; 48. See Spiegel (1969), p. 37. See also Maccoby (1982), p. 191.

15. Attis, according to Pausanias, was indirectly the son of Zeus (some

of whose semen, falling on earth produced Agdystis, whose severed genitals nourished an almond tree, a branch of which impregnated Attis's mother). Adonis was the son of an adulterous union of father and daughter; such a forbidden union had *mana*. Orpheus was the son of the Muse, Calliope; another account makes him the son of Apollo.

16. Harrison (1963).

17. Robertson Smith (1957), pp. 338-40 (quoting Nilus, *Nili opera quaedam*, Paris 1639).

18. For the concept that repentance and confession turn witting into unwitting sins, see Sifra, Ahare, 2.4; Tosephta, Yoma 2.1 (comm. Lieberman, *Tosefta Kifshutah*, ad. loc.); b. Yoma 86b. Milgrom argues that the concept is as early as the Bible; see Milgrom (1976), pp. 117-24.

19. In the Bible, the scapegoat of the Day of Atonement is said to bear the sins of the community (Lev. 16.21-22). In rabbinic thought, however, this was only when repentance and reparation had taken place beforehand (Mishnah, Yoma 8.9). See Maccoby (1988), pp. 89-92.

20. For an excellent study of these developments see Milgrom (1976).

21. For discussion of Paul's atavistic reading of Deut. 21.23 as placing a 'curse' on a hanged man, see p. 75.

22. E.g. Rowland (1985), p. 190.

23. See Vermaseren (1963), pp. 67-70.

24. Smith, J.Z. (1988), p.522.

25. In his important work, *Homo Necans*, Walter Burkert shows that the sequence of death and resurrection is integral to a vast variety of Greek myths and rituals, not only those of the mystery religions. The resurrection part of the sequence is often not explicit, since it formed part of an oral, secret initiation, but Burkert's method of interpretation leaves no doubt that resurrection, or, as he explains it, restitution, is the essential denouement of the sacrificial process. Burkert points out interestingly that reticence about the resurrection of the violently-dying deity is found even in the Gospels, where all the emphasis is on the story of the passion, the original version of Mark even lacking all reference to the resurrection.

26. See Mishnah, Pesahim 9.5.

27. See b. Yebamot 103b, statement of Rabbi Johanan.

28. For example, Gen. R. 33, where the sufferings of Rabbi Judah the Prince from a painful illness bring about a succession of good harvests. This implies that Rabbi Judah's sufferings act as vicarious atonement for the sins of the people. In the Bible too, Moses's offer (Ex. 32.33) implies a concept of vicarious atonement; but the offer is rejected with the statement, 'Whosoever hath sinned against me, him will I blot out of my book', an authoritative rebuttal of the doctrine of vicarious atonement.

The Jewish attitude appears to be that, while vicarious atonement sometimes occurs, it has no central importance. See Maccoby (1986). pp. 110-11. For a partial collection of passages relevant to vicarious atonement in the rabbinic writings, see Montefiore and Loewe (1963), pp. 225-29. For the 'sacrifice' of Isaac as an atonement, see Vermes (1961), pp. 193-227. This treatment, however, puts quite disproportionate weight on the subject, as remarked by E.P. Sanders (Sanders, 1977, p. 28). A passage often quoted to show the existence of vicarious atonement in first-century Judaism is IV Macc. 17.22: ' . . . they having as it were become a ransom for our nation's sin; and through the blood of these righteous men and the propitiation(*hilasterion*) of their death, the divine Providence delivered Israel.' This, however, like the examples cited above, does not express any central doctrine. Centrally, atonement was through repentance; but since one was always conscious of shortcomings in repentance, other aids were sought: the merits of the Fathers, the blood of martyrs (beginning with Isaac), the intercession of the saints – these could all help towards the acceptance of repentance, but never take its place.

29. See Maccoby (1988), pp. 195-97.

30. A passage sometimes adduced to prove that crucifixion entailed a curse is the speech to this effect by Trypho in Justin's *Dialogue with Trypho*, 89-90. It appears to be overlooked that this is not a speech by a Jew, but one put in the mouth of a Jew by a Christian author, who was no doubt influenced by Paul's formulation in Gal. 3.13. Even a Jew who took Deut. 21.23 literally would never confuse the death of a criminal by Jewish execution with a Roman act of murderous oppression, or think that the martyrdom of a Jew at the hands of idolaters could conceivably make him accursed.

31. Davies (1955), pp. 253-78.

32. The best known example in Greek legend is that of the three daughters of Leos, who willingly accepted death as sacrifices to avert a famine in Athens. Burkert (1983) shows also that details of Greek ritual in animal sacrifice were intended to indicate the willingness of the victim.

33. Schweitzer and other scholars have seen the clue to Paul's thought in the concept of 'eschatology', by which a strong link is perceived with the Jewish pseudepigraphic writings and the Qumran sect. But the question is, 'What kind of eschatology?' It was by no means only the Jews who had eschatological ideas; these featured prominently in the thought of both Orphism and Stoicism. The distinctive feature of Jewish eschatology was its this-world reference; and, by this criterion, Paul's views belong to Hellenistic eschatology. W. D. Davies has endeavoured to discern in Paul's thinking a distinction corresponding to the Jewish

distinction between 'the days of the Messiah' and 'the World to Come' (Davies, 1965, p. 72), saying that Paul regarded himself as 'living in the Messianic Age which preceded the Age to Come'. This, however, is most unconvincing, as the Messianic Age, in Jewish thought, was an age of earthly glory, presided over by the Messiah himself, not an insignificant and inglorious marking-time between the death of the Messiah and the coming of an other-worldly glory. On the other hand, Schweitzer's work on the Jewish-eschatological orientation of Jesus himself was valuable. It was vitiated, however, by failure to realize that Jesus envisaged a Messianic Age on earth, not a totally changed other-worldly condition. For an excellent criticism of Schweitzer's treatment of Jesus' apocalypticism, see Glasson (1980); though Glasson's view that Jesus had in mind, as the Messianic age, something like the Christian church, as it developed historically, goes too far in the other direction and is unacceptable. Jesus certainly envisaged an earthly state of affairs that would be continuous with the world he knew; but, in accordance with the prophecies of the Hebrew Bible, he saw this as a perfected state, in which war, poverty and injustice would no longer exist. That Jesus was rooted in Jewish tradition, in eschatological as in other matters, is incontestable; but this does not mean that Paul was too.

34. For Paul's conception of community in the 'body of Christ', see below, p. 82.

35. Porphyry, *Vit. Pythag.*, 17. See Harrison (1962), p. 597.

36. See Harrison (1962), p. 597.

37. See Harrison (1962), pp. 454-77.

38. Davies (1965), p. 103.

39. Davies (1965), p. 105.

40. See Maccoby (1986), pp. 62-71, and chapter 5 in this book.

41. For examples, see Burkert (1983), p. 136-43, 183. Burkert regards a 'comedy of innocence', by which responsibility for the death of the victim is disclaimed, as an ingredient in all Greek sacrifice.

42. See Maccoby (1982).

43. See Parkes (1934).

44. Ruether, (1974), pp. 106 ff.

45. For discussion of Gaston's exegesis of Rom. 11, see pp. 163 to 164.

4. Paul and the Eucharist

1. Loisy, (1908), ii, p. 532, n. 1.

2. Lietzmann, (1955), p. 255.

3. For bibliography, see Higgins (1952), pp. 25-26.

4. Jeremias (1966), p. 101.

5. Jeremias (1966), p. 202.

6. Schweitzer (1956), p. 266.

7. In what follows, I am treating the evidence of Acts as having historical weight. Acts, as most scholars agree, is a heavily tendentious work, in which a slanted picture of early church history is given. I myself have argued to this effect in *The Mythmaker*. But one must distinguish between material where the *tendenz* operates, and where historical distortions are to be expected, and material which is either neutral or against the *tendenz*. Here we have evidence that is actually against the *tendenz* of Acts, and which is therefore especially reliable historically. There was no motive for Luke, who believed in the validity of the eucharist and its Jesuan origin, to suppress its practice in the Jerusalem church. If anything, his inclination would have led him to invent such practice; if Acts gave a full description of eucharistic practice in the Jerusalem church, there would be grounds for discounting this as unhistorical. As it is, he testifies against his interest, and is therefore to be believed.

8. See Loisy (1948), pp. 231f. Chapter xiv of the Didache, which refers to 'breaking of bread' on the 'Lord's day' as a 'sacrifice', is clearly of later date, as has been pointed out by many scholars.

9. Jeremias (1966), p.118. See also Dibelius (1938), pp. 32-41.

10. Jeremias (1966), pp. 133-34.

11. Jeremias (1966), p. 158.

12. Jeremias (1966), p. 125.

13. Jeremias (1966), p. 134.

14. Jeremias (1966), p. 125, p. 129.

15. Jeremias (1966), pp. 132-36.

16. For John 6.53-58 as a later eucharistic addition, see R. Bultmann (1950), pp. 161f.

17. See A. Vööbus (1979), pp. 217ff.

18. David Flusser has argued that the bread-wine sequence was practised by the Qumran sect, or Essenes, by whom the Christian eucharist, he thinks, was influenced (Flusser, 1988, pp. 202-206). He cites Manual of Discipline VI, 4-6, and the Rule for all the Congregation (Messianic Rule) II, 18-20. He fails to notice, however, that these passages do not refer to festival meals but to week-day meals, when indeed a meal, even in Pharisaic and rabbinic usage, begins with a blessing on the bread, even when wine is included in the meal.

19. Even if we regard the Last Supper as a Passover meal (in which case there was an obligation to have four cups of wine, of which the grace-cup functioned as one), this obligation is of a much lesser order than the obligation of *qiddush* over wine.

20. This is not to deny that the eucharistic theme has its own apocalyptic aspect, which is expressed by Paul when he says, 'for every time you eat this bread and drink the cup, you proclaim the death of the Lord, until he comes' (I Cor. 11.26). I use the expression, 'the apocalyptic theme', however, to designate the theme that is *primarily* apocalyptic, i.e. Jesus's pledge to drink wine with his disciples at the messianic feast. This is usually called the 'avowal of abstinence', a designation which I reject. Paul excludes the apocalyptic theme (in this sense) entirely from his account of the Last Supper.

21. It has been argued that even Paul contemplates a wine-bread sequence in I Cor. 10.16 ('When we bless the cup of blessing, is it not a means of sharing in the blood of Christ? When we break the bread, is it not a means of sharing in the body of Christ?'). There is apparently a contradiction between this passage and Paul's firm statement of a bread-wine sequence in the next chapter, anchoring this sequence in the procedure of the Last Supper. Jeremias argues, however, (p.87, n.8) that Paul's expression 'the cup of blessing' can only mean the cup at the end of the meal for grace after meals, since the Hebrew *kos shel berakhah* has this meaning (see Billerbeck IV, 628, 630f. for examples). If so, Paul is still implying a bread-wine sequence, though for some reason he mentions the wine first. One may doubt whether Paul is being so technically precise. The real point is that Paul is concerned here with the meaning of the rite, rather than with its order.

22. For the Synoptics relations problem, see n.26.

23. See Maccoby (1980), pp. 139-49, and Maccoby (1986), p. 37.

24. *ouketi* is found in Mark 14.25. A few mss omit *ouketi*, some substitute *prostho* and some have *ouketi ou prostho*. Matthew 26.29 has *ou me pio ap' arti*, which is a little ambiguous, since it could be said either before or after drinking the wine. The same applies to Luke's *apo tou nun* (Luke 22.18), but in 22.16, *ouketi* is read by Epiphanius and many other sources, and seems to be the earliest reading. The tendency to substitute other phrases no doubt arises from the awkwardness felt in an expression that ran counter to the 'avowal of abstinence' scenario, which arose very early after Jesus' death, as can be seen from the practice of the Quartidecimani, who fasted on the first evening of Passover in purported imitation of Jesus (Eusebius, *Hist. Eccl.* 5.23.1-25): see Jeremias (1966), pp. 122-24.

25. Some play may be made with the fact that the Gospels do not actually portray Jesus as eating or drinking at the Last Supper, but rather as giving bread and wine to his disciples, after pronouncing a blessing. But this is the regular formula for the commencement of a meal: the presiding person is said to 'break bread' and offer it to the others, and it is taken for granted that he partakes of the bread first himself, for otherwise

his blessing over the bread would be a 'vain blessing' (*berakhah lebatalah*). Moreover, it was customary for those present to refrain from eating the distributed bread until they had seen the presiding person taste his own portion of bread (b.Berakhot, 47a).

26. Though the dependence of Luke on Mark is, in general, well established, it is also accepted by many that Luke, on occasion, (especially in the Passion narrative) ignores Mark and uses his own source (L) which may be earlier than Mark, and which he may elaborate in his own way. The Last Supper account in Luke is good corroboration of this, since it shows no dependence on Mark. See Streeter (1924), and many later scholars, for the theory of 'Proto-Luke'.

27. The word *kurios* (Hebrew, *adon*, Aramaic, *mar*) could refer, in Jewish usage to a human lord or king, as well as to God (see Vermes, 1973, pp. 113-16). But there is no such phrase as 'Lord's supper' in Jewish use. That the divine figures of the mystery cults were entitled *kurios* is attested in many sources, including I Cor. 8.5, ' . . . there are gods many and lords many.' See Bousset (1970).

28. The pioneer work of M. H. Segal on this topic was later refined by J. N. Epstein, H. Yalon and S. Lieberman.

29. Jeremias (1966), p. 186.

30. Jeremias says (p. 167), ' . . . in Greek the phrase is inoffensive. Since such postpositive attributes with the article are characteristic of the style of Paul (cf., e.g., II Cor. 7.12, *ten spouden humon ten huper hemon*; 9.3, *to kauchema hemon to huper humon*), the phrase *to huper humon* in I Cor. 11.24 can in this form go back to Paul himself.' I agree that the form goes back to Paul himself, but not that the form is 'inoffensive'. On the contrary, it is difficult and this is why the Gospels try to amplify it. The two allegedly illustrative phrases quoted by Jeremias are *not* difficult, because the words *spouden* and *kauchema* are natural antecedents to the word *huper*, while the word *soma* is not. It is perfectly natural to speak of having concern or pride for someone's sake, but not of having a body for someone's sake.

31. Jeremias (1966), p. 179.

32. For the Jewish derivation of both *eucharistia* (Heb. *todah*) and *eulogia* (Heb. *berakhah*), see Robinson (1964), p. 198.

33. According to Firmicus Maternus, the declaration of the initiate in the mysteries of Attis was, 'I have eaten out of the tympanum, I have drunk from the cymbal; I am an initiate of Attis.' (*de Errore Profanae Religionis*, ed. K. J. Ziegler, Leipzig, 1907, p. 57). Clement of Alexandria gives a similar formula (*Protreptikos* ii.21 (89)). In Mithraism, too, the sacramental meal consisted of bread followed by liquid (Justin Martyr, *Apol.* i.66, *Dial. c. Tryph.* 70, and Tertullian, *De Praescr.Haer.* 40). It is

unlikely that the Mithraist communion was copied from the Christian eucharist, since Pliny the Elder, writing about 65 CE, refers to a Mithraist sacramental meal (*Hist. Nat.* xxx.2 (6)). In the Samothracian mysteries, the priest broke sacred bread and poured out drink for the *mystae* (inscription, *Arch. epigr. Mitth.*, p. 8, no. 14, 1882).

34. Jeremias (1966), p. 68. See also note 37.

35. For the *agathos daimon*, see Harrison (1963), pp. 277–86. Suidas, s.v.*agathou daimonos*, says, 'The ancients had the custom after dinner (*meta to deipnon*) of drinking to the Good Daimon.'

36. Cf. Lake (1911), pp. 199f., 213f.

37. The theory of David Daube in his lecture 'He that Cometh', 1966, requires some comment. Daube argues (following R. Eisler) that the expression *aphiqoman* found in the Passover Haggadah, in reference to the piece of unleavened bread which is hidden and then brought out and eaten at the end of the Seder, means 'the Coming One' (Gk.*aphikomenos* or *ephikomenos*) and that this piece of bread thus symbolizes the Messiah. Daube is unable, however, to find in Jewish sources any other reference to the Messiah as symbolized by bread. He does find, however, references to the Messianic period such as 'the bread of the World to Come' (Gen.R. 82; Ruth R. on 2.14). Thus, even if his etymology of *aphiqoman* is correct (which is very doubtful, see below), it is much more likely to refer to the Messianic period than to the Messiah himself, who is never called 'the Coming One' in rabbinic literature. The expression 'the World to Come', on the other hand, is very common, and it is just possible that *aphikoman* is an abbreviation of *aion aphikomene* (Hebrew, '*olam ha-ba*). Daube points out that the expression in the Lord's prayer *artos epiousios* may well mean 'coming bread', and that this may be an eschatological expression; but even if this is correct, the context seems to point to the Messianic age rather than to the Messiah. The nearest Daube comes to showing that the Messiah, in Jewish thought, can be regarded as edible, is the view found in the Talmud (b. Sanh. 98b, 99a) that the Messiah has already come and that he was Hezekiah. This view is expressed as, 'They (i.e. Israel) have already eaten him (*akheluhu*) in the days of Hezekiah.' But even Daube lays little stress on this saying, since he is aware that it is merely an idiomatic expression meaning, 'they have enjoyed him'. Thus Daube's case that there was already a Passover custom of regarding the unleavened bread as symbolizing the Messiah, and that Jesus merely went further by identifying this messianic bread as himself, is flimsy indeed. Daube closes his eyes to the ideological gulf between Judaism and notions of 'eating the god'. But in any case, the most likely derivation of *aphiqoman* is from the Greek. *epikomazein* and *epikomion*, meaning 'after-dinner revelry', and the meaning of Mishnah Pesahim 10.8 is to forbid

such revelry as unfitting the solemnity of the Passover Seder, which it seeks to dissociate from the typical Greek *symposium* (on which, however, in many respects, the Seder is modelled). It is probable that it was only in mediaeval times that the term *aphiqoman* became wrongly attached to the piece of unleavened bread eaten at the end of the Passover meal to symbolize the paschal lamb. See Lieberman (1934), p. 521, Bokser (1984), p. 132, n. 62.

5. Paul and Pharisaism

1. This is the method of Alan F. Segal (Segal, 1990).
2. The Jewish scholar, Jacob Neusner, has contributed greatly to the view that the Pharisees form a quite separate and different movement from that of the rabbis. He distinguishes a layer of the Mishnah that stems from the Pharisees, but regards this as displaying preoccupations (chiefly ritual purity) that are much narrower than those of the rabbinic movement of the post-Destruction period. Moreover, Neusner discounts the Midrashic literature as irrelevant even to the Mishnah, much less to the Pharisees. These views stem from a severe (though not totally extreme) attitude towards the dating of material and the verification of attributed statements. Neusner's views have been very influential, and have had the beneficial effect of inducing scholars to be more careful than hitherto about datings and verifications. Recent scholarship, however, has been critical of Neusner's narrow criteria for datings and has cast much doubt on the picture of the Pharisees resulting from his work. See especially Sanders (1990), Maccoby (1984) and (1990).
3. This is fundamentally the view of W. D. Davies, who, while emphasizing that Pharisaism was not the same as Rabbinism, still regards the latter as a continuous development of the former. Thus, while drawing on the Pseudepigrapha for apocalyptic aspects, he stresses that these aspects are to be found in rabbinism too, and continues to regard the rabbinic writings as his most important source, even giving his book the title, 'Paul and Rabbinic Judaism'.
4. Jeremias (1972) writes, ' . . . Jesus' parables are something entirely new. In all the rabbinic literature, not one single parable has come down to us from the period before Jesus; only two similes from Rabbi (sic) Hillel (*c.* 10 BC), who jokingly compared the body with a statue, and the soul with a guest (Lev. R. 34 on 25.35). It is among the sayings of Rabban Johanan ben Zakkai (d. *c.* AD 80) that we first meet with a parable . . . As its imagery resembles one of Jesus' parables, we may well ask whether Jesus' model (together with other factors, such as Greek animal fables) did not have an important influence on the rabbi's adopting parables as a

narrative form' (p. 12). It is hard to see why Hillel's 'similes' are
characterized as jokes. As for Rabban Johanan's parable (b. Shabb.
153a), it constitutes (*contra* Jeremias's analysis, p. 188) an earlier version
than that found in Matt. 22.11-13. Further, many rabbinic parables are
found in anonymous form, and show every sign of being traditional; at the
least, they could be as early as the time of Jesus. The fact that Rabban
Johanan's parable is found attributed also to the later Rabbi Judah I
(Midr. Qohel. 9.8) shows that attributions are not hard-and-fast
indications of dating: a parable tended to be attributed to the person from
whom one heard it, even if it was traditional. It is said (b. Sukk. 28a) that
Rabban Johanan b. Zakkai was an expert in 'fox fables and washermen's
parables', and that this was part of his comprehensive grasp of religious
lore. This indicates that he was master of a whole corpus of parables and
fables, not just of one story derived from Jesus! It seems that parables
were not so carefully transmitted as other items of tradition (this is
indicated by the saying, 'Rabbi Meir had 300 parables of foxes, and we
have only three left', b. Sanh. 38b). They were probably regarded as
individual creations, or as folk-lore that could be useful for sermons,
rather than as items of Torah. This explains why so few survived as
explicit attributions to pre-Destruction figures. Probably the surviving
parables of Jesus form only a fraction of those he created or used.

    5. It may be objected that this argument, like the argument about Paul
criticized above (p. 132), is circular. This, however, is not the case. If a
characteristic not previously known to be Pharisaic is held to be proved so
because found in Paul, that is circular, since Paul's Pharisaic identity has
been assumed. If a characteristic *known* to be rabbinic is found in Jesus, it
is not circular to argue that this proves that rabbinic traits existed in
Temple times, and also that Jesus had something in common with
rabbinism.

    6. It might be argued that these expressions are merely idiomatic, and
might be used by any Palestinian Jew, not just by Pharisees or rabbis.
Indeed, the Talmud says explicitly that the saying about the dancing
camel was a folk-saying (*amri inshei*). But it was only the rabbis (and
before them very probably the Pharisees) who made a point of including
idiomatic language in their teaching and preaching. The use of parables
too was part of this policy and down-to-earth communication, which
cannot be discerned in any other religious group, and which receives
further testimony in Josephus's remarks about the popularity of the
Pharisees among the ordinary people.

    7. The permissibility of healing itself on the Sabbath by a method that
does not infringe the Sabbath (e.g. faith-healing, as practised by Jesus) is
never even questioned anywhere in the rabbinic literature. Questions

only arise when the method involves a forbidden 'labour' (e.g. making a fire, or grinding medicine); in which case, the answer is that this is permitted when the illness is serious.

8. Of course, Jesus, in keeping with the hostile attitude of John towards 'the Jews', is represented as the lone proponent of this ruling on Sabbath-healing, which was actually a characteristic item in rabbinic-Pharisaic law. At any rate, the ruling about circumcision on the Sabbath is *not* represented, in John, as anything but a well-known fact, and this aspect alone testifies to the existence of rabbinic law at this time.

9. The Mishnah states (Kilayim 9.4) that a corpse may be buried in a shroud containing a forbidden mixture of fibres (*sha'atnez*). The explanation given in the Talmud (b. Niddah 61b) is, 'Once a person is dead, he is free of all commandments.' The proof-text cited is Psalms 88.5, 'Free among the dead.'

10. Daube (1956), pp. 394-400.

11. Saying of Rabbi Ishmael ben Elisha, frequently quoted, e.g. Sifre on Numbers 15.31.

12. The other instances are Romans 6.19; Gal. 3.15; I Cor. 9.8.

13. See Stowers (1981).

14. O'Neill (1975), ad loc.

15. In order to avoid this difficulty to his theory, O'Neill, in the table on p. 66, shows Paul as quoting Ps. 14.3 followed by Ps. 14.2, followed by Ps. 14.3 again, instead of the natural order of 1,2,3. Such special pleading is amazing.

16. Deane (1942), p. 165.

17. An interesting example of spurious rabbinism is Paul's use of the injunction of the Torah, 'Thou shalt not muzzle the ox when he treadeth out the corn' (Deut. 25.4). In I Cor. 9.9, Paul deduces from this text that ministers of the gospel are entitled to receive pay for their services. In order to prove that this text should not be taken literally, Paul asks, 'Doth God take care for oxen?' Any Pharisee or rabbi would have answered this question with an emphatic, 'Yes'. The concern of the *halakhah* for the suffering of animals (*tsa'ar ba'alei hayyim*) would have made such a question impossible for a genuine rabbi.

18. The only exception to this is Paul's use of the expression 'through a glass darkly' (I Cor. 13.12), which is reminiscent of the rabbinical expression *ispaqlaria she-einah meirah*. See b. Sanhedrin 97b, where it is said that thirty-six people in each generation see God through a bright glass and eighteen thousand through a glass that is not bright. Paul's contrast, however, is between seeing 'through a glass darkly' and seeing God 'face to face'; and Paul is speaking apocalyptically, while the Talmud refers to 'every generation'. Nevertheless, the coincidence of expression is striking

and unusual; if this kind of coincidence were the rule rather than the exception in Paul's writing, the case for Paul's rabbinism would be much stronger. As it is, one can only suppose that he heard this phrase from some Pharisee preacher.

19. See Tabor (1986); Segal (1990).

20. It might indeed be argued that one phrase of Paul's excludes an affinity of his mysticism to that of rabbinism. He says that he was 'caught up' (*herpage*) into the third heaven. This suggests a sudden translation or ecstasy, and this accords with the story in Acts of Paul's vision on the road to Damascus (some scholars even regard the two passages as referring to the same mystical experience). In rabbinic mysticism, on the contrary, the picture is of careful preparation and an ordered progress through intermediate stages. Paul's mysticism, it might be argued, was closer to the prophetic experience of Isaiah and Ezekiel, who, however, did not talk in the theosophic style of numbered heavens. The rabbis, however, did not claim the prophetic experience.

21. Klausner (1942), p. 454.

22. Stowers (1981); White (1984); Elsom (1987). See also Sanders, J.T. (1962); Bahr (1966 and 1968); Doty (1969). For comparative material in the papyri, see Witkowski (1906).

6. The Gaston-Gager-Stendahl Thesis

1. Gaston (1970), Gaston (1979), Gaston (1987), Gager (1983), Stendahl (1976).

2. Gaston (1987), p.21.

3. Gaston (1987), pp. 35-37.

4. Gaston (1987), p. 71.

5. Gaston (1987), p. 79.

6. Gaston (1987), p. 79.

7. For an interpretation of this incident, see Maccoby (1986), pp. 147-50.

8. Rabbinic texts refer, for example, to the repentance or hoped-for repentance, of Adam and Cain (Lev. R., Tzav, 10, 5), the generation of the Flood (Mekh.de R. Y. p. 133), Balaam (Tanh. Balak, 70a), Pharaoh (Exod. R. Bo, 13,3). All these cases must refer to repentance within the Gentile covenant. A specific rabbinic reference to repentance and forgiveness in the Adamic covenant is Deut. R. Vaethanan, II, 25. Many other instances, of course, concern Gentile repentance leading to conversion to Judaism.

9. The work of David Novak (Novak, 1983) might be thought to support Gaston's contentions. Novak argues that the Seven Noachic

Laws cannot be attested before the second century. The 'Godfearers', however, he argues, are attested during the first century, but they are not to be equated with 'Noachites'. Novak's point is that the formulation of the Seven Noachic Laws was a *narrowing* of view, by which Gentiles were restricted to seven laws, as opposed to a previous more liberal attitude, in which they were encouraged to follow their own selection of laws of the Torah without restriction. Gaston, however, regards the alleged change from 'Godfearers' to 'Noachites' as a liberalization (since Gentiles now had a definite code instead of an anxious compulsion to add observances). Novak's view must be regarded with respect, since it is based on very thorough research; nevertheless, there are certain difficulties in it that require extended discussion. What is clear, however, is that his views do not support Gaston.

Bibliography of
Secondary Literature

Aland, Barbara (ed.) *Gnosis: Festschrift für Hans Jonas*, Göttingen 1978.

Angus, S., *The Mystery-religions and Christianity*, London 1925.

Bahr, G. J., 'Paul and Letter-writing in the 1st Century', *CBQ* 28, 1966, pp. 465ff.

Bahr, G. J., 'The Subscriptions in the Pauline Letters', *JBL* 87, 1968, pp. 27ff.

Bauer, Yehuda, *The Holocaust in Historical Perspective*, London 1978.

Bianchi, U. (ed.), *Le Origini dello Gnosticismo*, 1967.

Black, M., *An Aramaic Approach to the Gospels and Acts*, Oxford 1954.

Bokser, Baruch M., *The Origins of the Seder: the Passover Rite and Early Rabbinic Judaism*, Berkeley 1984.

Bousset, Wilhelm, *Kurios Christos*, (Eng. tr.), Abingdon 1970.

Bowker, J., *Targums and Rabbinic Literature*, Cambridge, 1969.

Brandon, S. G. F., *The Fall of Jerusalem and the Christian Church*, London 1974.

Bultmann, R., *Das Evangelium Johannes*, Göttingen 1950.

Bultman, R., *Theology of the New Testament*, 2 vols. London 1952.

Burkert, Walter, *Homo Necans*, (Eng. tr.) Berkeley 1983.

Campbell, Joseph, *The Masks of God: Occidental Mythology*, New York 1964.

Cumont, F., *Les Religions orientales dans le paganisme romain*, 4th ed., Paris 1929.

Dahl, N. A., 'The Arrogant Archon and the Lewd Sophia: Jewish Traditions in Gnostic Revolt', in Layton, 1982, pp. 599-712.

Dan, J. and Talmage, F. (ed.), *Studies in Jewish Mysticism*, Cambridge, Mass. 1981.

Dan, Joseph, 'Anafiel, Metatron and the Creator', *Tarbiz*, 52 (1983), pp. 447-57.

Dan, Joseph, *Gershom Scholem and the Mystical Dimension of Jewish History*, New York/London 1987.

Daube, David, *The New Testament and Rabbinic Judaism*, London 1956.

Daube, David, 'He that Cometh' (St Paul's Cathedral lecture), London 1966.

Davies, Alan T. (ed.), *Antisemitism and the Foundations of Christianity*, New York 1979.

Davies, W. D., *Paul and Rabbinic Judaism*, London 1965.

Davies, W. D., *Jewish and Pauline Studies*, London 1984.

Deane, Anthony C., *St Paul and his Letters*, London 1942.

Dibelius, M., 'Die Mahlgebete der Didache', *ZNW*, 37 (1938).

Doty, W. G. 'The Classification of Epistolary Literature', *CBQ* 31, 1969, pp. 183 ff.

Driver, S. L. and Neubauer, A., *The 'Suffering Servant' of Isaiah according the Jewish Interpreters*, Oxford 1877.

Elsom, Helen, 'The New Testament and Greco-Roman Writing', in *The Literary Guide to the Bible* (ed. Robert Alter and Frank Kermode), Cambridge, Mass. 1987.

Fallon, Francis T., *The Enthronement of Sabaoth: Jewish Elements in Gnostic Creation Myths*, Leiden 1978.

Flusser, David, *Judaism and the Origins of Christianity*, Jerusalem 1988.

Frazer, Sir J. G., *The Golden Bough*, 3rd ed., London 1907-13.

Friedländer, M., *Der vorchristliche jüdische Gnosticismus*, Göttingen 1898.

Fuller, R. H., *The Foudations of New Testament Christology*, London 1965.

Gager, John G., *The Origins of Anti-Semitism*, Oxford University Press, Oxford/New York 1983.

Gasparro, Giulia Sfameni, *Soteriology and Mystic Aspects in the Cult of Cybele and Attis*, Leiden 1985.

Gaston, Lloyd *No Stone on Another: Studies on the Significance of the Fall of Jerusalem in the Synoptic Gospels*, Leiden 1970.

Gaston, Lloyd, 'Paul and the Torah', in Davies, 1979, pp. 48-71.

Gaston, Lloyd, *Paul and the Torah*, Vancouver 1987.

Girard, René, *Violence and the Sacred*, (Eng. tr.) Baltimore/London 1977.

Glasson, T. Francis, *Jesus and the End of the World*, Edinburgh 1980.

Green, A. R. W., *The Role of Human Sacrifice in the Ancient Near East*, Missoula, Montana 1975.

Green, Henry A., *The Economic and Social Origins of Gnosticism*, Atlanta 1985.

Gruenwald, I., 'Aspects of the Jewish-Gnostic Controversy', in Layton, 1982, pp. 713-23.

Gruenwald, I., 'Jewish Merkavah Mysticism and Gnosticism', in Dan and Talmage (1981).

Guthrie, W. K. C., *Orpheus and Greek Religion*, 1935.

Halliday, W. R., *The Pagan Background of Early Christianity*, Liverpool 1925.

Harrison, Jane, *Prolegomena to the Study of Greek Religion*, London 1962.

Harrison, Jane, *Themis: a Study of the Social Origins of Greek Religion*, London 1963.

Hengel, Martin, *Between Jesus and Paul*, London 1983.

Hepding, H., *Attis, seine Mythen and sein Kult*, Giessen 1903.

Higgins, A. J. B., *The Lord's Supper in the New Testament*, London 1952.

Hubert, H. and Mauss, M., *Sacrifice: Its Nature and Function*, London 1964.

Jeremias, Joachim, *The Eucharistic Words of Jesus*, London 1966.

Jeremias, Joachim, *The Parables of Jesus* (rev. ed.), London 1972.

Jonas, H., *The Gnostic Religion*, (2nd ed.), Boston 1963.

Jonas, H., *Philosophical Essays: from Ancient Creed to Technological Man*, Englewood Cliffs 1974.

Kennedy, H. A. A., *St Paul and the Mystery Religions*, London 1913.

Kümmel, W. G., *The New Testament; the History of the Investigation of Its Problems* (Eng. tr.), London 1973.

Lake, K., *The Earlier Epistles of Paul*, London 1911.

Lake, K., and Cadbury, H.J. (ed.), *The Beginnings of Christianity*, London 1933.

Layton, B. (ed.), *The Rediscovery of Gnosticism*, Leiden 1982.

Leipoldt, J., *Sterbende und aufstehende Götter*, Leipzig 1923.

Lewis, Bernard, *Semites and Anti-Semites*, London 1986.

Lieberman, Saul, *Ha Yerushalmi Kiphshuto*, Jerusalem 1934.

Lietzmann, H., *Mass and Lord's Supper*, Leiden 1979.

Loisy, A., *The Birth of the Christian Religion* (Eng. tr.), London 1948.

Longenecker, R. N., *The Christology of the Early Jewish Christianity*, London 1970.

Maccoby, Hyam, *Revolution in Judaea*, New York 1980.

Maccoby, Hyam, *The Sacred Executioner*, London 1982.

Maccoby, Hyam, *The Mythmaker: Paul and the Invention of Christianity*, London 1986.

Maccoby, Hyam, *Early Rabbinic Writings*, London 1988.

MacRae, G. W., 'The Jewish Background of the Gnostic Sophia Myth', *Novum Testamentum*, XII (1970), pp. 86-101.

MacRae, G. W., 'Seth in Gnostic Texts and Traditions', *Society of Biblical Literature, 1977 Seminar Papers*, ed. P. K. Achtemeier, Missoula 1977.

MacRae, G. W., 'Why the Church Rejected Gnosticism', in Sanders (1980), pp. 126-33.

Maier, J., 'Jüdische Factoren bei der Entstehung der Gnosis?', in Tröger, *Altes Testament*, pp. 239-58.

Mansfield, J. 'Bad World and Demiurge: a "Gnostic" Motif from Parmenides and Empedocles to Lucretius and Philo'. In Van den Broek, R. and Vermaseren, M. J. (1981), pp. 261-314.

Meeks, W. A. (ed.), *The Writings of St Paul*, New York 1972.

Metzger, B., *Historical and Literary Studies*, Leiden 1968.

Ménard, Jacques E., 'Normative Self-Definition in Gnosticism', in Sanders (1980), pp. 134-50.

Milgrom, J., *Cult and Conscience: the Asham and the Priestly Doctrine of Repentance*, Leiden 1976.

Montefiore, C. G., and Loewe, H., *A Rabbinic Anthology*, 1938, New York 1974.

Moore, George Foot, *Judaism in the First Centuries of the Christian Era*, 3 vols, Cambridge, Mass. 1927.

Mosca, Paul G., *Child Sacrifice in Canaanite and Israelite Religion* (unpublished thesis), Harvard University, May, 1975.

Murray, Gilbert, *Five Stages of Greek Religion*, London 1935.

Nilsson, Martin P., *The Dionysiac Mysteries of the Hellenistic and Roman Age*, New York 1975.

Novak, David, *The Image of the Non-Jew in Judaism*, Lampeter 1983.

O'Neill, J. C., *Paul's Letter to the Romans*, Harmondsworth 1975.

Otto, Walter F., *Dionysos: Myth and Cult*, Bloomington 1965.

Pagels, Elaine, *The Gnostic Paul*, Philadelphia 1975.

Parkes, James, *The Conflict of the Church and the Synagogue*, London 1934.

Parrot, Douglas M., 'Evidence of Religious Syncretism in Gnostic Texts from Nag Hammadi', in Pearson (1975), pp. 173-89.

Patai, Raphael, *The Hebrew Goddess*, New York 1967.

Pearson, B. A., 'I Thessalonians 2: 13-16: A Deutero-Pauline Interpolation', *Harvard Theological Review* 64 (1971), pp. 79-94.

Pearson, B. A., 'Jewish Haggadic Traditions in the Testimony of Truth from Nag Hammadi', in *Ex Orbe Religionum*, Leiden 1972, pp. 456-70.

Pearson, B. A., 'Friedlander Revisited: Alexandrian Judaism and Gnostic Origins'. *Studia Philonica*, 2 (1973), pp. 23-29.

Pearson, B. A., (ed.), *Religious Syncretism in Antiquity: Essays in Conversation with Geo Widengren*, Missoula 1975.

Pearson, B. A., 'The Egyptian Seth and the Gnostic Seth', in *Society of Biblical Literature, 1977 Seminar Papers*, ed. P. J. Achtemeier, Missoula 1977, pp. 25-44.

Pearson, B. A., 'Jewish Elements in Gnosticism and the Development of Gnostic Self-Definition', in *Jewish and Christian Self-Definition*, Vol. 1, ed. E. P. Sanders, London 1980.

Pearson, B. A., 'Jewish Elements in Corpus Hermeticum I (Poimandres)', in Van den Broek-Vermaseren, 1981.

Pearson, B. A., 'Jewish Sources in Gnostic Literature'. In *Jewish Writings of the Second Temple Period*, ed. Michael E. Stone, Assen/ Philadelphia 1984.

Quispel, G., *Gnostic Studies*, I, Istanbul 1974.

Quispel, G., 'The Origins of the Gnostic Demiurge', in Quispel, 1974, pp. 213-20.

Reitzenstein, R., *Poimandres: Studien zur griechisch-ägyptischen und frühchristlichen Literatur*, Berlin 1904.

Reitzenstein, R., *Die hellenistische Mysterienreligionen*, 3rd ed., Leipzig/Berlin 1927.

Richardson, R. D., 'Supplementary Essay. A Further Enquiry into Eucharistic Origins . . . ', in Lietzmann (1979), pp. 217-27.

Robinson, James M., 'Die Hodajot-Formel in Gebet und Hymnus des Fruhchristentums', in *Apophoreta: Festschrift fur Ernst Haenchen*, Berlin (1964), p. 198.

Robinson, J. M. and Meyer, M. (ed.), *The Nag Hammadi Library in English*. London/San Francisco 1977.

Rowland, Christopher, *The Open Heaven: A Study of Apocalyptic in Judaism and Early Christianity*, London 1982.

Rowland, Christopher, *Christian Origins*, London 1985.

Rudolph, K., *Gnosis* (ed. R. McL. Wilson). Edinburgh/New York 1983.

Ruether, Rosemary, *Faith and Fratricide*, New York 1974.

Sanders, E. P., *Paul and Palestinian Judaism*, London 1977.

Sanders, E. P., *Jewish and Christian Self-Definition*, vol. 1: The Shaping of Christianity in the Second and Third Centuries, London 1980.

Sanders, J. T., 'The Transition from Opening Epistolary Thanksgiving to Body in the Letters of the Pauline Corpus', *JBL* 81, 1962, pp. 348 ff.

Schmidt, W., *The Origin and Growth of Religion* (Eng. tr.), 1931.

Schoeps, H. J., *Theologie und Geschichte des Juden-Christentums*, Tübingen 1949.

Scholem, Gershom, *Major Trends in Jewish Mysticism*, London 1955.

Scholem, Gershom, *Jewish Gnosticism, Merkabah Mysticism and Talmudic Tradition*, New York 1965.

Scholem, Gershom, 'Jaldabaoth Reconsidered'. *Melanges d'histoire des religions offerts a H. -C Puech*, Paris 1974, pp. 405-21.

Schweitzer, A., *The Quest of the Historical Jesus*, London 1948.

Schweitzer, A., *The Mysticism of Paul the Apostle*, London 1956.

Segal, A. F., *Two Powers in Heaven*, Leiden 1978.

Segal, A. F., *Paul the Convert*, New Haven 1990.

Smith, Jonathan Z., 'Dying and Rising Gods', *Encyclopaedia of Religion*, ed. Mircea Eliade, New York 1988.

Smith, W. Robertson, *The Religion of the Semites*, New York 1957 (2nd ed., first pub. 1894).

Spiegel, Shalom, *The Last Trial*, New York 1969.

Stendahl, Krister, *Paul among Jews and Gentiles*, Philadelphia 1976.

Stern, Menahem, *Greek and Latin Authors on Jews and Judaism*, Leiden 1974.

Stowers, S. K., *The Diatribe and Paul's Letter to the Romans*, Missoula 1981.

Streeter, B. H., *The Four Gospels*, 1924.

Stroumsa, G. *Another Seed: Studies in Sethian Gnosticism*, Leiden 1985.

Tabor, James D., *Things Unutterable: Paul's Ascent to Paradise in its Greco-Roman, Judaic and Early Christian Contexts*, New York 1986.

Tierney, Patrick, *The Highest Altar: the Story of Human Sacrifice*, New York 1989.

Tröger, K.-W., 'Frühjudentum und Gnosis', in *Literatur und Religion des Frühjudentums*, ed. Maier & Schreiner, Würzburg 1973.

Tröger, K.-W. (ed.), *Altes Testament-Frühjudentum-Gnosis*, Berlin 1980.

Tröger, K.-W., 'The Attitude of the Gnostic Religion towards Judaism', in Barc, *Colloque International*, Quebec 1981, pp. 96-98.

Van den Broek, R., and Vermaseren, M. J. *Studies in Gnosticism and Hellenistic Religions: presented to Gilles Quispel on the Occasion of his 65th Birthday*, Leiden 1981.

Van Unnik, W. C., 'Die jüdischen Komponents in der Entstehen der Gnosis', in Rudolph, *Gnosis und Gnostizismus*, Darmstadt 1975, pp. 476-94.

Vermaseren, M. J., *Mithras, the Secret God*, London 1963.

Vermaseren, M. J., *Cybele and Attis: the Myth and the Cult*, London 1977.

Vermes, Geza, *Scripture and Tradition in Judaism*, Leiden 1961.

Vermes, Geza, *Jesus the Jew*, London 1973.

Vokes, F. E., *The Riddle of the Didache*, London 1938.

Vööbus, A., 'A New Approach to the Problem of the Shorter and the Longer Text in Luke', *NTS* 15, (1968/9), pp. 457ff.

Wagner, Günter, *Pauline Baptism and the Pagan Mysteries*, Edinburgh/London 1967.

Weber, Ferdinand, *Jüdische Theologie auf Grund des Talmud und verwandter Schriften*, Leipzig 1897.

Wellhausen, J., *Prolegomena to the History of Ancient Israel*, Edinburgh 1885.

White, J. L., *New Testament Epistolary Literature in the Framework of Ancient Epistolography*, Aufstieg und Niedergang der Römischen Welt II 25.2, Berlin 1984, pp. 1733-51.

Whitely, D. E. H., *The Theology of Saint Paul*, Oxford 1971.

Williams, A. L., *Adversus Judaeos*, Cambridge 1935.

Wilson, R. McL., *The Gnostic Problem*, London 1958.

Wilson, R. McL., 'Gnostics and the Old Testament', in Widengren, *Proceedings of the International Colloquium on Gnosticism*, Stockholm 1977.

Witkowski, S. *Epistolae privatae Graecae*, 1906.

Yamauchi, E. M., *Pre-Christian Gnosticism, A Survey of the Proposed Evidences*, Grand Rapids and London 1973.

Yamauchi, E. M., 'Jewish Gnosticism?' in Van den Broek-Vermaseren, 1981, pp. 467-97.

Yarnold, Edward, 'Pagan Mysteries in the Fourth Century', *Heythrop Journal*, vol. xiii, No. 3, July 1972, pp. 247-67.

Yerkes, R. K., *Sacrifice in Greek and Roman Religions and Early Judaism*, London 1953.

Index of Quotations

HEBREW BIBLE

Genesis
1.3   39
1.28   161
2.7   62
2.16   174
4.25   16, 52
5   187 n.11
8.22   64
9.1–7   161
9.4   126, 174
10   186 n.10
15.6   146
15.16   86
19   60

Exodus
20.5   23
32.33   190 n.28

Leviticus
5.23   73
6.1–7   68
16.21–22   190 n.19
17.14   126
18.5   175
18.18   175

Numbers
12:7   8

Deuteronomy
4.12   42, 185 n.4
4.36   42, 185 n.4

21.23   75, 190 n.21, 191 n.30
25.4   199 n.17
29.28   82
30.11–14   57
32.2   162
30.12–14   151
33.1   8
33.2   185 n.4, 188 n.5

Joshua
14.16   8

Judges
13.16   60

II Samuel
5.6   14
12.18   186 n.8

I Chronicles
1   186 n.10
6.49   8
17.3   7
22.10   7
29.23   185 n.3

II Chronicles
20.7   8
24.9   8

Job
58

5.16   142

Psalms
5.9   142
10.7   142
14.1–3   142, 199 n.15
36.1   142
51.4   140
88.5   199 n.9
104.15   95
107.42   142
143.2   142, 144

Proverbs
1.16   142
8.3   61

Isaiah
6.9–10   23
41.8   8
53.12   120
53   76
59.7–8   142, 144
63.9   185 n.4, 188 n.5
65.20–22   81

Daniel
12.2   70

Zechariah
12.10   63

NEW TESTAMENT

Matthew
7.4   135
11.1   188 n.4
11.29   91
19.24   135
22.11–13   198 n.4
23.15   171
23.33–36   181
26.21–23   110
26.28–29   103
26.29   194 n.24
26.34   110
27.25   85

Mark
4.11   23
12.22–23   134
14 18.21   110
14.22   118
14.24   118, 121
14.24–25   103
14.25   194 n.24
14.30   110

Luke
3.13   188 n.4
8.55   188 n.4
22.14–19a 101
22.19b–20 101
22.15–16   103
22.16   110, 194
           n.24
22.17   104
22.17–18   103
22.18   194 n.24
22.19   105, 120
22.20   118, 120
22.21–23   110
22.31–34   110
24.21   109
24.25–27   111
24.53   98

John
1.10   9
6.47–71   114
6.51–57   116

6.53–58   94, 193 n.16
6.56   99
6.59–67   99
6.60   99
6.66   99
7.22–23   136
13.1   106
13.21–26   110
19.37   63
20.27   69

Acts
2.42   95, 97
2.46   97, 98
3.1   98
5   134, 178
6.7   100
7.38   42, 43
7.44   188 n.4
7.52–3   181
7.53   9, 10, 40, 41,
           42
7.58   41
15.1–2   45
18.2   188 n.4
20.7   95, 97
20.11   97
20.13   188 n.4
21.18–21   45
21.23–24   98
22.3   137
23.6   137
23.6–9   80
24.33   188 n.4
26.4–5   137
27.35   95

Romans
3.1–8   139–140
3.9–20   142
3.19   169
3.24   168
3.25   76
4   51, 145–146
5.8–9   76
5.10   164
5.17   146

6.1–4   128
6.19   199 n.12
6.23   147
7.1–6   138
7.7   48
7   59, 147–148
7.14–8.1   56
8   148
8.5   148
8.38   40
9   149–150
9–11   88, 163–165
9.5   59
9.13   188 n.9
9.6–21   164
9.22–23   165
9.30–33   165
10.5–10   150
10.12   171
11   88
11.7–8   87
11.11–12   87
11.28   163
11.25–28   87
12   151–152

I Corinthians
5.7   68
6.2   64
6.11–12   39
6.12–20   46
7.17   188 n.4
7.18–20   188 ch.3 n.1
8.5   195 n.27
8.6   59
9.8   199 n.12
9.9   199 n.17
9.20   189 ch.3 n.1
9.21   188 ch.3 n.1
10.1–2   52
10.2   83
10.3   125
10.4   153
10.16   194 n.21
10.21   123
11   97, 111, 112
11.22   124

11.23	92	2.11–14	45, 188 ch.3	*Colossians*	
11.23–30	91		n.1	1.7	91
11.24	116, 121,	2.14	170	1.16–17	59
	195 n.30	2.15–21	168	2.15	40
11.24–25	101	2.20–21	76	2.16–19	44
11.25	105	3.10	161	2.18	10, 185 n.4
11.26	194 n.20	3.13	75, 191 n.30		
13.12	199 n.18	3.15	199 n.12	*I Thessalonians*	
15.5	110	3.19	9, 10, 40, 41,	1	88
15.20	71		42, 160	2.13	92
15.24	40	4.3	46	2.14–16	86, 181
15.28	60	4.5	46	4.1	92
15.50–54	79	4.9–10	46		
		4.10	161	*II Thessalonians*	
		4.21–27	50, 160	3.6	92
II Corinthians		4.21–31	49, 161		
3.6–18	156–157	5.2	188 ch.3 n.1	*Hebrews*	
3.13–18	51	5.2–12	160		68
4.4	38	5.12	46	2.2	10, 40, 41,
7.12	121, 195				42, 43
	n.30				
9.3	121, 195	*Ephesians*		*James*	
	n.30	2.2	40	2.2	100
11.3	153			2.23	8
12.1–9	149				
		Philippians		*I Peter*	
Galatians		2.8	77		152
1.12	92	3.2–3	160		
1.14	137	3.5	137	*I John*	
2–3	169	3.21	69	5.19	40

APOCRYPHA AND PSEUDEPIGRAPHA

Apocalypse of Moses		7.19–29	58
	187 n.12	7.70–74	58
		7.116–18	58
		7.127–131	58, 189 n.6
II Baruch			
	58	*Jubilees*	
54.15–19	189 n.6		126
I Enoch		*Life of Adam and Eve*	
	189 n.7		187 n.12
IV Ezra		*IV Maccabees*	
3.21–22	57	17.22	191 n.28
4.30–32	57		

GNOSTIC TEXTS

Apocalypse of Adam		Second Treatise of the Great	
69	187 n.11	Seth,	
		VII, 2, 62–64	5–6
Apocryphon of John			
23–25	18	Sophia Jesu Christi	
24.34–25.7	189 n.8		185 n.5
Eugnostos the Blessed		Testimony of Truth	
	185 n.5	IX 3, 29–30	24
Gospel of the Egyptians		Testimony of Truth	
III, 2, 61	14	IX 3, 47–48	23
Hypostasis of the Archons		Testimony of Truth	
	185 n.7	X 3, 69–70	13

MISHNAH

Abot		Pesahim	
	152	9.5	190 n.26
Abot		Pesahim	
4.2	147	10.8	196 n.37
Berakhot		Yoma	
7.1	169	8.9	190 n.19
Kilayim			
9.4	199 n.9		

BABYLONIAN TALMUD

Abodah Zarah		**Gittin**	
22b	187 n.17	68b	14
Arakhin		**Niddah**	
16b	135	61b	199 n.9
Baba Bathra			
15b	135	**Sanhedrin**	
		34a	151
Baba Metzi'a		38b	198 n.4
38b	135	56–60a	174
		74b	175
Berakhoth		97b	199 n. 18
47a	195 n.25	98b	185 n. 3, 196 n. 37
55b	135		

99a	149, 196 n.37	Yebamoth	
		45a	135
Shabbath		46a	127
70a	68	103b	187 n.17, 190
145b–146a	187 n.17		n.27
153a	198 n.4		
		Yoma	
Sukkah		86b	190 n.18
28a	198 n.4		
52a	63		

OTHER RABBINIC WORKS

Canticles Rabbah		Pisha, Bo, 1	177
I.2	41, 185 n.4		
		Pesiqta Rabbati	
Derekh Eretz		15	185 n.3
	152		
		Pirqei de-Rabbi Eliezer	
Exodus Rabbah, Bo		22	186 n.10
13, 3	200 n.8		
		Ruth Rabbah	
Deuteronomy Rabbah, Va-ethanan		on Ruth 2.14	196 n.37
II, 25	200 n.8		
		Sifra	
Genesis Rabbah		Ahare, 2.4	190 n.18
19.13	187 n.17		
33	190 n.28		
50	65	Sifre	
82	196 n.37	on Numbers	
on Gen. 14.13	187 n.10	15.31	199 n.11
Hekhalot texts		Tanhuma B Behukkotai	
187 n.15		56b	189 n.13
Ecclesiastes (Qohelet) Rabbah		Targum Pseudo-Jonathan	
9.8	198 n.4	on Genesis 4.1	187 n.17
Leviticus Rabbah		Tosephta, Yoma	
34 (on 25.35)	197 n.4	2.1	190 n.18
Tzav, 10, 5	200 n.8		
Mekhilta			
Shabbeta on Exodus			
31.13	137		

OTHER WRITINGS

Clement of Alexandria		Didache	
Protreptikos		IX–X	95, 96
ii.21 (89)	195 n.33	XIV	193 n.8

Eusebius, *Hist. Eccl.*
ii.23   98
v.23.1–25   194 n.24

Firmicus Maternus, *De Errore*
   Profanae Religionis (ed. Ziegler)
57   195 n.33

Irenaeus, *Adversus Haereses*
30   6, 189 n.9
31, 1–2   187 n.16

Josephus, *Antiquities*
xv.135   41, 185 n.4

Justin Martyr
Apology
I.lx.6   123
I.lxvi   96, 195 n.33
I.lxvi.1, 2   97

Dialogue with Trypho
70   195 n.3

89–90   191 n.30

Manual of Discipline (Qumran)
                           152
VI.4–6   193 n.18

Messianic Rule II
18–20   193 n.18

Pliny the Elder, *Hist. Nat*
xxx.2(6)   196 n.33

Porphyry, *Vita Phythagorae*
17   192 n.35

Pseudo-Philo
                           153

Tertullian, *De praescriptione hereti-*
corum
40   195 n.33

General Index

a fortiori argument, 146
Abel, 1, 17, identification with
    Christian church, 49
Abraham, 5, 8, 48, 49, 51, 145, 174
Adam's sin, 58
Adam, 5, 17, 18, 19, 22, 23, 57, 174,
    176, 186 n.10, 187 n.11
Adiabene, 171
Adonis 65, 66, 71, 190 n.15
Agape, 96
agathos daimon, 124, 196 n.35
Agdystis, 190 n.15
Akiba ben Joseph, 131
Albigensians, 22
Aldabaoth, 17
Alexandria, 26, 28, 32, 52
Allogenes, 16
Angels, 60; man's superiority to, 65,
    189 n.13; death of, 65; and giving
    the Torah, 40–43, 160–61, 185 n.4,
    188 n.5; and the eucharist, 116
Animal sacrifice, role in Judaism, 72
Another seed, 16
Antinomianism, and Gnosticism, 4
Antisemitism, and Hellenism, 14;
    and Gnosticism, ch.1, passim; dif-
    ference between Gnostic and
    Christian, 23; influence of Christ-
    ianity of Gnostic, 25; Christian,
    33, 37; Gnostic prior to Pauline,
    38; and Church fathers, 49; cos-
    mic, 36; and Islam, 33–34; Paul
    and; 84–89, ch.7 passim
Aphiqoman, 196 n.37
Apion, 32
Apollo, 190 n.15

Aramaic, 117, 120
Aramaisms, 120, 122
Archon, 6, 10, 11
Aristotle, 29
Asmodeus, 14
Attis, 65, 66, 71, 78, 99, 189 n.15;
    resurrection of, 72, 125, 195
    n.33
Augustine, 49
'Avowal of abstinence', 107, 194
    n.20, n.24

Baal, 71
Bahr, G. J., 200 n.22
Baptism, 127
Barabbas, 85
Bathsheba, 14, 186
Bauer, Walter, 188 n.3
Billerbeck, Franz, 170
Black, Matthew, 120
Bokser, Baruch M., 197 n.37
Bousset, Wilhelm, 53
Bowker, J., 187 n.17
Bultmann, R., 38, 53, 170, 183, 188
    n.1, 193 n.16
Burkert, Walter, 189 n.12, 191 n.32,
    192 n.41; on resurrection aspect of
    sacrifice, 190 n.25

Cain, 15, 17, 19, 24, 85; identification
    with the Jews, 49, 187 n.17
Calliope, 190 n.15
Carpocratians, 47
Catharism, 30
Chaeremon, 32
Chief Archon, 17

Christian Gnosticism, 33; and the
    Hebrew Bible, 18; and the New
    Testament, 18; and Judaism, 18
Chrysostom, 49
Church fathers, 49
Clement, of Alexandria, 195 n.33
Cosmocrator, 7
Creator God of Genesis, identifica-
    tion of with Satan, 19
Crucifixion, whether incurring a
    curse, 75, 191 n.30; bringing
    atonement, 76
Cyril, of Alexandria, 71

Dan, J., 185 n.1, 187 n.15
Daniel, 8
Daube, D., 151, 152, 199 n.10; and
    the aphiqoman, 196 n.37
David, 7, 13, 14, 48, 95, 107, 186 n.8
Davies, W. D., 41, 59, 61, 76, 82, 83,
    130, 166, 185 n.4, 188 n.3, 189 n.4,
    n.5, n.10, 191 n.31, 192 n.38, n.39,
    197 n.3; and the Messianic age,
    191 n.33
Day of Atonement, 74
Deane, Anthony C., 188 n.6, 199
    n.16
Demiurge, 2, 15, 19, 25–26, 30, 34,
    36, 38–39, 47; as creator God of
    Genesis, 17
Didache, 65, 95–96, 152, 193 n.8
Dionysus, 71, 72, 80, 81, 83, 99, 125,
    189 n.12
Doty, W. G., 200 n.22
Driver, S. R., 189 n.11
Dying and rising gods, 64

Eber, 174
Eden, 19
Edomites, 162
Eisler, Robert, 196 n.37
Eleusinian Mysteries, 125
Eliezer ben Hyrcanus, 131
Elijah, 62, 70, 81
Elisha ben Abuyah, 29
Elisha, 81
Eloim, 17, 19
Elsom, Helen, 153, 200 n.22
Empedocles, 3

Enoch, 16, 62, 70, 174
Epistle to the Hebrews, 10
Epstein, J. N., 195 n.28
Esau, 50, 164, 171, 188 n.9
Eschatology, 191 n.33
Eucharist, origin of, ch.4 passim
Eve, 17, 19, 22, 23–24, 61; and
    Norea, 189 n.9
Exodus, 32
Ezekiel, 200 n.19, 27

Fallon, Francis T., 187 n.15
Female divinity, 30, 61
Firmicus, Maternus, 195 n.33
Flusser, David, and bread-wine
    sequence, 193 n.18
Fraser, J. G., 71, 72

Gager, John G., 150, 188 ch.3, n.1,
    200 ch.6, n.1
Galatians, 48
Gamaliel I, 131, 132, 177
Gamaliel II, 133
Gasparro, Giulia S., 72
Gaston, Lloyd, 88, 150, ch.6, passim,
    188 ch.2 n.9, ch.3 n.1, 192 n.45,
    200 ch.6, n.1, n.2, n.3, n.4, n.5, n.6
Glasson, T. Francis, 192 n.33
Gnosis, 2, 3, 4, 8, 51
Gnostic Saviour, 2
Gnosticism, antisemitism of, ch.1,
    passim, 180–181; and Judaism,
    12, 29; priority to Christianity, 1,
    9, 33–35; myth of, 1; acosmism of,
    2, 3; and the New Testament, 8–9;
    and Christianity, 9; and the Heb-
    rew prophets, 10; and angels, 9;
    and the Hebrew Bible, 6, 8, 10, 23,
    28; and Rabbinic writings, 19; and
    the Torah, 21, 24, 25, 48; com-
    pared with polytheism, 29; differ-
    ent schools of, 31, 44; derivation
    from Judaism, 26–28; and Hellen-
    ism, 30; precursor of Christian
    antisemitism, 37; and biblical
    commandments, 22; and pleroma,
    30
Gnostics, identity of, 31, 32
Godfearers, 15, 32

Grant, Robert M., 187 n.19
Green, Henry A., 26, 187 n.20

Hadrian, 29
Hagar, 49, 50, 162
Harrison, Jane, 66, 71, 72, 189 n.12, 190 n.16, 192 n.35, n.36, n.37, 196 n.35
Haustafeln, style of participles in, 152
Healing on the sabbath, 198 n.7, n.8
Hebdomad, 5, 7
Hebrew Bible, and human sacrifice, 66
Hekhalot literature, 28, 187 n.15
Hellenism, Jewish, 16
Herford, Travers, 170
Hesiod, 161
Hezekiah, 7, 185 n.3, 196 n.37
Higgins, A. J. B., 192 ch.4, n.3
Hillel, 131, 185 n.3, 197 n.4
Hippolytus of Rome, 97
History-of-religion-school, 53
Homiletic Midrashim, 131
Human sacrifice, 68

Idumaeans, 171
Impassibility of God the Father, 64, 80
Irenaeus, 189 n.9, 6, 187 n.16
Isaac, 5, 8, 50, 68; sacrifice of, 66, 174
Isaiah, 200 n.19, 27
Ishmael ben Elisha, 131, 199 n.11
Ishmael, 50
Ishmaelites, 162
Islam, 34

Jacob, 5, 8, 14, 164, 188 n.9
James, 98
Jeremiah, 27, 69
Jeremias, Joachim, ch.4, passim, 192 n.4, 193 n.5, n.9, n.10, n.11, n.12, n.13, n.14, n.15, n.16, 194 n.21, n.24, 195 n.29, n.30, n.31, 196 n.34; on Jesus' parables, 197 n.4
Jerome, 71
Jerusalem church, 44, 45, 46, 91, 94, 95, 97, 98, 99, 100, 110, 113, 152, 158, 167, 184; and resurrection of Jesus, 71

Jerusalem, 13, 14
Jesus, 7, 34, 99, 102, 107, 108; as sacrifice, whether grounded in Judaism, 68, 70; as martyr, 77; and use of parables, 134, 135
Jewish Apocalypticism, 28
Jewish Gnosticism, 27, 32
Jewish mysticism, 30, 98, 149
Jews, as representatives of Demiurge, 4; as chosen people, 16; symbolized by inferior figures in Bible, 49, 50, 51
Johanan ben Zakkai, Rabban, 131, 197 n.4
Johanan, Rabbi, 175
John the Baptist, 5
Jonah, 177
Jonas, H., 187 n.22
Joseph, 174
Josephus, 13, 32, 41, 132, 133, 171, 185 n.4, 198 n.6
Joshua ben Hananiah, 131
Joshua, 48
Judah, Rabbi, the Prince, 190 n.28
Judas Iscariot, 85, 110, 113
Jupiter, 29
Justin Martyr, 96, 195 n.33

Kabbalah, 60
Kittel, R., 188 n.3
Klausner, Joseph, 150, 151, 200 n.21
Koran, 33
kuriakon deipnon, 116, 123

Lake, K., 196 n.36
Last Supper, ch.4, passim
Layton, B., 187 n.18
Lazarus, 70
Lazarus, 81
Leos, 191 n.32
Lewis, B., 187 n.23
Lieberman, Saul, 197 n.37, 195 n.28
Lietzmann, H., 192 ch.4 n.2, 91, 92
Loewe, H., 191 n.28
Loisy, A., 192 ch.4 n.1, 193 n.8, 91, 92
Long Text and Short Text of Luke, 94

Lord's Supper, 67; and mystery
cults, 67
Lysimachus, 32

ma'aseh bereshit, 28
Maccoby, Hyam, 185 n.4, 188 n.8,
188 ch.3 n.1, 189 n.11, 189 n.14,
190 n.19, 191 n.28, n.29, 192 n.40,
n.42, 194 n.23, 197 n.2, 200 ch.6
n.7
MacRae, G. W., 39, 188 n.2, 189 n.8
Maenads, 65
Maimonides, 173, 174, 175
Manetho, 13, 32
Manichees, 22
Manfield, J., 185 n.2
Maranatha, 96
Marcion, 102
Maximinus, 49
Meir, Rabbi, 175, 198 n.4
Melchizedek, 10, 14, 48, 62
Ménard, Jacques E., 185 n.5
Messiah, 7, 196 n.37; in Christianity,
63; son of Joseph, 63; son of David,
63; and the Elect One, 189 n.7
Methuselah, 174
Midrash, 12, 131, 133, 186 n.10, 189
n.13
Milgrom, J., 190 n.20
Mishnah, 131, 133
Mithraism, 71, 195 n.33
Mithras, 71
Montefiore, C. G., 191 n.28
Moore, George Foot, 170
Moses, 5, 7, 8, 10, 32, 48, 51, 62, 92;
and vicarious atonement, 190 n.28
Mot, 71
Mount Sinai, 162, 174
Muhammad, 33, 34; attitude to
Bible of, 49
Muslim antisemitism, 34
Mystery cults, 66–67; and resurrec-
tion of deities, 71, 73; Paul and,
ch.3 passim
Myth, difference between Christian
and Gnostic, 26

Nag Hammadi, 10
Nazis, 25

Neubauer, A., 189 n.11
Neusner, Jacob, 197 n.2
New Testament, and Gnosticism,
23; and the Hebrew prophets, 9,
10
Nilus, 190 n.17
Noachic laws, 170, 173, 176, 177, 200
n.9
Noah, 15, 174, 176, 186 n.10, 187
n.11
Norea, 61

O'Neill, J. C., 199 n.14, n.15
Og, 186 n.10
Origen, 71, 62
Original Sin, 189 n.6
Orpheus, 65, 66, 81, 190 n.15
Orphism, 63, 83; influence on Paul,
78; view of resurrection of, 191
n.33
Osiris, 65, 66, 71, 72, 81

Paran, 162
Parkes, James, 170, 192 n.43
Parmenides, 3
Parrot, Douglas M., 185 n.5
Pascal lamb, 72
Passover meal, four cups in, 193 n.19
Patai, Raphael, 187 n.21
Paul, views of on God and Satan, 38,
39, 40; christology of, 59, 60, 61,
66, 67; and antisemitism, 38, 46,
84–9, ch.7 passim; attitude to biblical figures of, 51; as Gnostic
thinker, ch.2, passim; as Pharisee,
56, 69, ch.5, passim, 198 n.6, 199
n.17; doctrine of original sin of, 59;
Pastoral Epistles of, 21, 92, 102;
and the eucharist, ch.4 passim;
and the Torah, 10, 39, 47, 49;
allegorical method of, 51, 52; concept of faith of, 81, 82; and baptism, 128; doctrine of salvation of,
54, 55; influence on of mystery
cults, 53, 67; importance to, of
divine sacrifice, 55, 56, 78, 80, 83;
and interpretation of Bible, 49;
and moral pessimism, 58, 59; view
on resurrection, of, 79, 80; view on

angels giving the Torah, 40, 42,
43, 44; his concept of fellowship
compared with Jewish concept,
82; influence of Judaism on, 69; his
view of circumcision, 46; his view
of Torah compared with that of
Gnostics, 43; and salvation for
non-Jews, 188 ch.3 n.1; and
alleged curse on hanged man, 190
n.2, 1
Paulinism, whether derivable from
Judaism, 62, 63, 64
Pausanias, 189 n.15
Pearson, Birger, 185 n.6, 186 n.9, 187
n.14, 12
Perrin, Norman, 135
Peter, 134, 168
Pharisaism, 57, 58, 99
Pharisees, 25, 130, 131, 197 n.2;
connection with rabbinic move-
ment, 133
Philo, 15, 16, 28, 29, 52, 186 n.10
Plato, 29, 30, 63
Pleroma, 30, 72
Pliny the Elder, 196 n.33
Prayer of Joseph, 62
Procopius, of Gaza, 71
Pseudepigrapha, 19, 39, 57, 133, 183,
191 n.33, 197 n.3
Pythagoras, 80

qal va-homer argument, 146
Qiddush, 95, 96, 102, 104, 105
Quartidecimani, 194 n.24
Qumran literature, 38, 39, 57, 133,
183
Qumran sect, 152
Qur'an, 49, 187 n.23

Rabbinic Judaism, and original sin,
75; and vicarious sacrifice 75; mystical aspect of, 2, 3, 133; view of
human psyche of, 56, 57
Rabbinic literature, 38
Reitzenstein, Richard, 54
Rejudaization, 74, 116, 117, 135
Resurrection of Jesus, 69, 71;
whether Jewish precedent for, 70;

and Pharisaism, 70, 78, 79; and
Gnosticism, 72, 73; Jewish con-
cept of, compared with Pauline, 81
Ruether, Rosemary, 192 n.44, 88
Rhea, 71
Robinson, 195 n.32
Rowland, Christopher, 190 n.22

Sacred Executioner, 85, 183
Sadducees, 132
Saklas, 18
Salem, 14
Sammael, 18, 187 n.17
Samothracian mysteries, 196 n.33
Samuel, 48
Sanders, E. P., 170, 189 n.3, 191
n.28, 197 n.2
Sanders, J. T., 200 n.22
Satan, 19, 38
Saturn, 30
Scapegoat, 85, 190 n.19
Scholem, Gershom, 2, 19, 133, 185
n.1, 187 n.15
Schürer, Emil, 170
Schweitzer, A., 92, 148, 191 n.33,
192 n.33, 193 n.6
Seder, 124, 197 n.37
Segal, Alan F., 197 ch.5 n.1, 200 n.19
Segal, M. H., 195 n.28
Seir, 162
Semitisms, 115, 116, 117, 118, 122
Septuagint, 69, 150, 151
Seth, 6, 8, 10, 12, 16, 18, 19, 186 n.10,
187 n.11, n.12, n.14
Sethian seed, 14, 15
Sethian-Ophites, 6
Shabbetai Zevi, 127
Shammai, 131
Shechem, 14
Shem, 174
Simon Magus, 13
Sinai, 50
Sins, witting and unwitting, 190 n.18
Smith, J. Z., 71, 72, 190 n.24
Smith, Morton, 188 n.3
Smith, W. Robertson, 190 n.17
Solomon, 5, 7, 8, 12, 13, 48, 107, 185
n.3, 186 n.8; as Messiah, 7; power
of, over demons, 14

Son of God, 7, 55
Son of Man, 5, 7, 8
Sophia, 18, 61, 189 n.9
Stendahl, K., 150, 188 ch.3 n.1, 200 ch.6 n.1, ch.6, passim
Stoicism, 191 n.33
Stowers, S. K., 153, 200 n.22, 199 n.13
Strack-Billerbeck, 188 n.3
Stroumsa, Gedaliah, 12, 185 n.7, 186 n.10, 187 n.13, 187 n.17, 189 n.9
Suffering Servant, 61, 76; as Messiah, 62; as Jewish people, 62; as martyr, 77

Tabor, James D., 200 n.19
Talmud, 131
Tannaitic Midrashim, 131
Targum, 62, 133
Tarsus, 72, 115
Tatian, 102
Tendenz, 193 n.7
Tertullian, 49, 195 n.33
Testimony of Truth, 13
Titans, 65, 71
Torah, 4, 5, 21, 27, 37, 40; in Jewish tradition, 42, 43, 50; whether given by angels, 40, 41, 42

Trinity, 64
Triumphal entry, 67

Valentinianism, 22, 37, 47, 187 n.18
Vermaseren, M. J., 72, 190 n.23
Vermes, Geza, 191 n.28, 195 n.27
Vicarious atonement, 77, Jewish attitude towards, 190 n.28
Vööbus, A., 193 n.17

Weber, Ferdinand, 170, 189 n.2
Wellhausen, J., 189 n.2
White, J. L., 153, 200 n.22
Windisch, H., 189 n.10
Wisdom, 61
Witkowski, S., 200 n.22

Yaldabaoth, 7, 17, 18, 19, 187 n.15
Yallon, H., 195 n.28
Yave, (Yahveh), 17, 19

Zechariah, 27, 107
Zeus, 80; identification of, with Jewish creator God, 29
Ziegler, K. J., 195 n.33